INTERNATIONAL REVIEW OF COMPARATIVE PUBLIC POLICY

Volume 7 • 1996

SOCIAL COSTS OF ECONOMIC TRANSFORMATION IN CENTRAL EUROPE

PART II. ECONOMIC POLICY, REGULATION AND SOCIAL CHANGE: SOCIAL (IN)EQUALITY

PART III. UNEMPLOYMENT, DECENTRALIZATION OF SOCIAL POLICY AND HEALTH CARE REFORM: CASE STUDIES OF THE TRANSFORMATION

CONTENTS

INTERNATIONAL REVIEW OF COMPARATIVE PUBLIC POLICY

SOCIAL COSTS OF ECONOMIC TRANSFORMATION IN CENTRAL EUROPE

Series Editor: NICHOLAS MERCURO
Department of Economics and Finance
University of New Orleans

Volume Editor: JÁNOS MÁTYÁS KOVÁCS
Institute for Human Sciences
Vienna, Austria

VOLUME 7 • 1996

Emerald

United Kingdom – North America – Japan –
India – Malaysia – China

Emerald Group Publishing Limited
Howard House, Wagon Lane, Bingley BD16 1WA, UK

First edition 1996

Published by Emerald Group Publishing Limited in 2008

First published by Elsevier in 1996

Reprints and permission service
Contact: books@emeraldinsight.com

British Library Cataloguing in Publication Data
A catalogue record for this book is available from the British Library

Printed and bound in Great Britain by
CPI Antony Rowe, Chippenham and Eastbourne

ISBN: 978-0-7623-0153-9

ISOQAR QUALITY ASSURED ISO 9001 UKAS QUALITY MANAGEMENT 026
Certificate number 1985

Awarded in recognition of Emerald's production department's adherence to quality systems and processes when preparing scholarly journals for print

INVESTOR IN PEOPLE

Andrzej Rychard	Professor of Sociology and Director Institute of Philosophy and Sociology Polish Academy of Sciences, Warsaw
Ágnes Simonyi	Department of Social Policy Eötvös Lorand University, Budapest
Julia Szalai	Deputy Director, Institute of Sociology Hungarian Academy of Sciences President of the Active Society Foundation, Budapest
István György Tóth	Associate Professor of Sociology Budapest University of Economics Director, Social Research Informatics Center (TARKI), Budapest
Jiří Večerník	Research Director, Institute of Sociology Czech Academy of Sciences Chairman of the START Foundation, Prague
Peter Vince	Senior Research Fellow Institute for Market Research and Informatics Ltd. (Kopint Datorg), Budapest

LIST OF CONTRIBUTORS

Leszek Balcerowicz	Professor or Economics Warsaw School of Economics President of Poland's Union of Freedom Party and former Deputy Prime Minister and Finance Minister of Poland
Michal Boni	Director of the Social Policy Program Institute of Public Affairs, Warsaw Former Minister for Labor and Social Policy of Poland
Elżbieta Drogosz-Zabłocka	Assistant Professor Institute for Educational Research, Warsaw
Zsuzsa Ferge	Head of the Department of Social Policy, Eötvös Lorand University, Budapest
Lena Kolarska-Bobinska	Director, Public Opinion Research Center CBOS, Warsaw
Petr Matějů	Research Director, Institute of Sociology Czech Academy of Sciences; Director, START Foundation, Prague
Iveta Radičová	Professor of Sociology and Deputy Director, Academia Istropolitana, Bratislava; Executive Director, SPACE Foundation

STATEMENT OF SCOPE

The *International Review of Comparative Public Policy* is interdisciplinary and dedicated to publishing original scholarly contributions that systematically analyze international public policy issues. It is a nationally referred, annual jointly sponsored by the University of New Orleans and the University of Innsbruck. Each yearly edition will be devoted to a different public policy issue that can benefit from comparative political, legal, economic, and social scientific examination. The topic, together with the volume editor(s), will be selected through a competitive prospectus-selection process.

An individual who is interested in editing a future volume of the *International Review of Comparative Public Policy* should submit three copies of a 5-7 page, double-spaced, typed prospectus to the series editor. Each prospectus must include: (1) identification of the issue/topic and a prospective title of the volume; (2) a detailed description of the international dimensions of the particular policy issue; (3) a statement as to why and how the chosen issue can benefit from a comparative political, legal, economic, and social scientific examination; and, most important, (4) a list of potential contributors along with tentative titles of their contributions.

Each edition is expected to contain contributions from scholars from both the United States and abroad.

Please note that the Series Editor does not accept individual manuscripts for publication consideration.

Nicholas Mercuro, *Series Editor*
Department of Economics and Finance
University of New Orleans
New Orleans, LA 70148
Tel: (504) 286-6270
Fax: (504) 286-6397

ACKNOWLEDGMENTS

I gratefully acknowledge the help of Iveta Radicova, Andrzej Rychard, Julia Szalai and Jiri Vecernik who recommended contributors. Thanks are especially due to Helen Addison for coordinating this publication project and editing the papers. Finally, I wish to express my gratitude to Karin Slamanig and Elisabeth Zickbauer who carefully prepared the manuscript for publication.

János Mátyás Kovács

INTRODUCTION:
OUT OF THE INCUBATOR

János Mátyás Kovács

The premature welfare state of communism—the term coined by the Hungarian economist from Harvard, János Kornai—has enormous popularity in East-Central Europe today. Neophyte followers of free-market orthodoxy and nostalgic communists are making efforts to interpret the metaphor of the early-born baby according to their own taste. While the neoliberals opt for active euthanasia, that is, they would like to accelerate the death of the struggling baby, their adversaries try to keep the incubator working even if the baby died. Between the two extremes represented by a few radicals there are a great number of social scientists and policymakers with diverse convictions who do their best to combine the virtues of both approaches without reinforcing their vices.

Indeed, can the communist welfare regimes be transformed and modernized without falling into the trap of (a) conserving the dirigism, inefficiency and pseudo-egalitarian character of the old system of social policy; (b) targeting an end-state which has become unsustainable even in the Western world during the past two decades; (c) seeking new forms of collectivism in welfare policy along the "Third Roads" leading to somewhere between capitalism and communism; and (d) triggering popular discontent (that may in turn block the entire transformation process) by dismantling the old welfare regimes too rapidly, in a haphazard way, without compensation, and so forth?

* * *

It was with these questions that we turned to our colleagues in the Czech Republic, Hungary, Poland and Slovakia in 1992 when launching our SOCO (Social Costs of Economic Transformation in Central Europe) project at the Vienna Institute for Human Sciences.[1] In the framework of this long-term comparative research program we wanted not only to address the vital social issues of post-communist transformation but also to formulate policy recommendations for the new governments.

The current situation in East-Central Europe presents a rare opportunity for a comparative analysis of economic liberalization, its social costs and the options for policy reform. Focusing especially on labor market problems and social welfare deficiencies, our project aims to contribute to the success of the democratic transition from communism, as well as to the reinforcement of social policy research in the region—a systematically neglected discipline under the old regime. Also, an important objective of the program was to promote dialogue between scholars and politicians from the East and the West;[2] a dialogue from which also the Western partners can profit by learning what is "boiling" in the huge laboratory of social transformation in the former East-Bloc countries. In order to facilitate East-East and East-West communication in social policy thought, we have established the first comprehensive data base of the social consequences of post-communist transformation in East-Central Europe.

The four national research teams are encouraged to elaborate a common framework for analysis, investigate similar problems and, where feasible, share methodological approaches. The more than fifty sub-projects currently underway fall into four areas:

1. Factual analysis of the social problems arising from economic liberalization, with emphasis on labor market issues;
2. Potential preventive policies and new institutions designed to improve the labor market and thus reduce social tensions;
3. Ameliorative policies that provide social safety nets and general social support systems such as health and pensions;

4. Changes in the locus of delivery and budgeting of social services, including decentralization of social policy among levels of government and between firms and other entities.

The SOCO program lays a special emphasis on "small policies," that is, on the understanding of how individuals and families cope with the difficulties of economic transformation. We would like to help identify not only the losers but also the winners of this process. In this sense the project seeks to specify the social benefits of the transformation, not exclusively its social costs.

* * *

The papers in this volume represent the large variety of social philosophies and economic/sociological methodologies, which have been applied by our colleagues in studying the transitional welfare systems of the post-communist democracies. The authors also show a great diversity in terms of profession and scholarly discipline. Among them the reader will find ministers and ngo leaders, university professors and directors of polling agencies, labor economists, political scientists and social policy experts.

The volume consists of three parts. The first part covers some general issues of social theory and politics ranging from the chances for social-liberalism under post-communism, through a new dichotomy of the transforming societies, to the birth of neo-socialism in the region. The chapters in the second and third examine economic policies and regulation schemes from the perspective of social change. In the second one four papers are devoted to new inequalities, a burning problem of social thought in East-Central Europe. The third part chapter includes four independent case studies of vocational training, long-term unemployment, local welfare policy and health insurance with a view to providing first-hand information on the daily workings of the new social systems.

* * *

When organizing the research program, we promised ourselves to avoid easy answers to the dramatic questions raised by the social transformation in the region. Before accepting or formulating any (neo)liberal, social-democratic, corporatist, and so forth, advice, or any of their blends, we wanted to understand the actual processes of the transition of the communist welfare regimes. Dissatisfied with the idea of "the unprecedented transformation," as well as with the pessimistic prediction of inevitable clashes between the principles of economic liberalization and the provision of social welfare (and of the subsequent Latin-Americanization of East-Central Europe), we were interested in (a) the similarities of the transformation of welfare regimes in the East and the West; (b) the dissimilarities of the post-communist country cases and the multitude of mixed answers to the social questions; (c) the success (at least, non-failure) stories of the transition in social affairs.

Obviously, the reader will decide whether the following papers convince him or her about the flaws of binary argumantation: either retaining communist social policy or eradicating welfare as an interventionist legacy. Maybe he or she will be disappointed at the sight of a great number of intermediary, "unclean" welfare institutions and policies emerging after 1989. In order to reassure the reader (and to defend the social transformers of East-Central Europe), let us briefly enumerate some of the frustrating starting conditions of social transformation.

1. The new democracies have inherited extremely inefficient, interventionist, expensive, unjust and corrupted welfare systems, which display great inertia by sustaining huge interest groups and generating high expectations in the population concerning public social services. Political liberalization reveals most of the hidden social maladies of communism and, at the same time, reinforces the bargaining power (or at least the voice) of those suffering from these maladies. Egalitarian nostalgia (which is not completely unfounded) may be exploited by populist political discourse.

2. The dismantling of the old welfare regimes should be accompanied by the creation of new, costly social schemes (unemployment insurance, poor relief, etc.) as well as by the modernization and/or marketization of others such as the pension system and health care. These require major initial investments amidst a lasting crisis of state finances (cf. falling revenues, galloping inflation, increasing foreign debts, etc.), while the new tasks may legitimize the old welfare bureaucracies with their obsolete skills.

3. The social systems are not only burdened by the inefficiency of the old ("Eastern") schemes and by the financing of services related to economic liberalization but also by the performance of tasks (protection of refugees, drug prevention, etc.) which are relatively new even in the "Western" world.

4. The principle of marketization of social services was compromised by large-scale corruption under the old regime. The fact that paying for the formerly free services (e.g., in health care) does not necessarily involve quality improvements may be seen by the people that they are exposed to a new form of taxation. Thus, free riding and bribe may remain the rational strategy of coping with social difficulties.

5. The deconstruction of the old welfare regimes cannot be centrally managed because a large share of social services under communism were enterprise-based and public administration after 1989 has been rapidly decentralized. Owing to the holes in the regulation system, whole social groups (long-term unemployed, disabled, gipsies, etc.) may fall through the social net. The new private sector—the "winner" of the transition—is not directly interested in repairing the safety net.

6. The "no longer state—not yet market" gap in social transformation can be immediately bridged neither by community-based self-help arrangements nor by the charity of the new rich due to the lack of such traditions in the region. Ngo-s are only making first steps, social work is also underdeveloped, so the coping strategies of those in need are typically based on the family and the shadow economy.

* * *

Considering these points of departure of the social transition, it would be too much to believe in "first-best" solutions. The incubator of the premature welfare state of communism is broken. Life outside the incubator is painful but not impossible. The baby is bound to adjust...

NOTES

1. Supported by grants from the Ford Foundation, the Pew Charitable Trusts, the Austrian Federal Chancellery, the German State of Saxony, the Robert Bosch Foundation and the Austrian National Bank, IHS has established independent national research teams in Hungary, Poland and the Czech and Slovak Republics.

2. The SOCO International Expert Committee is chaired by Richard Freeman, Professor of Economics, London School of Economics and Harvard University. Members: Leszek Balcerowicz, President of Poland's Freedom Party; Professor of Economics, Warsaw School of Economics; Michael J. Dowling, Former Commissioner, New York State Department of Social Services; Zsuzsa Ferge,

Professor of Sociology, Head of the Department of Social Policy, Eötvös Lorand University, budapest; Georg Fischer, Advisor to the Austrian Federal Minister of Finance; Hans Geisler, Minister for Social Affairs, Health and Family of the German State of Saxony; Ira Katznelson, Professor of Political Science and Constitutional Law, Columbia University; János M. Kovács, Professor of Economics, Member of the Institute of Economics, Hungarian Academy of Sciences; Permanent Fellow of IHS; Claus Offe; Professor of Sociology, Humboldt University of Berlin; Andrzej Rychard, Professor of Sociology, Diretor of the institute of Philosophy and Sociology, Polish Academy of Sciences; Frantisek Sebej, President, Macro-Economic and Social Analysis Center, Bratislava; Julia Szalai, Professor of Sociology, Deputy Director of the Institute of Sociology, Hungarian Academy of Sciences; Jiri Vecernik, Sociologist, Institute of Sociology, Czech Acadmey of Sciences.

PART I

THEORY AND POLITICS: STATE AND MARKET IN POST-COMMUNIST WELFARE SYSTEMS

SOCIAL SECURITY THROUGH ECONOMIC GROWTH

Leszek Balcerowicz

It is always with some hesitation that I voice my opinion on any subject matter with the word "social" attached to it. This is not due to the fact that I generally underestimate social issues as such; I have simply noticed that the very word "social" contains a few traps.

The first trap is that many people have a tendency to accept—without further reasoning—any solution which happens to be labeled "social" whether or not it really is better than the other solutions presented. The word "social" belongs to a category of expressions that seem to disable thinking.

For example, the expression "social market economy" has gained extreme popularity in Poland. Introduced in the 1940s by West German liberals (and applied to their own country), it denoted a free market capitalist economy with a relatively minor element of welfare state. In Poland, however, it is generally associated with a high, and

International Review of Comparative Public Policy,
Volume 7, pages 3-17.

ISBN: 0-7623-0153-8

even increasing, level of social expenditure. This is true, regardless of the fact that Poland, unlike West Germany, does not yet have an efficient capitalist economic system, but it is also burdened with the heritage of excessive welfare spending.

Moreover, I think that many people in Poland consider "social" policy to be the most important aspect of a state's general policy. In the communication between the Polish Ministries of Finance and Labor, numbers and people are set against each other in the name of social policy even though there are only people on both sides. Theirs are simply two points of view, two different perspectives for perceiving one and the same: people.

The second trap I associate with the word "social" is that it is extremely elastic. Any discussions under this headline may pertain to virtually anything—including nothing at all. To limit this elasticity, I will assume that the word "social" denotes here non-physical phenomena concerning many *individuals* at the same time.

Obviously, the number of such phenomena is great. I will therefore concentrate upon the following matters:

1. the issue of a social deal in Poland;
2. an overview of different means of political activity (socio-techniques) used in the transition period from one political and economic system to another;
3. the criteria for shaping so-called "social policies."

ON THE SOCIAL DEAL

On the face of it, nearly all people in Poland agree that Poland should strive toward democracy and a non-socialist market economy. Nobody advocates socialism in the economy, even the "market variety" of socialism suggested in the 1980s (excluding or considerably limiting the private sector). Nonetheless, I think that this agreement is only on the surface rather than real, at least as far as the economic system is concerned. In the first place, some people who claim to support an efficient non-socialist economy, hinder or block progress in that direction. In particular, they block privatization. The danger there is that by doing so, Poland may get stuck in something often referred to as the "Latin-American model;" comprising a considerable number of inefficiencies and distortions produced by a large public sector and multi-branched state interventionism. This very model belongs more and more to the past even in Latin America itself. Many of these same countries have been privatizing their economies and are trying to learn from their own mistakes.

Secondly, different variations of market economies have different influences upon the rate of economic development and, in consequence, on people's living conditions. Consequently, making general statements is not enough: one has to clearly state his or her preferences as to a given variation. I would like to elaborate on that a little.

A rational approach to determining preference includes three consecutive stages: (1) defining criteria for the choice of the ultimate system, (2) identifying a system which meets the criteria at the highest degree, (3) defining political means, that is, political actions that will lead to the implementation of this system in a given socio-political reality.

I will present my opinions on issues 1 and 2, first with regard to economy, then—more briefly—with regard to the political system. As for point 3, I will discuss the matter later.

It is worth noting that as a society, Poland has finally been given the opportunity to choose the kind of social system she wants. For a few years now, we have been fully independent. In my opinion, in order to make good use of our independence, we have to employ two criteria for the choice of an economic system:

- fast economic growth,
- the greatest possible equality of opportunity.

"Fast" in our case means a much faster growth than that in the West. By economic growth I understand a process that results in *creating an increasing number of productive jobs.* (*It is the only effective way of defeating poverty.*) So understood, economic growth is something Poland needs very badly. First of all, because we have dozens of years to make up for. And second, because within the next few years a vast number of young people will appear on the labor market looking for suitable work (that makes Poland an exception among all post-communist countries). Irrespective of his or her intentions, whoever impedes Poland's economic growth by increasing unemployment and emigration will be responsible for the failure of a whole young generation.

As I understand it, equality of opportunity is a situation in which people with similar mental capacities and motivations have similar chances to achieve their life-goals. Needless to say, full equality is an ideal that cannot be reached; it is impossible to eliminate the chance factor. This includes an individual's good or bad luck, the stratificatory influence of informal social ties and the advantages and disadvantages received from one's own family background.

What does the degree of realization of the "equal opportunity" goal depend on? It depends mainly on three factors. First, *free entry* into economic life and a homogeneous legal and administrative system. Financial results of enterprises and individuals should not depend on the lobbying power they can exert upon the state. *State interventionism is always contradictory to the principle of equal opportunity.* A second factor is the availability of high-quality education. Differences in the financial situation of families should not limit the access of children and youth to the high-quality education that allows for social equality between generations. Finally, a third factor specific to countries progressing toward a non-socialist market economy can be the programs of "enfranchising citizens" by mass privatization. Strangely enough, such programs were faced with general resistance even from political parties professing socialist ideas.

I would like to stress that the two criteria, fast economic growth and the greatest possible equality of opportunity, *are convergent to a large extent*. By this I mean that certain factors facilitating fast economic growth facilitate the equality of opportunity as well. At the same time, certain variants of the economic system inhibiting fast economic growth increase the disparity of opportunities (and incomes as well). I would now like to identify the system which enables fast and long-term economic growth. My opinion is based on research comparing different economic systems as well as my reading of economic theory, development economics in particular. A system of fast economic growth meets seven conditions that can be termed *foundations for fast economic growth* and are listed below:

1. Macro-economic stability, that is, low inflation.
2. Free entry onto the market. Of course, competition is contradictory to the widespread system of corporate tax relief and special licenses. It also requires a mechanism to eliminate state-supported business enterprises that do not function

properly on the market. Any state which supports permanently insolvent enterprises nullifies the customers' verdict, thus undermining the principle of competition.

3. Dominance of the private sector. There is no reason for the so-called "strategic" sectors to be excluded from the scope of privatization. Besides, what does "strategic" mean, after all?
4. Strengthening the links with the external world instead of practicing isolationism. Incentives for export should not be weaker than those for home market production. This is in contrast to strong protection of the home market: protection weakens *relative* export incentives. In the economy—and life—it is the relative incentives that count; incentives associated with one activity *compared* to benefits resulting from other activities.
5. A flexible job market fostering development, that is, a situation in which profits of business enterprises are protected against increases in surpasssing the growth of productivity. Profits are re-invested, thus creating higher real wages and new jobs. For countries like Poland, which are abandoning socialism for good, the most important means of development-oriented labor markets is privatization of the economy. It adds strength to the party representing profits in the process of wage bargaining. At the same time, due to increased average efficiency of private business enterprises, it enables faster increase in real wages. Another important condition is trade unions. Even a dynamic and stable private market economy can be impaired by trade unionists pushing ahead their scheme of pay raises at any cost. Long-lasting increases in real wages can only result from increased productivity.
6. A relatively low ratio of taxes and budget expenditures as compared to national income (relatively low means lower than the current one in Poland). In the countries which experienced extremely fast economic growth, the ratio of taxes and expenditure to national income was below average. Another important factor is that of social overheads (such as pension fund contributions) attached to wages. These additional expenses increase labor costs and hinder the increase in employment. In extreme cases, they can lead to slow economic growth and large-scale unemployment. In fact, West European countries are now facing this problem.

7. Political stability enabling the politicians to lay the above foundations, and not only to formulate the goal in itself. Political stability and poor economic policy results in situations like that in North Korea; South Korea's present stage of development is the outcome of political stability combined with good economic policy.

Each of the above-mentioned conditions is gradable, that is, can assume a different degree of intensity. There are no countries in the world with ideal foundations for economic growth. The differences between countries with regard to the number of fundamental conditions that are being met and the extent of their fulfillment are enormous. These differences are linked with the speed of economic growth. The more solid the foundations and the more conditions that have been met, the higher the tempo of economic growth. Countries in which the economic system differed greatly from the one presented above developed slowly. Indeed, one cannot find a single example of an economy that differs considerably from the model discussed which would experience long-term economic growth faster than the countries closer to the model. In this sense, the economic growth foundations hypothesis meets the falsification criterion of Karl Popper.

Slow long-term growth affects those countries which differ considerably from the fundamental conditions in the following points:

- The economy is dominated by the public sector, a sector which is associated with lack of competition and extreme protectionism. This is the case in former socialist countries.
- There is a large public sector in the economy which is in principle capitalist, combined with protectionism and extensive state interventionism. Until recently, this was the case in the Latin American countries, most of which suffered from high inflation. All-powerful interventionism also paralyzed the economic growth of India.
- The economy is burdened with budget expenditures for consumption; excessive taxation results. For many years, this has been the problem of many "over-socialized" Western European countries. Apart from that, they suffer from various restrictions in the job market (regulations severely limiting the

> possibilities of dismissing an employee, high obligatory severance pay, legal limitations imposed on flexible contracts between employers and employees, etc.). All this contributes to the fact that Western Europe, compared to, say, the United States, has a relatively low potential for creating new jobs and, as a result, a high degree of structural unemployment.

In the post-communist countries there is no room for typical social-democratic policy. This is understood as increased redistribution of income through the budget or even redistribution kept at the past level which exceeds the redistribution level in capitalist countries with a similar per capita income. Just the opposite is needed: rationalizing reforms of the state budget are among the basic conditions to maintain fast economic growth of the economy. Furthermore, we have to adopt an extremely cautious approach toward all possible kinds of "social charters" introduced in Western European countries in which the level of economic development is much higher before the harmful consequences of oversocializing the economy becomes apparent.

Among the countries which have the strongest foundations and where the fundamental conditions have been met to the largest extent are the Asian tigers: Japan, which came first; then Taiwan; South Korea; Hong Kong and Singapore; and, finally, Thailand; Malaysia and Indonesia. It is no wonder that the rate of economic development has been higher in these countries than anywhere else in the world since 1960: three times as high as in Latin America and with much smaller income discrepancies. Anybody willing to attribute this spectacular achievement to some kind of special interventionism would be wrong. Whatever has been gained, it is due to the particularly broad foundations of growth. Although these countries differ with regard to outward forms of the state's involvement in the economy, fast economic growth is common to all of them. Secondly, the scale of state interventionism is on the average smaller than in the Third World. Last but not least whenever this scale happened to increase in Southeast Asia (which in the 1970s was the case in South Korea which went through a period of investment expansion in heavy industry), it quickly turned out to be harmful and was abandoned.

Let us come back to the large degree of convergence of the two main criteria for the selection of the economic deal: fast economic growth and the greatest possible equality of opportunity. This convergence is due to the fact that some factors are extremely important for the realization of *both criteria at the same time*. As we have already mentioned, access to good education is one of the basic criteria that have to be met in order to approach the ideal of equality of opportunity. Education is also important for the development of the economy provided that the foundations listed above are also present. Otherwise, development of education results in frustration by people who cannot make proper use of the knowledge and skills acquired in the education process because of faults within the economic system. An unrestricted entry to the market is important for fast economic growth and it is also relevant from the point of view of equal opportunity. A system in which profits do not depend on market performance but on the access to politicians and state employees both impedes growth and increases inequality of opportunity as well as income discrepancies.

As far as the political system is concerned, I will say only a few words. Of major importance is the stability lack of stability has a detrimental effect upon economic policy and economic growth. Moreover, it lowers the legitimization of democracy as perceived by the society. In extreme cases, it can even lead to elections without the electorate, that is, to failing governments and passive citizens.

The political system should contain provisions against harmful influence of populist policy. This is where *a constitution* can play a significant role. A constitution should protect the stability of money, competition and other economic freedoms. On the other hand, a constitution should not contain such social rights which sound nice but are either void because there is no real money to implement them, or are harmful, because they require the imposition of high taxes and constitute a threat to the stability of money.

Last but not least, it is important to base the democratic institutions on the *principle of subsidiarity*. The right to make decisions should be vested to the highest levels only in those matters which, as if by nature, exclude the lower levels (e.g., national defense) or in such cases when the higher level can be definitely more efficient. *Broad competencies should be granted to the local governments.* There are three reasons why this is more important in young democracies than in the countries where democracy is well-established. Local government, being close to the voters, is a good school of democracy and good for managing common resources. Locally, the connection between taxes and expenditure is more clear than on the national level. Finally, local government can exercise better control over suppliers of educational and other services financed from the budget.

SOCIO-TECHNIQUES OF THE GREAT TRANSITION

I will now discuss the political actions to implement this system in a given socio-political reality.

One can label these means as "socio-techniques of the transition." In this case, the word "socio-techniques" is neutral, not pejorative. Let us begin with three kinds of *misunderstandings:*

(1) It is a common error to concentrate mainly on *the risk of triggering social protest* by introducing radical economic measures to say nothing of a similar risk connected with the *abandoning* of such measures. In a dramatic economic situation similar to that of Poland in 1989, both implementing radical means and abandoning them were risky. Implementing them, however, gave us a chance to overcome economic disaster.

(2) A similar error is linking the notion of "*social costs*" to economic reforms only, especially to radical ones as if the costs of abandoning these reforms were not even higher. Let us compare the changes that have occurred within the last few years in Poland or Estonia with the situation in Russia or the Ukraine.

(3) The third error is to blame the result of elections unfavorable for the party advocating change on radical economic reforms. This explanation was cited after the Polish elections of 1993 regardless of the fact that there is no clear cause and effect link between the type of implemented economic program and the results of the elections. The results were even worse for the governing parties in Lithuania and Hungary where economic reforms were less radical than in Poland.

I would like to present an overview of means employed by different political forces for the purpose of realizing the social deal. Some of these means, local government for example, should be a permanent element of this deal.

I will distinguish four kinds of socio-techniques:

(1) *Finding a scape-goat.* Different political groups suggested different categories of "lightning rods." In fact, some of them, such as Konfederacja Polski Niepodleglej, KPN, and Ruch dla Rzeczpospolitej mentioned all categories at one time.

Among the groups attacked, the communists and their collaborators were mentioned most often. Without analyzing the moral aspect of the issue, one can say that the matter is practically no longer relevant. In fact, this was largely due to the actions taken by the "decommunizators" and inspectors themselves. Of course, the necessity of creating a mechanism that would enable the state to check the political past of people aiming at high official positions is still on the agenda.

Extensive use was also made of the "*swindlers*" category. Here, again, results were totally opposed to intentions. People developed a false conviction that all entrepreneurs were crooks thereby lowering the reputation of the capitalist system being aimed at. In my opinion, some right-wing political groups rendered special services to this cause.

(2) *Information policy and persuasion.* This kind of political activity deserves a more serious treatment than the previous one because it does not have dubious moral implications. Besides, explanations concerning the meaning of reforms are much in demand. The results of informative and persuasive activities depend on their economic and political context. I find it hard to accept that the first two governments in Poland after 1989 had, at their disposal, a kind of information policy which could have changed the actual political outcomes, that is, the fall of the liberal governments. After all, in political pluralism, which is a precious thing in itself, public opinion is constantly exposed to streams of information based on different values. Unfortunately, in Poland, where until recently, election campaigns were held very often, people, many of them disoriented and lost, were treated with huge doses of demagogy and populism.

The Czech Republic is often cited as an example to show that information policy can be either the main or even the only factor that contributes to maintaining the popularity of radical reforms and politicians associated with them. This argument, however, is questionable because in the Czech Republic the economic context was much more favorable for these reforms. Already at its starting point, the Czech economy was exceptionally stable compared to other post-communist countries. It did not have to pay the costs of hyper-inflation. The inherited economic structure generated less unemployment. There have been no aggressive and strong trade unions, and the populist opposition has been weak. To realize the importance of the context for the efficiency of information policy toward reform, it is enough to take a look at Slovakia. During the first three years of the transformation, the economic policy implemented there was identical to the Czech Republic's, yet the unemployment rate in 1992 was four times as high. In the Slovak elections of 1992, the party of Vaclav Klaus got only 4 percent of the votes; the majority of votes went to the opposition criticizing the radical economic program.

All I have written so far does not mean, of course, that I neglect the informative and persuasive activities toward reform. In fact, most of my working life is occupied by such activities. I think, however, that they should be treated as a long-term investment.

(3) *The widest possible participation.* One has to define what the main institutional planes where this participation can develop are. I myself can see two. One of them is local government; I have already discussed its importance. The other plane is that of non-governmental organizations; private but non-profit organizations established with an aim to achieve specific goals identified by the members of these organizations. The former minister of labor and social affairs, Jacek Kuroń's SOS Foundation, or the Foundation For Economic Education, of which I myself am an associate, can serve as examples here.

(4) *Social deals.* Here again we see the magic word "social," so some distance seems essential. National deals can be divided into those of a permanent character, and extraordinary solutions. Each advocate of social deals should make it clear from the beginning which of these he or she supports.

Deals as permanent structures serve as a mechanism for reaching agreement upon decisions, or as preliminary attitudes toward a wider or narrower range of subjects between organizations of entrepreneurs, employees and the government. According to widespread expectations such deals can be efficient, especially when they concern a wide range of issues. Experience shows, however, that such solutions are effective only in very specific conditions that are hard to meet in general and are quite different from the Polish conditions. Thus, one cannot reproach the opponents of social deals with lack of realism ("without deals the people would revolt"). Secondly, permanent structures in Poland would be a dangerous solution, particularly if it pertains to a wide range of issues and takes the shape of definitive decisions. It would mean establishing corporative structures with labor union oligarchies and employers' representations. Such structures could lead to the limiting of competition and to the creation of decision making mechanisms with strong veto elements. The question also arises: what range of issues would then be left to the free market and the democratic organs of the state?

All in all, I think that social deals as durable structures should be treated skeptically, both in terms of their realism and consequences.

I think though that Poland needed (and still needs, in fact) a single deal increasing the tempo of privatization.

*

Apart from the four socio-techniques discussed above, I would like to focus on some other political actions toward reforms which usually get less attention:

(5) *Strengthening the pro-reform groups within the party system.* Particularly important was the fusion of Unia Demokratyczna (Democratic Union) and Kongres Liberalno-Demokratyczny (the Liberal and Democratic Congress) into the Union of Freedom. Also important is the position of the liberal wing in parties which call themselves right-wing (even if not always accurately) and in Sojusz Lewicy Demokratycznej—The Alliance of the Social-Democratic Left.

(6) *Certain elements of the economic reform itself* might have contributed to the ultimate economic goal:

- The radical character of reforms just after the political turnover in 1989 allowed for covering a large part of the distance to the ultimate goal, yet some of the solutions introduced at that time were designed as protective measures against turning back (e.g., independence of the central bank, exchangeability of the currency, large participation of the private sector). Without these radical reforms the present situation of the Polish economy would be much worse. The chances for further reforms would be few and social discontent would probably be greater although for different reasons (more inflation and queues, more hidden, less overt unemployment, weaker tendencies toward economic growth).

- *Privatization itself can set in motion the forces supporting economic reforms.* It is characteristic that people already employed in the private sector evaluate privatization much higher than those still working in the public sector. It means that first-hand experience can neutralize the political propaganda against privatization. Accelerating privatization can be the best way to overcome anti-privatization attitudes and gain support for further changes.
- Establishing banks specializing in granting *commercial* investment credits for poor people and modeled on the Grameen Bank in Bangladesh. Its equivalents have also been established in much richer countries.

THE CRITERIA OF SHAPING SOCIAL POLICY

It should be noted first that the criteria distinguishing social policy from other policies, including the economic one, are flexible and, in fact, arbitrary. The distinction is largely due to the fact that scientists—just as people—need specialization and they have the habit of attaching separate labels to areas they specialize in. Saying that social issues are more relevant for people than, for instance, monetary or tax policy is not a good criterion for distinguishing social policy. As a matter of fact, I do not see any clear and logical criterion: the distinction is based on a certain habit or convention. Keeping to this convention, one can say that among the issues usually included in the scope of "social policy" are:

- the issue of *social insurance*, that is, insurance related to old age, unemployment and illness;
- the issue of *"social" consumption* (collective). This name should not imply that the society as a whole consumes something; consumption is done by individuals on a massive scale. "Social" here means—however inadequate—that the services are financed from the budget: education and medical care. It would be more appropriate to speak of consumption financed through taxes. For these services, people pay as tax-payers and not purchasers. Charges in the form of taxes are

not an iron rule: these goods can be financed in different ways. Taxation is the only possibility in the case of public goods such as defense, which, as if by nature, cannot be purchased and consumed piece by piece. Conventional services included under "collective consumption," because they are financed through taxes, do not have to be rendered by state-owned public institutions such as schools and hospitals. It is possible to reconcile public financing with competition by different suppliers of different ownership structure.

Employment, unemployment, job market. These are central issues of the classical economic policy. Treating them mainly or solely from the perspective of social policy may bring about undesirable results. In the case of unemployment benefits, for example, creating safety through benefits may force out the creation of safety through development.

I would now like to concentrate on the first two issues, as the third one is closely connected with the foundations of growth already discussed.

(1) *Solutions with regard to social policy should not be contradictory to the condition of fast economic growth.* Accepting this criterion means the necessity of lowering the ratio of expenditures (and taxes) to national income.

Comparative research shows that the cost of each additional 10 percent points of increase in the budget expenditure/national income ratio equals 1 percent point of the rate of annual economic growth, other factors remaining equal. One percent point is a great number. In the course of many years it means huge discrepancies in the level of consumption and employment between countries differing with regard to the burden of budget expenditure.

(2) The necessary rationalization of expenditure for social policy depends to a large extent on *increasing the role of local governments.* Completing the local government reform not only constitutes an important element of the ultimate social deal in Poland, but serves as a means to reduce the conflict between solutions within the social sphere and the requirements of fast economic growth.

(3) *The suppliers of social services should be subject to competition.* It is technically possible to combine financing of certain services through taxes with competition between suppliers (education vouchers or other solutions, linking budget money with the recipient

of services without providing automatic financing for their producers).

(4) In shaping the solutions within the social sphere, *a series of economic analyses* should be performed. *The resulting of those analyses will help establish rational limits for the social sphere.*

It is obvious that adopting market solutions is impossible in some cases. For example, a chronically ill person could not insure him- or herself in accordance with the principles of market economy. This leaves room for the actions of the state.

Still, employing rules of economic analysis also means that all expenditure, irrespective of the emotional power of their justification, have to be analyzed from the perspective of their social consequences as a whole. And one of the consequences of social expenditures above a certain critical point is that they reduce the rate of economic growth and increase unemployment.

(5) It is a good idea to *learn from other people's mistakes.* It is one of the few advantages of being a country trying to catch up. By mistakes I mean the already mentioned "over-socializing" of the economy in most West European countries. Over-socializing had three harmful consequences. The first was lowering the tempo of economic growth by disturbances within the sphere of public finances; the second—increase in structural unemployment; the third— demoralization and decline of the family.

(6) Last but not least, it is worth learning from our own mistakes. In the first stage of Poland's economic reform the problem of "over-socializing" the economy was not faced clearly; we did not say explicitly what should be done. In the then existing conditions we were thinking more about how to quickly establish new elements of social protection—such as unemployment benefits—and to intensify social welfare directed at specific groups.

FREEDOM AND SECURITY

Zsuzsa Ferge

Frequently, essence can only be expressed as hyperbole. On occasion, however, hyperbole entails precisely the loss of essence. I have been entertaining this suspicion vis-à-vis a new intellectual vogue which regards security as irreconcilable with freedom.

Jacek Kuron (1994) writes: "The socialist state was the system of centrally managed economy and society, and, consequently, of centralized redistribution. It can be stated that it realized the intentions of its ideologists: it established an order of maximum social security in a country, where all citizens were employees of the state. In practice, the workplace provided unlimited services. Theoretically, wages only had to cover food and clothing. Housing, electricity, heating, medical care, crèches, nurseries, schools, books, children's holidays, holidays for the people were (also theoretically) free of charge. The state guaranteed to every worker an old age pension, health insurance and disability provision. Thus, the system guaranteed security, albeit at the same time it divested workers of their freedom and of their autonomous self-determination: prison guarantees the greatest security."

International Review of Comparative Public Policy,
Volume 7, pages 19-42.

ISBN: 0-7623-0153-8

Peter Ambros (1994) believes that the concept of freedom can be infinitely stretched, even to the liberation of acts of destruction. It is possible, therefore,

> To be free to rip off the ladybird's wings
> To be free to starve
> To be free to hate (others or ourselves)
> To be free to fear and to spread terror...

Why must this important value be safeguarded, especially when the situation in currently democratizing states is deteriorating and "liberation is bringing populism, intolerance and war in its wake?" Ambros protests against either justification or acceptance of destructive freedoms. Should he reject them, he "would thereby justify those, who nostalgically crave for the return of the former period of stability, predictability, and of unequivocal captivity in the Eastern half of Europe." He therefore offers further explanations. "It is no coincidence if we can describe the period of captivity using the terms 'stability' and 'predictability'—in other words 'security.' Indeed we can even identify this period with it. 'Freedom' and 'security' stand in unresolvable contradiction with each other." When the object of the aspiration toward security is property which a person "sits on" (an image coming from the German 'besitzen' = to possess), this entails restriction of the person's freedom of movement. Hence thesis No. 1.: "The freedom of the individual aspiring toward security is restricted by this very aspiration." Indeed, if the aspiration is fulfilled, then this (thesis No. 2.) "amounts to relinquishing with a single decision all future decisions." The situation is no better when the individual does not rely on his/her own resources to maintain security but resorts to those of a go-between (e.g., compulsory social insurance). The same holds if the individual makes the decision of his/her own free will—as for instance in the former Federal Republic of Germany where freedom and security were regarded "as being equal in value and equally worthy of aspiring toward." Security saves people "the worry of having to come up with the means necessary for existence," that is, security divests the people of continuous existential decisions, thereby demoting them to the status of children. Hence thesis No. 3.: "Freedom is related to adulthood to the same extent as security is to dependency." The relinquishing of freedom and adulthood is thus characteristic not only of Eastern Europeans, but also of citizens living in welfare states—the phenomenon is only more conspicuous in the East. In order to reject the truly repulsive, destructive and self-destructive freedoms, Ambros declares without any particular argumentation that these are not "genuine" freedoms.

OVER-STRETCHING THE MEANING OF VALUE

I believe that all values of humankind could be rendered meaningless and discredited if we interpret abstract concepts in an absolutist way and project them onto reality without interpretation.

Opponents of equality have always been able to say with a clean consciousness that to demand equality is meaningless. In an abstract sense, equality is indeed exactly that. Thus, for instance, Letwin, a particularly conservative author, maintains that egalitarianism is based on three ideas. "1. all persons should be equal; 2. all existing inequalities can be reduced if not utterly eradicated by actions of governments; and 3. all other political objectives must give way to equality, if any conflict arises between it and them" (Donnison 1984). According to Donnison, Letwin does not back up his assertions with a single reference "for the good reason that no one ever said anything so silly." After all, it is profoundly true that "the idea of a perfectly egalitarian society is not only unrealistic: it is terrible. [This] utopia is the home of total terror or absolute boredom" (Dahrendorf 1969, p. 42). Those who have spent the last 40 to 70 years under "existing socialism" have accumulated considerable experience of terror and boredom even though their societies remained fundamentally unequal in many respects (such as the distribution of power and of physical and social life chances) (Ferge 1969). It was precisely the contradiction between the zealously advocated ideal of equality and real life that led to the discrediting of equality as a value.

Moreover, it is almost impossible to assess the situation in which we are genuinely equal, even if the criteria of equality are simple and apparently unambiguous. The concept of "income equality" appears to be a simple one, but, what exactly do we mean by it? Do we mean that all families have the same income, or that their per capita income is equal? Do we mean that their opportunities for consumption, their standard of living, if you like, is "identical," whatever that means? Who can decide that incomes are "equal" (from the viewpoint of opportunities for consumption) given an old age pensioner living in the countryside as compared to a skilled worker in the capital? For someone healthy and someone physically handicapped? For a vegetarian and a meat-eater? Is it sufficient to compare current incomes, or must property also be taken into consideration as a potential source of income that can be mobilized on occasion?

There are, of course, even more complicated phenomena. If, say, we were to advocate the "equality" of human abilities, then the differences between us could only be abolished with a Huxley-style negative "test tube baby" utopia. However, even Huxley built social castes into his system. In sum: equality as an abstract social ideal—as a liberating dream—has played a major role in European culture and in all of the world religions for over 2000 years. However, as an abstract concept, it does not lend itself easily to a theoretical interpretation, and as a practical demand, it either entailed distorted consequences or was implemented with only a partial or particular meaning.

Thus, it either meant (worst case scenario) that a specific kind of equality (e.g., the abolition of private property) was forced onto society producing countless new inequalities, injustices and restrictions, or else (best case scenario) that politics did not strive for "equality" but only for the reduction of certain inequalities. The latter goal is, for instance, served by the reduction of those inequalities, from housing to health care, which affect physical or social life chances the most strongly.

The situation is no better in case of another value, tolerance, which in an extended, unconditional interpretation also contains the need for tolerating intolerance. This extended interpretation is philosophically unmanageable. Rawls' theory of justice regards, in the interest of freedom, the tolerant's obligations in respect of toleration as almost unlimited. He finds only one circumstance, when "the tolerant sects have a right not to tolerate the intolerant, namely, when they sincerely and with reason believe that intolerance is necessary for their own security. This right follows ... since, as the original position is defined, each would agree to the right of self-preservation. Justice does not require that men must stand idly by while others destroy the basis of their existence."

If the threat is not direct, then "just citizens should strive to preserve the constitution with all its equal liberties as long as liberty itself, and their own freedom are not in danger... when the constitution is secure, there is no reason to deny freedom to the intolerant." Thus, when an intolerant sect or group emerges but does not immediately gather sufficient muscle to force its will on everybody, or does not grow very fast, then it can be hoped that it will gradually become aware of the superfluousness of tolerated intolerance. But this takes time. "Of course, the intolerant sect may be so strong initially or growing so fast that the forces making for stability cannot convert it into liberty. This situation presents a practical dilemma which philosophy alone cannot resolve." (Rawls 1971, p. 217 ff.).

Thus, in practice, tolerance may lead to its own fatal negation, or to a life and death struggle between the tolerant and the intolerant. János Kis comes to a similar, but politically and not philosophically formulated, conclusion when he says that the constitutional state can only survive "if civic intolerance against intolerance starts to operate long before state coercion becomes permissible" (Kis 1994).

The abuse of the concept of freedom is poignantly illustrated by Ambros' examples. In his conception, positive freedom is freedom to something (voting or destruction), while negative freedom is to be free of something (suffering, coercion). In the most generally accepted interpretation of freedom, according to which the limit of my freedom is another person's freedom, the freedom to destroy is conceptually excluded. A. Sen (1992) puts forth an almost reverse interpretation of the two freedoms, extending their interpretation, and (in my opinion) not over-stretching their meaning. Sen holds that negative freedom is exemption from constraint. For example, my vote is not constrained either by a political rule which, say, would exclude my participation in the vote on account of the color of my skin, or by hooligans blocking my path or beating me up when I go to vote. Positive freedom means in his conception everything that one can or cannot do. By way of illustrating the point, he says, "if I cannot walk freely in a park because I am disabled, then this is a constraint on my positive freedom, but there is no indication that anyone acted violently toward my negative freedom. If, however, it is not on account of my disability that I cannot walk in the park, but because hooligans beat me up if I do so, then this is a violation of my negative freedom—and not only of my positive freedom... If we consider it important that people be capable of a lifestyle that they would choose for themselves, then there are arguments to address the general category of positive freedom." In this rationale, poverty in itself does not violate negative freedom since it is not necessarily the consequence of another's direct intervention (or legal intervention). At the same time, however, the fact that a poor person cannot do a host of things—cannot feed his family properly, cannot buy the necessary heating fuel or medicines—is a constraint on his positive freedom. Similarly, the lack of positive freedom may compel the poor to take on work detrimental to their health and their chance of living longer. "While there is a real distinction between the positive and negative aspects of freedom, ...to concentrate only on one or the other is not only ethically incomplete, but can also be socially disjointed. The social commitment to individual freedom has to be concerned with both positive and negative freedoms and with their extensive interconnections" (Sen 1990).

In this system of thought the relationship between various values is addressed even if in an indirect way. It almost compels one to reexamine how freedom and equality (or, rather, the reduction of inequalities), freedom and tolerance, or, for that matter, freedom and security are related (see also Sen 1992).

ON SECURITY

Security has many different meanings. One important security is public security—the extent to which we can walk safely in the park. Here I believe the two constraints which Sen deals with—in connection with negative freedom—have to be clearly distinguished. One issue is legal violence, on account of which the (secret) police can take anybody away from the park. This is a serious restriction of my negative freedom, and simultaneously, it is an obvious threat to my public security. There may be a political pretext to my arrest (and if this is the case, then naturally they can take me away, not only from the park, but also from my home or workplace and perhaps this belongs less to the category of public security). Or the pretext may simply be that the police considers my behavior a "threat" to the public. In the latter event, the police's move is again based on legalized political tyranny, since the "safe-guarding of public security" is carried out with the help of elastic regulations. (It may give rise to lawful police intervention if I am unable to prove on the spot that I have a job, a home or money, or even if this may be suspected based on my outward appearance.) This is the political curtailment of my negative freedom.

At the same time, the danger that hooligans will beat me up in the street is reduced precisely on account of "preventive" police intervention and due to stringent punishment. Indeed, in dictatorial-totalitarian systems, it is police omnipresence and fear of tough or unpredictable retaliation, and so forth, that curtails street violence. In this sense public security can be said to be good. Paradoxically, the fragility of negative freedom of a political character can strengthen "everyday" negative freedom. It follows from this that the concept of constraints, and of negative freedom in general, must be refined. I would make a distinction within negative freedom between a threat from state power and from fellow citizens because it is true especially of the former that it is "interference of others in one's personal life (which) has offensive—perhaps intolerable—features going well beyond the resulting failure of positive freedom" (Sen 1990).

Alongside public security, "private security"—the security and predictability of everyday life and its different components—are also worthy of attention. It is precisely this interpretation of security that is currently dominant and which has prompted views equating security with prison. I believe that there can be other less pejorative interpretations of security.

Actually, it is rather strange when somebody denies the importance of existential security. I suspect that only those whose security has never been in jeopardy can do it.

The Hungarian poet János Arany writes somewhere that "happiness" can come simply from "the absence of suffering." By way of analogy, I would say that security is the absence of anxiety. A child cannot rid itself of its more elemental anxieties. It cannot develop properly if it lacks the mother or at least a permanent, security-giving care-provider stepping in her place. We can feel anxious over the health or life of our loved ones (or of ourselves), over the stability of our relations with people, over the risks of losing much of what we have, or over the opportunity to secure our everyday bread. All of these—applying Freud's conceptual system—are real anxieties (that is, not pathological or neurotic symptoms); it is always painful to experience them. "... The kind of situation in which anxiety arises naturally largely depends on the degree of our knowledge, and on how powerful we consider ourselves in relation to the outside world." Realistic anxiety is, however—Freud continues—neither rational nor expedient because "it paralyzes all action...." It would be expedient, rather, "to size up coolly one's own strengths in comparison with the magnitude of the threat, and then to decide whether to escape or defend ourselves, or perhaps an attack itself would provide more chance for everything to end well" (Freud 1986, p. 321).

The problem is that in the case of a good part of our realistic anxieties our knowledge cannot be adequate. For instance, there may be no cure for the illnesses we are afraid of. But it may also be that the knowledge which could help build up the necessary protection is missing only in some (or many) individuals or groups and that this ignorance is not distributed at random across society. Similarly, for many, the problem is not that they "feel" powerless but that they are genuinely powerless in relation to the outside world. When knowledge and power are absent, then there is practically no opportunity for an escape, defense, or attack, by means of which "things could turn out well." After all, drinks and drugs and "subsistence crime," that is crime to make ends meet, are all forms of escape, but their consequences are neither rational nor expedient.

For the majority of socially "real" paralyzing anxieties there have always been expedient solutions. When (with the advent of capitalism) the former agents of security—such as the family, the locality, the church, or the whole system of feudal privileges, bonds and obligations—weakened, new institutions emerged. The most important ones were the insurance companies. These risk-sharing communities have their roots in the middle ages, and spread alongside capitalism, both as market ventures and as associations of mutual help.

Every form of insurance serves to avert material losses, that is, to provide material security. One of the important developments, "invented" at the end of the last century, is social insurance itself. The market failures of the insurance market (Barr 1990, 1994), and the financial weakness of the small solidaristic communities, made imperative the creation of an institution in which the state assumes some responsibility in handling the risks. Indeed, social insurance is a societal response to the new anxieties about income losses connected with industrialization. Anxiety over inability to pay for medical care brought into being state health care provision systems, or similar insurance-type solutions. All these systems, collectively called social security, developed to a high level in Western European welfare states.

SECURITY AND THE WELFARE STATE: QUESTION MARKS

The welfare state always had opponents. Since the mid-seventies theoretical writings as well as practical policies bear witness to a series of onslaughts, initially timid, then increasingly aggressive, against the welfare state. Admittedly, the impact of these onslaughts has barely been discernible on welfare expenditures, whose real value is continuously increasing in most countries. Ratios, too, have changed favorably for welfare since 1975 or 1980 (OECD 1994). Up until the most recent years, these attacks were mainly based on the adverse impact, as it were, of social policy on the economy. To this was added the accusation—going back to the debates in the late nineteenth century—that excessive security undermines morals, divesting people of their independence (e.g., Hatzfeld 1971; Ferge 1986). In recent years, this has been accompanied with the allegation that security (paternalism) is irreconcilable with freedom.

Here I cannot address the economic arguments in detail; a host of books and studies have already dealt with this (Korpi 1985; Castles 1988; Pfaller et al. 1991; Pierson 1992). I would merely note that the genuine cause of the economic attacks is probably different from the avowed one. Although the GDP continues to rise in practically all the advanced market economies (OECD 1993), the pace of economic growth has slowed down. Also, international competition is becoming fiercer. Thus, the former situation, whereby everyone in the society could gain despite the increasing centralization of incomes by the welfare state, cannot be upheld any more. If social policy were to markedly increase its resources (e.g., to the extent justified by action to combat protracted unemployment and poverty on the rise), those with a good income position ought to make genuine sacrifices. These are—understandably, maybe—resisted. Another important reason for the diminishing efforts to improve or uphold welfare standards in the West is that the "social policy contest" between the two world systems became meaningless upon the collapse of the Eastern Bloc.

Regarding accusations concerning paternalism, these provide food for thought. Paternalism has at least two faces. A paternalistic higher power "takes care" of those under its authority—of its subjects—without the latter having any say. The higher power makes them happy even against their own will. In other words, paternalism as unchallenged authority is anti-democratic. The other side of the coin is that one may think of a kind of benevolent paternalism, implying that—even if undemocratically—the higher power does provide basic securities. One may ask whether state paternalism is inevitably antidemocratic? Or, whether non-state benevolence necessarily avoids anti-democratic paternalism? And of course, in a more general way, one has to ask whether basic securities indeed undermine moral strength.

If we affirm that state paternalism is inevitably non-democratic, this practically amounts to saying that the state in general cannot operate democratically. This danger is indubitably great. Even in a smoothly functioning parliamentary democracy, many operations of the government are hidden from the public and the control of citizens over the state is often weak. Welfare bureaucracies, whose clients belong to the most deprived and least vocal groups, may be specifically prone to non-democratic practices (Niskanen 1973). However, efforts toward decentralization, toward self-government and local community solutions (the growing role of citizens organizations in initiation and control) can significantly reduce these dangers (Culpitt 1992; Donnison 1991).

Paternalism is not a specific feature of state benevolence. Private charity is certainly not immune to this problem. Curiously enough, neo-liberals and conservatives who wish to minimize the state's role do not reject all forms of paternalism out of hand. Neo-conservatism (including the Catholic Church) over-emphasizes the benefits and beauties of family paternalism. After all, focusing on maternity as a vocation, advocating motherhood as a full-time occupation can hardly have a consequence other than the father becoming the family's provider. It is the father who takes care of his family. Neo-liberalism stands up for the rights of women and speaks out against the authoritarian family. Having said that, it nonetheless finds nothing objectionable in certain forms of entrepreneurial paternalism, namely the pension or health funds set up by companies. These are not the mutuality-type insurance funds widespread in France which can operate totally democratically. Company insurance schemes are less democratic: monitoring the rules of operation and the control over the investment of capitalized contributions is usually not possible. Frequently, company management even decides who can join these schemes. ("Less important" or uneducated employees, for example, are often not covered under these insurance schemes. OECD 1993.) Similarly, the New Right often emphasizes without reservation the advantages of private charity. Indeed, it is often recommended that public social policy, or at least social assistance, be replaced by private charity. Perhaps there is no particular need to prove that private donations are "more paternalistic" or that they lay greater emphasis on the hierarchical superiority of the donor and create greater vulnerability than social insurance provision or even modern statutory (predictable, subject to legal redress) state/local authority social assistance. In the case of the latter—even if they do not function democratically—at least the warmhearted donors do not expect humble gratitude. In fact, private charity cannot assure rights (entitlements) and guarantees or controls of any type. Without these, modern citizenship is devoid of sense. My objections to undemocratic paternalism cannot, incidentally, be extended to self-help organizations that come into being upon genuine citizen initiative. "Unfortunately," they cannot be mandatorily established everywhere, that is, they cannot replace, they can only complement, state-managed provision.

The positive aspect of paternalism is the provision of security. The question now is whether security of livelihood is of itself destructive to character, reducing the citizen into the status of the child, whether it is really irreconcilable with the free choice of one's own fate, with free decisions, or, generally speaking, with freedom.

THE NEGATIVE AND POSITIVE IMPACT OF EXISTENTIAL SECURITY

I do not deal with precapitalist societies in which every kind of paternalism—ranging from the "pater familias" through Church charity to the feudal lord's "noblesse oblige" obligations—was considered "natural." These mechanisms assured—theoretically at least—that the needy were taken care of from the cradle to the grave, albeit on a rather modest level.

In modern market economies, and especially in the welfare states, the main components of social security are social insurance, social assistance and social services. Some brief comments are in place concerning their paternalism or their relationship to democracy. It seems to me that:

- their emergence in the West, or at least their post-Second World War development, was in harmony with the democratic rules of the game, that is, it is hard to accuse them of authoritarian paternalism;

- once institutionalized, they may easily develop unfavorable traits. In the absence of active societal control, sooner or later any system may become bureaucratic, turning from service provider into a higher authority. In addition, social assistance, which can never totally rid itself of the negative traits of paternalism, often constrains the individual or the family into a situation where they give up all effort to improve their own fate;
- existential security may instill idleness or imprudence—both in the rich and the poor;
- and finally, if we take democracy seriously, then what citizens think about legally guaranteed existential security cannot be disregarded. Despite the intensive onslaughts on the welfare state over the past 15 years, the majority of people still consider security-providing systems indispensable, indeed they believe these systems should be further developed.

Public commitment notwithstanding, all the components of the developed welfare state are under continued criticism. The social insurance schemes seldom invite the accusation of being of a destructive character, since one of their important constituents is the "purchased right" to benefits, an eminently market-conform arrangement. Indeed, the reform proposals of the New Right concerning social insurance rarely recommend its abolition. Rather, they advocate modifications such as minimization of its compulsory level, restrictions on eligibility, a switch from a pay-as-you-go to a funded system, and the privatization of the already accumulated funds (e.g., Fox 1994). A further proposal is the possibility of contracting out from the compulsory system which may fundamentally alter the societal, solidaristic character of social insurance. The Chilean scheme implementing most of these proposals has a mixed record (Barr 1994, pp. 221-223).

As for in-kind services—nurseries, schools, health care—recommendations for marketization are frequent. The aim is to restrict state responsibility to the financially insolvent, the rest providing for their own provision with or without private insurance. (For a recommendation to transform Eastern European health care systems in this manner, see, e.g., Ehrlich-Révész 1993: World Bank 1994.)

The above proposals concerning social insurance and services reduce either eligibility, or the level of service provision, or both. The intended effect is to increase the individual's responsibility for him-herself, and his/her freedom of choice. The question is what will happen to the minority or majority who do not have the means to join a non-compulsory scheme. Indeed, many of the poor have the utmost difficulty to make ends meet today. It is unrealistic to expect from them to save money for long-term goals voluntarily. The probable consequence of lowering the standards of the compulsory schemes and of marketizing services is the appearance of a two-tier system (one paying, one for the poor), the squeezing out of many from one or more systems of provision, and—perhaps most importantly—the emergence of a large-scale old-age poverty (Korpi-Palme 1994).

Unlike social insurance, social assistance has many imperfections which in fact entail negative moral and social consequences on a large scale. Abuses are widespread—the only question being whether the loss of society on this score is as high as the loss incurred from other kinds of abuse. Tax fraud, for example, breeds less prejudice against the well-to-do than assistance-abuse breeds against the poor. The unemployment (or poverty) trap is a well-known negative consequence which implies that there is no incentive to improve one's situation by his/her effort. What the state budget can gain from the withdrawal of the assistance may be less than its loss. The unemployed are interested in receiving assistance and, simultaneously, engaging in the black economy—a practice detrimental for fiscal policy and for the moral stance of both employees and employers. If one knows that the majority of the unemployed cannot count on "good" jobs, it is not only worthwhile to ask why some prefer to live on social assistance rather than work, but also why so many people accept tough and badly paid jobs instead of trying to live on assistance. (See also Hirschman 1991.) Interestingly enough, despite the genuine "moral hazards" of social assistance, and despite the fact that this is a kind of benefit which is the farthest removed from any market logic, it seems to be more acceptable for the New Right than any other form of social benefits.

To come back to our central question: does security really harm freedom, does it deprive me of choosing my own fate? It is indeed possible to abdicate one's right to decision making, either voluntarily or under constraint. Existing socialism did divest its subjects of many kinds of freedoms. It prohibited the freedom of enterprise, of thought, of movement and of association, together with other civic or political freedoms; it also severely limited the freedom to choose a school, a vocation, the type of house one could build, often going as far as to limit the choice of such trifles as a hairdo or jeans. It also imposed severe constraints, starting with the constraint of compulsory engagement in paid employment. These lacks of freedom were, however, not caused by the welfare provisions.

I emphatically deny that the society's "prison character" was due to existential security. Firstly, it has to be made clear that social policy provisions "from cradle to grave" never existed. The principle of "they who do not work should not eat" was strictly enforced, leaving, for instance, the unemployed (who always existed, even if their number was low) without any provision whatsoever. Also, in the event of a host of misfortunes—low wages or unemployment entailing poverty, homelessness, home care for the permanently ill or disabled, all sorts of distress—no state help was available (social work and social assistance being absent). Secondly, the anti-democratic character of social policy, ranging from its non-participatory operation to some built-in constraints (such as the fact that access to benefits was linked to employment), was the effect rather than the cause of the lack of freedom.

It may occur, even under democratic conditions, that one accepts the curtailment of some freedoms. I guess that, in this case, there is a trade-off. If social insurance is compulsory, then the "social contract" once concluded binds everybody in a given moment. Since it cannot be reviewed too often, the commitment may also affect those who had not, indeed could not, participate in hammering out the contract. This is, no doubt, a loss of freedom, even if in a democratic regime the loss may be controlled, or the bargain renewed. The voluntary abdication of (some degree of) freedom is countered by more existential security, sometimes on a high level. Since this is a mostly voluntary trade-off, it is worthwhile to look into what is gained.

Existential security appears to mean that it is not necessary to perpetually obey the existential constraints of the moment in choosing a job, a school, a home, or the next meal. It means that children's life course can be mapped out and prepared for in the best possible way. It means that in every respect individual and family autonomy grows, in shaping lifestyles or in choosing a life-path. It means that life is less anxiety-ridden. Existential security provides an opportunity (and perhaps only this provides an opportunity) for the realization and development of individual abilities, for the conscious planning of life. To put it into less high-flown terms: if I do not know whether I will still have my job tomorrow, or whether I will be able to repay my loans, how can I start building a home, buying furniture, or educating my children for a long period of time?

Existential security—security of income, security of housing, security of health care—are definitely freedom-enhancing. By comparison, the obligation to pay taxes or social contributions are a rather small price. Were this not so, why would the best-off strata have always aspired to buttress their own, their family's and their children's security on all sides with property or individual or other forms of insurance, and why, despite all counter-propaganda, do existing welfare systems in the West resist the attacks? True, certain members of the society turn out to be wastrels. However, if in any walk of life we look at the successful—entrepreneurs or scientists, doctors or politicians, or even quite a few of artists and athletes—then we shall find that the majority succeeded because they profited from the freedoms of choice underpinned by lasting security. No doubt, affluence has turned some into weaklings and has demoralized them. But the chances that people's lives may go wrong seems incomparably greater at society's opposite pole.

The other pole—poverty—has survived in practically all the welfare states, sometimes to a high degree, and it is now on the increase almost everywhere. In the majority of countries, rural poverty used to be such a deep-rooted tradition that the village poor were mostly resigned to suffering fatal poverty and insecurity of existence in a submissive way. The majority of the urban poor (or rural poverty without rural traditions) can only adapt to the unpredictable and the uncertain in a different manner. What is (rightly or wrongly) called the culture of poverty, includes among other things the abdication of long-term rationality in the choice of ways of life (including schooling for the children, the choice of a profession, etc.)—because the probability of the realization of such plans is so low that it makes planning irrational. Instead, the desire for immediate gratifications, and, on occasion, the acceptance of deviancy as a way out of the unacceptable (alcohol, certain type of crimes), offer "rational" strategies of survival and of making life worth living at least for the brief moments of satisfaction.

Whether we need to speak in this context of character weakness or only of life strategies chosen under constraint can be a matter for individual judgment. It is, however, certain that the behaviors and life strategies thus emerging do not fit in with the rationality of a market economy. In these marginal situations, the property (of others) may not be regarded as sacrosanct and contracts are not necessarily respected.

THE EVALUATION OF FREEDOM AND SECURITY BY THE PUBLIC

People mostly value what they do not have—but they seldom aspire to the impossible or the unknown. Under state socialism, citizens responded to the lack of civic liberties in different ways. Many, albeit probably not a majority, gave up their demand for more freedom. However, a sort of "fight for freedom" was never abandoned and found most diversified forms of expression ranging from films or novels with coded messages, through diverse forms of gray and black economies, to genuine illegal oppositions producing "samizdats." After 1989, previously suppressed or repressed feelings, thoughts and attitudes were liberated.

From the perspective of our topic, there was a significant change in the open endorsement of the value of freedom. It was only after 1989 that citizens realized what the state's intervention into private life—regarded for a long time as natural—had previously meant. The ratio of those in Hungary who thought that "the state should not interfere with the private life of people" has jumped from 50 to 80 percent. There is a smaller, but significant increase in the ratio of those who consider that "the free association of people for protecting their interests" is important. Since about ninety per cent of citizens regarded security under both the previous and the new regimes being of maximum importance, the change in this field was much less marked (see Table 1, Simon 1993).

For many, the positive experience of gaining freedoms cannot offset the crumbling of existential security. The majority of citizens do not accept the withdrawal of the state. It is strongly felt that the state should not give up its responsibilities for social and cultural matters—especially under the conditions of an economic crisis and massive impoverishment. Thus, for instance, in surveys conducted

Table 1. Rank Order of 12 Social Values Index Points on a Scale of 100

How important is it in life that:	*1985*	*1989*	*1991*	*1985-1991*
People can freely tell their opinion	79	83	88	9
Are not exposed to authorities' will	69	80	90	21
Everybody can have a say in public matters	62	61	76	14
The state does not interfere with people' private life	50	66	84	34
People can freely establish organizations to defend their interests	49	57	77	28
People can live without worries	93	93	94	
All people can work	90	90	93	3
People are well-off	86	86	90	4
People can learn, accede to culture	85	86	91	6
People are equal	72	72	83	11
People can have rest, entertainment	71	76	84	13
There are no great income differences	65	65	90	25

Source: Simon (1993).

in 1990 and in 1991, 96 percent of respondents claimed that the state should provide everybody with health care provision; 88 percent called for universal education (state-provided, free of charge); 81 percent regarded it the state's responsibility to reduce income inequalities; and 89 percent believed it to be the state's duty to ensure jobs for all (Sági 1993). The demand for state responsibility has been growing in the course of the transition. This can be illustrated by opinions related to family allowance. 25 percent of respondents in a 1984 survey believed that child care was entirely the parents' duty. By 1993, this ratio dropped to 5 percent. The ratio of those, however, who hold that society (the state) ought to contribute as much or even more than parents to the cost of child raising has increased from 28 to 55 percent (see Table 2, Nagy 1993).

Table 2. Who Should Cover the Costs of Children?

	1982	*1984*	*1987*	*1993*
Parents alone	19	25	18	5
Mainly parents, but to some extent also society (state)	50	47	47	34
Parents and society should share equally	24	23	27	48
Mainly society, but to some extent also the parents	3	2	2	6
Society exclusively	1	1	1	1
Others and N.A.	3	3	5	5
Total	100	100	100	100

Source: Nagy (1993).

A panel study (directed by the present author) throws some more light on the attitudes toward freedom and security.[1]

The subjective importance of existential security grew rapidly between 1991 and 1992. Thus, for instance, to an open question as to what good and bad things had happened in the country during the past period, 10 percent of the respondents in 1991, and 43 percent of the same respondents in 1992 said that insecurity of livelihood had increased.

Appraisal of both freedoms and securities continues to be high, but the importance attached to security is significantly higher than that of freedom both in 1992 and in 1993 (compare Tables 3a and 3b). The means for instance (always on a scale of 7 grades) range between 3.6 and 6 in case of freedoms, while securities, with one exception, are near the maximum figure of 7.

The difference in appraisal becomes particularly marked when the distribution of opinions is examined. Securities were regarded as enormously important almost unanimously. (The overwhelming majority, 84-92 percent indicated the top mark of 7 on a scale of 7.) In the case of freedoms, fewer respondents used mark 7 (at most 60%), and the number of those who regarded a good many types of freedom as "not important" was not negligible (see Tables 4a and 4b).

Table 3. The Evaluation of Freedoms and Securities
Means Based on a Scale of 7 Grades

	1992 *n = 295*	*1993*	*1993/1992* *n = 735*
3A. How Important are the Various Types of Freedom			
Choice of Style of Life	5.92	6.01	101.5
Freedom of opinion	5.78	5.87	101.6
Freedom of travel	5.78	5.92	102.4
Freedom of choice of doctor	5.38	5.52	102.6
Freedom to own property	5.38	5.33	99.1
Freedom of enterprise	5.38	5.45	101.3
Freedom of press	5.35	5.51	103.0
Political freedom	4.98	5.07	101.8
Freedom of religion	4.33	4.42	102.1
Freedom of association	4.28	4.36	101.9
Freedom of forming political parties	3.60	3.57	99.2
(In decreasing order of means in 1992, not following the order of the questionnaire)			
3B. How Important are the Various Types of Security			
Housing Security	6.83	6.86	100.4
Security of family life	6.80	6.86	100.9
Security of the future of children	6.77	6.82	100.7
Economic (financial) security	6.72	6.70	99.7
Job security (only active)	6.82	6.73	98.7
Security of health care	6.69	6.70	100.1
Calculability of politics	5.47	5.48	100.2
3C. To What Extent Do Various Types of Security Exist			
Housing security	5.51	5.68	103.1
Security of family life	6.03	6.08	100.8
Security of the future of children	5.22	5.11	97.9
Job security (only active)	3.96	4.51	113.9
Economic (financial) security	3.25	3.58	110.2
Security of health care	3.69	3.96	107.3
Calculability of politics	3.15	3.33	105.7
(In decreasing order of means of 1992, not following the order of the questionnaire)			

Among the less valued freedoms is, in both years, the freedom to form political parties, which seems to point more to a revulsion from party politicking rather than political indifference. (Other political freedoms are highly valued.) At the same time, a host of freedoms pertaining to the private domain (choice of lifestyle, travel, etc.) scored outstandingly high values, especially among active earners (that is, not pensioners). The significant exception is freedom to own

Table 4. The Evaluation of Freedoms and Securities
The Percentage of Those Choosing the Extremes in Households
Headed by Active or Inactive Earners

Table 4a. How Important Are the Various Types of Freedom

	Not important at all (1)			Very important (7)		
	Inactive	*Active*	*Together*	*Inactive*	*Active*	*Together*
1992 Autumn, 295 Households						
Style of life	4.7	3.1	3.8	49.2	67.5	59.5
Opinion	6.2	3.7	4.8	54.3	58.6	56.8
Travel	12.2	3.1	7.2	45.0	64.6	56.0
Choice of doctor	3.9	6.8	5.5	41.9	39.8	40.9
Property	9.3	6.9	7.9	38.8	47.5	43.8
Press	10.2	6.8	8.2	43.8	46.9	45.7
Enterprise	18.6	4.9	11.0	38.8	56.2	48.6
Political freedom	20.5	11.9	15.6	37.8	46.9	43.1
Religion	16.0	21.6	19.0	39.7	21.6	29.9
Association	26.2	16.5	20.7	27.0	22.8	24.9
Political parties	35.9	24.4	29.4	17.2	16.9	17.3
1993 Autumn, 735 Households						
Style of life	5.7	2.9	4.0	54.4	68.5	62.8
Opinion	5.6	2.4	3.5	49.7	55.1	52.9
Travel	10.8	4.0	6.8	50.7	64.0	58.6
Choice of doctor	5.9	3.8	4.6	46.2	42.4	43.9
Property	*12.4*	*4.7*	*7.8*	33.9	43.4	39.6
Press	8.8	2.9	5.3	42.8	44.5	43.8
Enterprise Politi-	16.3	5.9	10.1	37.6	53.6	47.2
cal freedom	21.4	11.0	15.2	40.7	44.7	43.1
Religion	16.3	19.7	18.3	36.0	25.4	29.7
Association	25.9	12.4	17.8	20.6	24.1	22.7
Political parties	35.4	24.6	29.0	17.5	13.4	15.1

Table 4b. How Important Are the Various Types of Security

	Not important at all (1)			Very important (7)		
	Inactive	*Active*	*Together*	*Inactive*	*Active*	*Together*
1992 Autumn, 295 Households						
Housing	0.8	0.0	0.3	87.9	94.4	91.5
Family life	3.0	0.0	1.4	85.6	95.3	91.5
Future of children	2.6	0.0	1.1	84.5	94.3	90.1
Economic sec.	1.5	0.0	0.7	81.8	88.9	85.8
Job security	*	1.6	*	*	89.2	*
Health care	1.5	0.0	0.7	80.3	86.4	83.7
Politics	2.5	7.5	9.7	47.7	55.9	52.1

(*continued*)

Table 4b. (*Continued*)

	Not important at all (1)			Very important (7)		
	Inactive	*Active*	*Together*	*Inactive*	*Active*	*Together*
	1993 Autumn, 735 Households					
Housing	0.0	0.0	0.0	89.6	91.2	90.6
Family life	0.0	0.2	0.1	87.7	93.3	91.1
Future of children	2.1	0.5	1.1	88.1	92.7	91.0
Economic sec.	0.0	0.0	0.0	79.9	85.2	81.4
Job security	*	15.3	*	*	83.8	*
Health care	0.0	0.0	0.0	82.4	80.3	81.2
Politics	13.2	6.8	9.4	43.9	47.0	45.7

Table 4c. To What Extent Do Various Types of Security Exist

	Not important at all (1)			Very important (7)		
	Inactive	*Active*	*Together*	*Inactive*	*Active*	*Together*
	1992 Autumn, 295 Households					
Housing	4.5	7.4	6.1	57.6	46.9	51.7
Family life	4.6	1.2	2.7	60.3	59.3	59.9
Future of children	1.6	3.8	2.8	41.1	30.0	34.8
Economic sec.	18.9	16.8	17.7	8.3	3.1	5.8
Job security	*	18.6	*	*	16.6	*
Health care	17.1	19.1	18.2	13.5	8.6	11.0
Politics	20.8	27.9	24.6	9.2	8.2	8.6
	1993 Autumn, 735 Households					
Housing	1.7	4.7	3.5	56.4	45.9	50.1
Family life	1.8	1.7	1.7	60.4	58.2	59.1
Future of children	1.4	1.9	1.7	31.3	24.4	27.2
Economic sec.	12.5	9.5	10.7	5.9	3.8	4.6
Job security	*	10.1	*	*	17.1	*
Health care	9.6	11.8	10.9	13.0	8.6	10.3
Politics	19.6	16.7	17.8	5.5	6.1	5.9

property—which even slightly decreased. Even though the differences between the two years are not significant, the importance of private freedoms increased slightly more than that of political ones.

The majority perceives the erosion of securities, although not to the same extent in every instance. Strongest is the faith in family security which belongs to the domain of private life and which is little

Table 5. The Comparison of the Importance of Security and Felt Degree of Security 1992-1993

	1992			*1993*		
	Importance (1)	*Felt Degree (2)*	*2/1 (3)*	*Importance (4)*	*Felt Degree (5)*	*5/4 (6)*
Housing security	6.83	5.51	80.7	6.86	5.68	82.8
Security of family life	6.80	6.03	88.7	6.86	6.08	88.6
Security of the future of children	6.77	5.22	77.1	6.82	5.11	74.9
Economic (financial) security	6.72	3.96	58.9	6.70	4.51	67.3
Job security (only active)	6.82	3.25	47.7	6.73	3.58	53.2
Security of health care	6.69	3.69	55.2	6.70	3.96	58.2
Calculability of politics	5.47	3.15	57.6	5.48	3.33	60.8

affected directly by politics. In addition, in both years, people perceived housing and children's future as relatively secure. At the same time, that is in the third year after 1989, people experienced financial and job security as being most threatened. It is important to note that there is a slight increase in optimism concerning securities—with the significant exception of trust in children's future (see Table 5).

Opinions and values are influenced by innumerable factors. The impact of the social situation (age, gender, type of work, school qualifications, etc.) is seldom perceivable directly with significant force. By involving a few more subjective variables, far more can be explained from the total diversity of opinions. Thus, for instance, the feeling of poverty, the feeling of existential insecurity, and so forth, sometimes reveals more about the appraisal of freedom and security than do the "hard" background data (the results of the multivariate analyses are not presented).

Instead of a summary, let me add a post-script in the wake of the Hungarian elections in 1994. The prehistory of Western welfare systems was an ongoing struggle for security. Against the acquired securities, a frontal offensive is presently underway, not only in the East, but also in numerous traditional Western welfare states. It appears that the majority of citizens do not agree with the undermining of their securities. The most elemental conclusion from this is that if the neo-socialist governments in Eastern Europe want not only to acquire legitimacy, but also to retain it, then they cannot disregard the citizens' will in this respect.

NOTE

1. The panel started in 1991, only among urban households with a random sample of 1000. In 1992, we returned only to 300 households, and in 1993 to the whole sample. In 1993, only 735 households could be found from the original 1000. The tables present the results for the 295 households in 1992 and the 735 in 1993. We calculated the results also for the comparable 280 households between 1992 and 1993. The results are almost similar to that of the whole sample, and therefore we preferred to show the data for the whole sample which are more reliable.

REFERENCES

Ambros, P. 1994. "Szabadság Vagy Biztonság (Freedom or Security). *Magyar Lettre Internationale*, Spring.

Barr, N. 1987a. *The Economics of the Welfare State.* London: Weidenfeld and Nicolson.

———. ed. 1994. *Labor Markets and Social Policy in Central and Eastern Europe. The Transition and Beyond.* Oxford: Oxford University Press.

Castles, F.G., and S. Dowrick. 1988. *The Impact of Government Spending Levels on Medium-Term Economic Growth in the OECD, 1960-1986.* Discussion Paper. Canberra: The Australian National University, Centre for Economic Policy Research.

Culpitt, I. 1992. *Welfare and Citizenship. Beyond the Crisis of the Welfare State?* London: Sage.

Dahrendorf, R. 1969. "The Nature and Types of Social Inequality." In *Social Inequality*, edited by A. Beteille. Harmondsworth, Middlesex: Penguin

Donnison, D. 1984. "Social Policy: An Egalitarian View." *Community Care* (October 11).

Donnison, D. 1991. *A Radical Agenda. After the New Right and the Old Left.* London: Rivers Oram Press.

Ehrlich, E., and G. Révész 1993. *Present and Feasible Future in Hungary.* Prepared in the framework of "Eastern and Central Europe 2000." Project, First draft, September.

Fekete, G. 1993. "Contribution to the Social Insurance Debate in the Hungarian Journal." *Társadalmi Szemle* (Social Review), 11.

Ferge, Z. 1969. *Társadalmunk Rétegződése* (The Stratification of Hungarian Society). Közgazdasági és Jogi Kiadó

_______. 1986. *Fejezetek a Magyar Szegénypolitika Történetéből* (Chapters from the History of Hungarian Politics of Poverty). Budapest: Magvetö.

Fox, L. 1994. "What To Do about Pensions in Transition Economies?" *Transition*, 5(2-30.

Freud, S. 1986. *Introduction to Psychoanalysis* (in Hungarian). Budapest: Gondolat.

Hatzfeld, H. 1971. *Du Paupérisme... la Securité Sociale*. Paris: Librairie Armand Colin.

Kis, J. 1992. *Erkölcs, Hit, Tolerancia* (Morality, Faith, Tolerance). Kritika.

Korpi, W. 1985. "Economic Growth and the Welfare State: Leaky Bucket or Irrigation System?" *European Sociological Review* 1(2).

Korpi, W., and J. Palme. 1994. *The Strategy of Equality and the Paradox of Redistribution*. Stockholm: Swedish Institute for Social Research.

Kuron, J. 1993. "Soziale Gerechtigkeit als Soziale Bewegung." *Transit* (6).

Nagy, L.G. 1993. *Változások a Szociálpolitikai Kérdések Megitéléseben, 1982-1993* (Changes in the Appraisal of Social Policy Issues, 1982-1993). Based on the data of the Hungarian Gallup Institute. Budapest. Compiled with the support of the ATA Foundation.

Niskanen, W. 1973. *Bureaucracy: Servant or Master?* London: Institute of Economic Affairs.

OECD. 1993. *National Accounts*. Paris: OECD.

OECD. 1994. "New Orientation for Social Policy." *Social Policy Studies* No. 12. Paris: OECD.

Pfaller, A., I. Gough, and G. Therborn. 1991. *Can the Welfare State Compete?* Macmillan.

Pierson, C. 1992. *Beyond the Welfare State? The New Political Economy of the Welfare State*. Cambridge-Oxford: Polity Press.

Rawls, H. 1971. *A Theory of Justice*. Cambridge, MA: The Belknap Press of Harvard University Press.

Sági, M., and P. Robert 1993. *Dismantling the Welfare State. [How the Welfare State Discards its Responsibilities.]* Paper prepared for the European Research Conference on from European Societies to European Society: the national welfare states and European Integration. St. Martin, Germany, November 22-26.

Sen, A. 1990. "Individual Freedom as Social Commitment." *The New York Book Review* (June 14).

Simon, J. 1993. "Post-paternalist Political Culture in Hungary: Relationship Between Citizens and Politics During and After the 'Melancholic Revolution'." *Communist and Post-Communist Studies* XXVI(2).

World Bank. 1994. *Reform Issues in Social Policy*. Unpublished Manuscript.

IN SEARCH OF EXPLANATIONS FOR RECENT LEFT-TURNS IN POST-COMMUNIST COUNTRIES

Petr Matějů

INTRODUCTION

The results of the September 1993 parliamentary elections in Poland were striking to many observers of social and political developments in post-communist countries. Although in the case of Poland the label "left-turn"—a label both journalists and political scientists tend to attach to the electoral success of left-wing political parties in some post-communist countries—may not be entirely appropriate,[1] it seems far more suitable for the outcomes of the Hungarian parliamentary elections held in May 1994, as well as for the December 1994 election victory of post-communists in Bulgaria.[2]

What is more, Poland, Hungary, and Bulgaria are not alone in turning left. If we look at recent political developments in some other post-communist countries, we see a similar picture. The Ukrainian

International Review of Comparative Public Policy,
Volume 7, pages 43-82.

ISBN: 0-7623-0153-8

elections of April 1993 returned communists and their allies to the parliament as the largest bloc, while the Lithuanian former Communist Party, after transforming itself into the Democratic Labor Party, recently returned to power as the leading party. The October 1994 elections in Slovakia brought victory to a party with quite a strong anti-reform and nationalist orientation ("Movement for Democratic Slovakia"), which was able to create a government coalition from two parties operating at the peripheries of the political spectrum: one from the extreme left (Marxist) and the other from the extreme right (nationalist). These events may indicate that an emerging trend in post-com munist countries is the return to power of former communist parties, their successors and their allies.

Our intent here is not to analyze the political mechanisms behind the individual left-turns, nor to speculate about their potential political and economic consequences. Instead, we attempt to contribute to a sociological understanding on a broader theoretical level of social change in formerly communist countries. The principal objective of this chapter is to examine the social causes of the increasing preference of voters for left political parties. The central thesis of the chapter is that besides specific historical, economic and political circumstances, the left-turns in post-communist countries share common ground in the increasing social costs of the transformation and the challenged legitimacy of the growing socio-economic inequality.

We propose that *subjective* factors of social stratification are more important in explaining the "left-turns" in post-communist countries than the *objective* criteria of location in the class structure. In other words, we argue that studying *relative* social and economic deprivation and the perception of change in factors determining life-success may be an important key to better understanding why voters in post-communist countries are increasingly preferring parties of the left.

REFLECTIONS ON RECENT LEFT-TURNS

A popular explanation for the recent left-turns is that voters are responding to the failure of the governments in post-communist countries to redirect the national economies from a protracted decline toward prosperity.[3] In our view, this explanation, although not without some merit, is over-simplified and potentially even misleading.

To understand current political developments in post-communist countries, we must not overlook the great variety of economic, political and social circumstances that led to the establishment of communist regimes in the individual countries, the conditions that caused their collapse and the legacies these regimes left behind. There is no doubt that whether the communist regime was imposed on a relatively advanced capitalist system or on an underdeveloped economy with limited democracy determined the political and economic developments following the collapse (of the communist regime). In the former case, the communist regime interrupted the ongoing modernization process in countries such as the Czech Republic and the GDR, while in the latter case, the era of "building socialism" coincided only with the beginning of postwar modernization (such as in Hungary and Poland). Of equal importance is whether at the time of its collapse, the communist system had already disintegrated (as, for example, in Hungary or Poland) or remained largely unaffected by political democratization and economic liberalization (for example, in Czechoslovakia and East Germany). We may also expect that typical patterns of behavior and responses to profound changes in life-conditions both have deep cultural and religious roots.

To avoid misleading conclusions, it is equally important to understand that the transformation process is governed by "revolutionary simultaneity" rather than "historical causality" (Offe 1991; Sztompka 1992), and that introducing capitalism by "political design" (Offe 1991) necessarily creates unprecedented social and political dilemmas (Sztompka 1992). Thus, we have to be very cautious when applying traditional sociological concepts and theories.

Two issues should be emphasized in this respect. First, the ties between political, economic and social processes are much stronger in societies undergoing deep change than in relatively stable societies. In formerly communist countries, the unusual speed and complexity of changes increases the difficulty of maintaining an accord between the three main dimensions of the transformation (political, economic and social) as well as between the dominant and "off-center" goals at each stage of the transformation. A further complication is that changes in political, economic, and social systems occur with incongruent time scales (Dahrendorf 1990). "What we are facing here," Dahrendorf argued as early as in 1990, "is one of the more vexing issues of modern history, which is the relationship between *political* and *economic* reform, with *social* change thrown in at both ends" (Dahrendorf 1990, p. 82).

Second, the development and perception of inequality is a crucial issue in understanding the socio-economic background of political behavior. A strong link between popular views on inequality and the legitimacy and stability of the political system has been one of the central assumptions in both sociology and political science (see, for example, Della Fave 1986a, 1986b; Habermas 1975; Shepelak 1987; and others). We may assume that if perceptions of inequality and related issues of distributive justice shape the political climate in essentially stable systems, their effect would be even stronger in post-communist countries.

In this respect, three issues seem to be crucial: (a) the trans formation of a dominant distributive ideology (Matějů 1993a; Kluegel and Matějů 1995), (b) the effect of one's social position on attitudes toward inequality (Kluegel and Smith 1986) and (c) the perception of factors generating socio-economic inequality and its growth (Wnuk-Lipinski 1992).

Regarding the role of the dominant distributive ideology, we may assume that in relatively stable systems, beliefs about inequality and distributive justice stem from the well-crystallized dominant distributive ideology (Huber and Form 1973; Kluegel and Smith 1986). In post-communist countries, the formerly dominant distributive ideology that had originated in the *egalitarian* interpretation of distributive justice and re-distributive practices is being substituted by a new dominant distributive ideology based on an *inegalitarian* and meritocratic interpretation of distributive justice. The transition between the two ideologies strengthens the tendency to confound different normative elements in the subjective evaluation of growing inequality and distributive justice (Matějů 1993a; Kluegel and Matějů 1995). This creates a social base for political instability, since people can easily succumb to election campaigns that appeal to conflicting attitudes toward inequality and distributive justice.

Another source of potential instability in attitudes toward inequality in post-communist countries are the changes in the social structures of these societies. At least two processes are relevant in this respect: (a) intragenerational mobility specific to a profound social transformation (Matějů 1993b; Matějů and Řeháková 1993) and (b) changes in the relevant attributes of occupations caused by the transformation of normative principles of social stratification.

Individuals who experience different intragenerational occupational mobility or different changes in their position within relevant social hierarchies (socio-economic status, power, prestige, income, life-chances, etc.) develop quite different beliefs about inequality and distributive justice. Consequently, extensive intragenerational mobility and changes in social stratification very likely strengthen the link between attitudes toward inequality and one's position in the social structure.

As new economic inequalities become visible and absolute or relative deprivation grow, the subjective interpretation of changes in factors determining life-success becomes an issue of high political potential. From the very beginning of the transformation, there was no doubt that the dismantling of the communist system would mean the loss of the relative advantages of living in an egalitarian and state-paternalist distributive system. At the same time, however, expectations were generated (intentionally or spontaneously) that the newly created system would be based on "equal opportunity" and meritocracy in income and wealth distribution. In other words, people expected that while they might not be rewarded as equally in the new system as in the old, they would have equal opportunity for higher rewards, and they believed that both opportunity and rewards would be more firmly linked to traditional meritocratic criteria such as edu cation, skill, ability and effort.

Unlike the first stage of the post-communist transformation, which was characterized by enormous enthusiasm, high speed and social solidarity, its second stage is generating deep disillusions and high social tensions. It is a time when "the incompatible time scales of political and economic reform become relevant, and each threatens the other" (Dahrendorf 1990, p. 85). At this very stage, the inegalitarian (meritocratic) distributive ideology is supposed to take over from the old (egalitarian) one. Consequently, socio-economic inequality and equal opportunity become central political issues. Since the growth in inequality is accompanied by a general decline in the standard of living (meaning that many people experience both *relative* and *absolute* deprivation), the second stage of the transformation is creating severe contradictions and conflicts, particularly the contradiction between the tasks of implementing market principles and preserving democracy (Offe 1991; Sztompka 1992). The legitimacy of the new system is questioned in particular when people find that it raises both the inequality of reward *and* the inequality of opportunity. Unless the various forms of informal networks and/or political assets strengthen, those who find themselves unable to cope with the consequences of the market reform or who feel disprivileged by the new "rules of the game" are very likely to reject the new inegalitarian ideology. They may become an electorate of political parties offering the restoration of a more egalitarian distributive system.

As shown in the literature, the transition to a new social structure usually causes a crisis of legitimacy, especially if the new system is unable to sustain the expectations raised in the earlier stages of the social change (see, e.g., Lipset 1981). Accordingly, the second stage of the post-communist transformation brings about a *crisis of legitimacy*, especially if the emerging system of inequality does not offer socio-economic success to sufficiently large segments of the population and shows a correlation between economic success and the assets accumulated during the previous regime (political capital, informal networks, etc.). One may ask (a) whether there is a sufficiently strong popular belief that the new system of inequality grows from the principle of equal opportunity, and (b) whether the growing differences in income and wealth have sufficient justification by meritocratic arguments. In other words, the popular acceptance of the increase in inequality largely depends on the compatibility between the growth of inequality and the progress in establishing its link to equal opportunity and meritocracy.[4]

With regard to the theoretical explanations for support of "leftist" politics, the existing literature provides equally convincing arguments for two principal explanations.[5] First of all, there is overwhelming evidence from electoral studies that political parties operating on the left side of the political spectrum receive support especially from lower social classes whose members experience higher economic insecurity and, consequently, are strongly affected by the presence or absence of governmental redistributive policies. Since redistributive policies are a part of the agenda of most parties on the political left, both individuals with lower education and members of the working class are more likely to support the left. One of the most recent sociological analyses of data from electoral studies addressing this particular issue (Heath 1990) shows that, indeed, "objective class" predicts voting preferences for the left quite sharply. In fact it shows that in Britain the logit coefficients for a vote for the Labor Party range from −.35 among professionals and higher controllers to 0.41

among the working class and do not change even after controlling for earned income (Heath 1990, p. 169).

Besides the evidence supporting the idea that "objective class" has a strong effect on left-voting, there is equally convincing support—both theoretical and empirical—for the thesis that left-voting is a typical political reaction to *relative social deprivation*, stemming from the perception that the current distributive system produces or maintains illegitimate differences in relative life-chances. There is no reason to regard the two theoretical perspectives as mutually exclusive. On the contrary, both provide a relevant theoretical framework for the analysis of voting behavior. A distinction should be made, however, regarding the *relative* explanatory power of each of these perspectives in different social and historical situations: the *objective* parameters of class location might have a stronger impact in a relatively stable system with a well crystallized class structure, while *relative* social deprivation will dominate in systems undergoing deep and rapid change.

In view of these theoretical assumptions, we posit two general theses: First, we suggest that right-wing political parties, that is, the actual "designers" of the market reforms in post-communist countries, lose their electorate if they underestimate the social costs of the transformation and fail to develop comprehensive policies reducing the negative impacts of the transformation on a large segment of the population (that is, increasing the *number* of 'losers').[6] We also argue that support for the "Left" grows if the system fails to provide sufficient evidence that the transformation is opening space for equal opportunity and is not reducing the space for the operation of non-meritocratic mechanisms of economic success (that is, permitting differential and unequal *strategies* for economic success among 'winners'). In other words, under certain circumstances a strong feeling may grow that it would be better to restore an egalitarian system based on centralized redistribution than to allow a highly inegalitarian system based on unequal opportunities. Since political parties on the left traditionally uphold various forms of redistribution aimed at greater equality, such a feeling would lead to their reelection.

Four operational hypotheses may be derived for the analysis:

1. Countries escaping communism differ substantially in the number of individuals who feel *relative* social and economic deprivation.

2. Individuals who feel that the transformation has led to a *relative* deterioration in their social and/or economic position are more likely to vote for the left than people who feel that their relative position in the society has remained unchanged or has improved.
3. Individuals who believe that ascriptive (non-meritocratic) factors and informal (political) ties as factors underlying economic success have increased in importance are more likely to vote for the left than individuals who believe that such factors have been gradually replaced by meritocratic factors of life-success.
4. During the post-communist transformation, the above mentioned "subjective" factors of social stratification play a more important role in determining voting preferences for the left than the traditionally strong "objective" criteria of class location.

THE DATA, VARIABLES, AND DESIGN OF THE ANALYSIS

Data Files

The data analyzed in this paper is drawn from the research project "Social Stratification in Eastern Europe after 1989," namely from "General population surveys" conducted in 1993 in six post-communist countries: Bulgaria, the Czech Republic, Hungary, Poland, Russia and Slovakia.[7] If available, matching variables from other surveys were used to show the change over time.

General population surveys (GPS) were conducted on samples of about 5,000 respondents representative for the population aged from 20 to 69 years. Stratified random sampling was adopted by all participating countries.[8] After weighting that brought the distributions of the most important variables closer to the census data (community size, age, sex, education) and after elimination of respondents of out-of-range ages, national data files have the following number of cases: Bulgaria 4907, the Czech Republic 5620, Hungary 4286, Poland 3520, Russia 4734, and Slovakia 4876.

Dependent Variable

For all nations the question as to which political party the respondent would vote for if elections were held "next Sunday" was

Table 1a. Distributions of Selected Variables (Percentages and Adjusted Residuals*)

	BUL	CZR	HUN	POL	RUS	SLO
CLASS:	Respondent's class position (current or last occupation)					
PROF	18.8	23.2	19.1	20.0	31.2	24.3
	(-7.2)	(0.5)	(-6.4)	(-4.4)	(14.3)	(2.3)
NONM	9.2	15.1	13.5	17.1	11.1	15.4
	(-9.0)	(3.9)	(0.0)	(6.4)	(-5.2)	(4.1)
SELF	3.1	3.7	5.4	7.2	2.0	3.2
	(-2.9)	(-0.8)	(5.1)	(10.5)	(-7.5)	(-2.9)
SKLD	17.7	21.2	24.8	21.0	25.7	24.1
	(-8.2)	(-2.5)	(4.0)	(-2.1)	(5.8)	(3.0)
UNSK	33.0	30.0	28.5	21.2	22.0	24.7
	(10.0)	(5.8)	(2.5)	(-7.8)	(-8.0)	(-3.6)
FARM	18.2	6.8	8.7	13.5	8.0	8.3
	(18.7)	(-9.6)	(-3.5)	(6.6)	(-5.6)	(-4.8)
TYPMOB:	Type of mobility between 1989 and current class position					
PRIV	3.7	7.8	5.0	7.2	1.6	5.4
	(-4.2)	(8.8)	(-0.2)	(5.2)	(-10.3)	(1.0)
UPWD	4.9	6.1	6.1	6.9	7.0	5.3
	(-2.9)	(0.3)	(0.1)	(1.9)	(2.7)	(-1.8)
STAB	57.5	62.7	53.3	62.7	76.4	64.5
	(-7.4)	(-0.7)	(-11.7)	(-0.5)	(17.6)	(1.8)
DOWN	5.2	6.3	5.5	6.0	6.6	5.3
	(-1.8)	(1.5)	(-0.8)	(0.4)	(2.1)	(-1.4)
RETR	15.2	15.3	17.6	7.3	6.8	12.8
	(4.7)	(5.4)	(8.3)	(-8.1)	(-11.4)	(0.1)
UNMP	13.5	1.7	12.5	9.6	1.6	6.6
	(15.9)	(-14.8)	(12.1)	(4.7)	(-13.8)	(-1.4)
CPTEVER:	Ever member of the Communist Party?					
yes	13.5	15.0	10.4	10.9	10.9	14.4
	(1.9)	(5.7)	(-4.8)	(-3.4)	(-4.1)	(3.8)
no	86.5	85.5	89.6	89.1	89.1	85.6
	(-1.9)	(-5.7)	(4.8)	(3.4))	(4.1)	(-3.8)

Notes: See the text for the explanation of categories.
* Adjusted residuals were computed for tables "variable" by COUNTRY.

used to define the dichotomous dependent variable LEFTVOTE classifying respondents in two categories: 1 = would vote for the left political party, 0 = would vote for another political party.[9] Table 1 shows the distribution of a variable VOTE, combining categories of the variable LEFTVOTE (categories "left" and "other") with a variable showing the proportion of people who did not respond to the question or said they would not participate in an

Table 1b. Distributions of Selected Variables (Percentages and Adjusted Residuals)

	BUL	CZR	HUN	POL	RUS	SLO
SUB-SOC:	Perceived change in respondent's position in social status hierarchy between 1989 and 1993.					
downward	64.2	36.6	56.4	46.1	51.0	49.5
	(20.7)	(-22.5)	(8.5)	(-5.3)	(.9)	(-1.4)
no change	27.5	45.9	33.7	34.9	39.6	37.7
	(-14.6)	(15.3)	(-4.7)	(-2.6)	(4.0)	(1.3)
upward	8.2	17.5	9.9	19.0	9.4	12.8
	(-10.1)	(11.7)	(-6.0)	(11.7)	(-7.1)	(0.2)
SUB-INC:	Perceived change in respondent's position in income hierarchy between 1989 and 1993.					
downward	58.8	32.0	42.2	49.5	56.0	41.0
	(19.2)	(-23.1)	(-5.5)	(4.4)	(14.7)	(-7.7)
no change	33.1	52.9	51.0	37.5	34.0	48.0
	(-15.3)	(16.1)	(11.1)	(-7.2)	(-13.7)	(7.4)
upward	8.1	15.1	6.8	13.0	10.0	11.0
	(-6.4)	(11.5)	(-8.9)	(4.5)	(-1.8)	(0.7)
VOTE:	Voting preferences (including potential no-voters).					
left	17.8	10.2	9.8	24.8	3.7	12.8
	(11.8)	(-6.2)	(-6.0)	(23.1)	(-20.4)	(2.2)
other	24.9	46.8	44.8	30.8	36.1	38.5
	(-19.9)	(16.3)	(10.9)	(-8.7)	(-2.0)	(6.7)
no	57.3	43.0	45.4	44.5	60.2	48.6
	(11.4)	(-11.7)	(-6.5)	(-7.0)	(15.5)	(1.9)
LEFTVOTE:	Voting preferences (potential voters only).					
left	41.6	17.9	18.0	44.6	9.2	24.9
	(18.6)	(-10.9)	(-8.9)	(21.2)	(-17.3)	(-0.4)
other	58.4	82.1	82.0	55.4	90.8	75.1
	(-18.6)	(10.9)	(8.9)	(-21.2)	(17.3)	(0.4)
Total	4907	5620	4286	3520	4734	4876

Notes: See the text for the explanation of categories.
* Adjusted residuals were computed for tables "variable" by COUNTRY.

election (NOVOTE). For two countries (the Czech Republic and Slovakia), the variable LEFTVOTE was checked against the answer to the question concerning the respondent's self-placement on a scale representing a left-right political continuum (1 = extreme left, 10 = extreme right). As expected, the two variables reveal a very strong association.[10]

Independent Variables

To assess the effect of class location and mobility between 1988 and 1993, two variables were created: CLASS and TYPMOB. Variable CLASS is a slightly modified version of the EGP class classification scheme.[11] The modification resulted in a six-class analytical scheme: professionals (PROF), routine non-manuals (NONM), self-employed (SELF), manual supervisors and skilled workers (SKLD), semi-skilled and unskilled workers (UNSK) and farm occupations (FARM). Type of mobility (TYPMOB) was created by comparing respondents' class in 1988 and 1993 (using the original nine-category class scheme). All classes except "self-employed" were treated as being in a hierarchical order. For both tech nical and substantial reasons, a move from any class to the category of "self-employed" was coded as a specific type of mobility (with a special relevance in post-communist countries). This operation resulted in six types of mobility: self-employment (PRIV), upward mobility (UPWD), stable (STAB), downward mobility (DOWN). To keep all segments of the population in the analysis (potential voters), we created two special categories for individuals who had no class at the time of the survey but had one in 1988: became retired (RETIR) or unemployed (UNMP). Other independent variables entering into the analysis were: the respondent's age in years (AGE), the respondent's highest completed education categorized to four levels: elementary, vocational, secondary and tertiary (EDUC), and household income (QHSHL) (for comparability categorized in quintiles defined separately for each country). To control for the effect of Communist Party membership, the variable CPTEVER was created, assessing whether the respondent was ever a member of the Communist Party.

To define "losers" and "winners," we used two pairs of variables assessing the subjective interpretation of one's position in two important social hierarchies: in social status and household in come in 1993 and, retrospectively, in 1988.[12] Since identical questions were asked in 1991 in the questionnaire of the "International Social Justice Project," three points in time were available for the analysis.[13] Because the ISJP project also includes Western countries, we may evaluate the distance between "East" and "West" (Germany, the Netherlands and the USA). The distributions of these variables in individual countries in 1988, 1991 and 1993 are displayed in Figures 1 and 2.

For further analyses, two additional variables were defined assessing a change in the respondent's "subjective social status" and "subjective income" between 1988 and 1993. These two variables (SUB-SOC, SUB-INC) have three categories: −1 = a downward shift in the subjective evaluation of the respondent's position on a particular scale, 0 = no change; 1 = an upward shift. Table 1 shows the distribution of the two variables.

In order to assess the effect of beliefs about mechanisms underlying life-success, namely the hypothesized effect of ascription and informal networks, a new variable ASCRIP was created by means of principal component analysis. A set of respondent's evaluations of life-success determinants (wealth, education, ambitions, hard work, informal networks, political connections, risk) in 1988 and 1993 was analyzed. Seven new variables measuring the difference between the 1988 and 1993 evaluations for each determinant were created (see the Appendix for details regarding the questions and construction of the variables). These seven variables entered principal component analyses performed separately for each country as well as on pooled data. As expected, all analyses proved the existence of a factor representing the belief that "ascriptive criteria" (wealth, connec tions, networks) played a stronger role in 1993 than in 1998 (see Factor 2—ASCRIP in the Appendix).

Four other independent variables were defined for analyses: CPTEVER (the respondent's membership in the Communist Party at any time in his or her life), AGE (the respondent's age in years), EDUC (respondent's highest completed education categorized to four levels: elementary, vocational, secondary and tertiary), and QHSHL (household income - for comparability categorized in quintiles defined separately for each country).

Design of the Analysis

Two analytical strategies were chosen to elaborate our four hypotheses empirically. We start with a *descriptive* approach to show the major differences between the compared countries in *potentially* significant *social* causes of voting preference for the "Left": (a) a perceived change in one's position in two important social hierarchies (subjective social status and subjective income); (b) a subjective interpretation of the change in the role of factors underlying life-success (the role of ascription).

We then proceed with an *explanatory* analysis. The same variables used for descriptive cross-national comparisons enter the analyses designed to predict an individual's voting behavior, namely the decision to vote for the "Left." In addition to the variables used for descriptive comparisons (the perceived change in respondent's social status and income, the perceived change in the role of factors underlying life-success), seven other independent variables were included in the explanatory model: class, type of mobility, age, education, household income, Communist Party membership and nation.

Since the dependent variable is dichotomous, we use *binomial logistic regression* to test the effects of individual independent variables on voting behavior. Two equations for binomial logistic regression can be written in general form, one for *log-odds*:

$$\log\left[\frac{p}{1-p}\right] = B_0 + B_1 X_1 \ldots + B_n X_n \qquad (1)$$

another one in term of *odds*:

$$\frac{p}{1-p} = e^{B_o} +^{B_1X_1} + \ldots {}^{B_1X_1} = e^{B_o} e^{B_1 X_1} \cdots e^{B_nX_n} \qquad (2)$$

where p is the probability of casting vote for the left, B_o is the intercept, and B_i is the logistic regression coefficient for the independent variable X_i. For the interpretation we use both logistic regression coefficients (B) and so-called odds multipliers (factors). The *odds multiplier* can be obtained by raising e to the power of B_i (see equation 2); it represents the factor by which the odds change when the jth independent variable increases by one unit. The SPSS logistic regression procedure was applied with a so-called "deviation contrast" for categorical variables (nation, class, type of mobility, change in subjective social status, change in subjective income).[14] Other independent variables in the equation were treated as continuous.

Four nested models were built for testing: a model that includes only "objective' characteristics (nation, age, education, income, class), but excludes the type of mobility (Model I). In the next step, the type of mobility was added to the previous objective dimensions of social standing (Model II). Model III incorporates the entire "subjective" dimension of the respondent's situation, namely his or her perception of a change in social status and income between 1988 and 1993. At this stage, the perception of 'ascription' also entered the analysis. The last model (Model IV) added only the Communist Party membership. The idea behind comparing the last two models (Model III and Model IV) was to establish whether Communist Party membership is an important predictor of voting for the left, and if so, whether it overrides or even nullifies the effects of other independent variables. If we find that party membership significantly overrides the effects of various dimensions of the subjective interpretation of direct consequences of the social transformation for one's position in the society, we may conclude that negative interpretations of the change, which are assumed to increase the probability of voting for the left, are biased evaluations typical among "political losers." If, on the contrary, the effect of Communist Party membership does not eliminate the effects of the variables measuring subjective evaluations of the change, we may conclude that, indeed, there are *direct* political consequences both of the social costs of the transformation and the lack of expected change in determinants of life-success.

The four models were tested both on an international data set (pooled data) and separately for individual countries. The analysis of the international data set was performed to find the general patterns of determination as well as the net effect of nation on voting behavior.

THE RESULTS

The results of the simple descriptive analysis of change in the subjective social status (subjective evaluation of one's position in the social status hierarchy) and subjective income (the evaluation of one's position in the income hierarchy) between 1988 and 1993 are displayed in Figures 1 and 2. These results give a clear picture of the cross-national differences in the development of distributions of the perceived social status and income between 1988 and 1993. Given the elementary theoretical assumption that the feeling of descent within relevant social hierarchies usually results in relative social deprivation, we may read these figures as indirect evidence of the potential social base for egalitarian distributive ideologies and redistributive policies (see, e.g., Fave 1986a, 1986b; Ritzman and

Tomaskovic-Devey 1992). From this point of view two general tendencies have been present in all countries: (a) an overall growth in differentiation (the distributions becoming less concentrated around the mean), (b) an overall shift toward the bottom of the two social hierarchies (subjective social status and subjective income).

However, the dissimilarity between countries has grown. The F-ratio for the differences between country means of subjective social status has increased from 27.3 to 232.9 between 1988 and 1993 (for subjective income, there was a similar increase from 46.4 to 233.7). As shown in Figures 1 and 2, a great deal of the increase in heterogeneity between countries was due to a unique development in the Czech Republic, where the differentiation process has not produced such a strong feeling of relative deterioration in life-conditions as in other post-communist countries.[15]

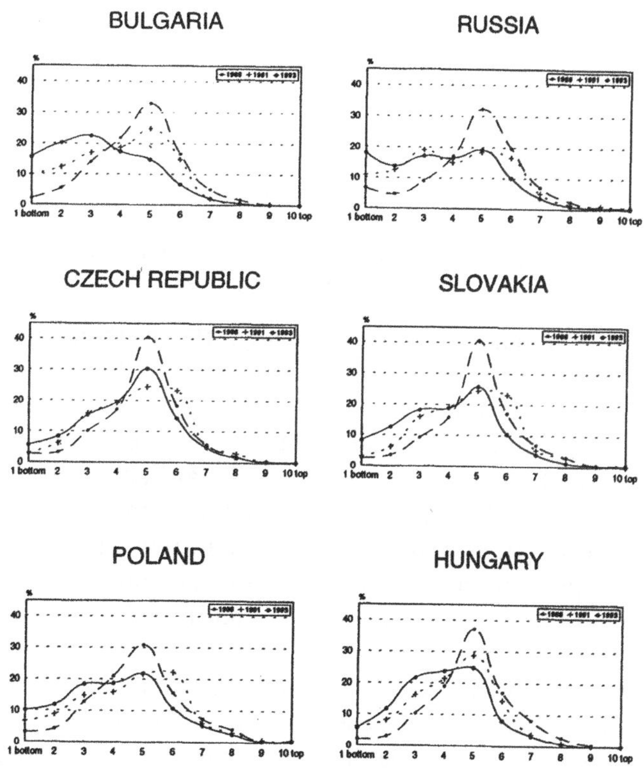

Figure 1. Distribution of Subjective Social Status in 1988, 1991, and 1993

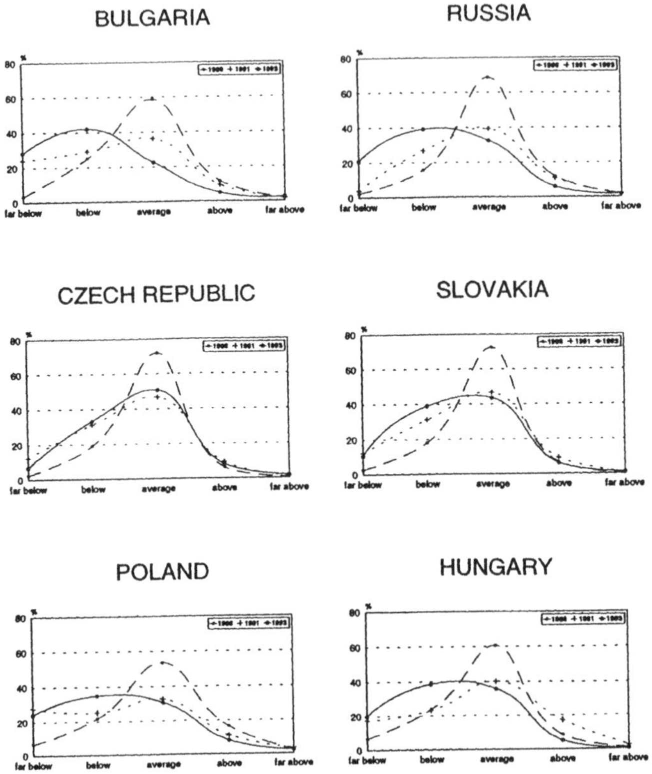

Figure 2. Distribution of Subjective Income in 1988, 1991, and 1993

Simple comparisons with Germany, the Netherlands and the United States (Figure 3) show that subjective reflections of the two social differentiation dimensions (subjective social status and subjective income) differ substantially between post-communist countries and Western democracies. Regarding social status, the distributions in Western countries—despite some interesting cross-national distinctions—show an overall shift toward the upper social strata. In post-communist countries, on the contrary, respondents tend to locate themselves toward the bottom of the two hierarchies.

The effects of selected independent variables on voting for the left are displayed in Tables 2a and 2b. Simple crosstabulations show some interesting association patterns. First, the tables for both education and class seem to challenge the traditional view that more educated people and people from higher social classes show a much weaker propensity toward left-voting. In all countries except Poland and

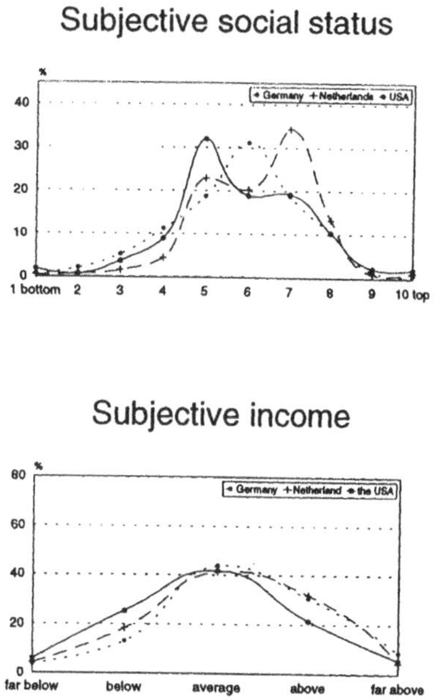

Figure 3. Distributions of Subjective Income and Subjective Status in 1991 Germany, the Netherlands, and the United States

Russia, individuals with tertiary education (college, university) show quite a similar tendency as people of lower education (secondary and vocational) to vote for the left. Regarding the effect of class, the picture does not differ much from that of education: there is no common and strong tendency among higher social classes to disfavor left political parties. In all countries except Russia professionals show no significantly weaker propensity toward left-voting than the rest of the population. Nor does the type of mobility between 1988 and 1993 show a strong effect. Only one mobility pattern shows significant negative deviation, namely the move to self-entrepreneurship.

As predicted, relative social and economic deprivation and evaluation of change in the role of ascriptive factors of life-success play a much stronger role in predicting left-voting than the objective criteria of location in the stratification system. The perception of change in the respondent's position in income and social hierarchies has a very significant effect on left-voting; the same holds for perceptions of "ascription." Finally, there was no doubt that ever being a Communist Party member has a very strong effect on voting for the left, even after the collapse of the communist regime. The last section of Table 2b proves that this assumption holds true.

Table 2a. Proportions of "Left-votes" in Categories of Independent Variables (Percentages and Adjusted Residuals)

	BUL	*CZR*	*HUN*	*POL*	*RUS*	*SLO*
EDUC:	Respondent's education					
PRIM	48.4	19.2	18.1	46.8	11.4	23.5
	(5.7)	(1.1)	(0.1)	(1.2)	(1.7)	(-1.1)
VOCAT	35.9	17.8	17.1	49.3	11.8	24.9
	(-1.2)	(-0.1)	(-0.7)	(2.6)	(2.4)	(0.0)
SECND	34.2	16.4	17.8	42.0	7.5	24.7
	(-5.3)	(-1.4)	(-0.2)	(-1.7)	(-1.9)	(-0.2)
TERT	41.8	19.0	20.4	36.2	6.1	29.7
	(0.1)	(0.6)	(1.1)	(-2.7)	(-2.1)	(1.9)
CLASS:	Respondent's class position (current or last occupation)					
PROF	37.8	18.5	21.4	40.3	5.9	26.4
	(-2.0)	(0.2)	(2.0)	(-2.2)	(-3.3)	(1.0)
NONM	43.0	15.9	18.9	43.8	9.9	25.3
	(0.2)	(-1.4)	(0.2)	(-0.4)	(0.5)	(0.2)
SELF	43.1	4.61	4.23	7.5	0.0	15.3
	(0.1)	(-4.1)	(-1.3)	(-1.7)	(-1.6)	(-1.8)
SKLD	36.7	22.7	19.0	47.9	12.7	23.7
	(-2.3)	(3.4)	(0.4)	(1.4)	(3.3)	(-0.8)
UNSK	46.0	18.4	16.7	46.6	8.3	24.9
	(2.2)	(0.2)	(-1.2)	(0.8)	(-0.4)	(0.0)
FARM	46.0	14.9	15.8	50.5	12.7	26.7
	(1.5)	(-1.2)	(-0.9)	(1.9)	(1.5)	(0.6)
TYPMOB:	Type of mobility between 1989 and current class position					
PRIV	29.5	8.4	12.9	40.9	0.0	17.8
	(-2.0)	(-3.9)	(-1.9)	(-1.1)	(-1.8)	(-2.1)
UPWD	34.0	17.5	15.5	45.0	8.9	23.1
	(-1.3)	(-0.4)	(-1.3)	(-0.3)	(-0.4)	(-1.0)
STAB	41.2	17.9	19.4	47.0	9.8	25.9
	(-0.3)	(-1.4)	(-1.0)	(0.3)	(-0.7)	(-1.8)
DOWN	33.6	27.7	22.3	44.5	10.9	37.5
	(-1.5)	(2.9)	(0.5)	(-0.4)	(0.3)	(2.2)
RETR	48.5	24.4	28.9	42.9	18.3	33.5
	(2.4)	(3.1)	(3.6)	(-0.8)	(2.8)	(2.3)
UNMP	44.2	20.0	19.0	55.1	3.6	32.3
	(0.8)	(0.2)	(-0.5)	(1.8)	(-1.1)	(1.2)

Notes: See the text for the explanation of categories.
* Adjusted residuals were computed for tables "variable" by LEFTVOTE by COUNTRY.

To evaluate statistically the effects of individual independent variables on the probability that a person would vote for the left

Table 2b. Proportions of "left-votes" in Categories of Independent Variables (Percentages and Adjusted Residuals)

	BUL	*CZR*	*HUN*	*POL*	*RUS*	*SLO*
SUB-SOC:	Perceived change in respondent's position in social status hierarchy.					
downward	48.2	28.3	21.5	50.9	11.8	28.7
	(7.7)	(11.2)	(5.0)	(4.8)	(4.3)	(4.2)
no change	34.4	14.1	14.0	42.2	7.2	21.2
	(-4.0)	(-5.0)	(-3.4)	(-1.6)	(-2.0)	(-3.3)
upward	21.0	8.2	12.1	35.9	1.6	21.6
	(-6.4)	(-7.1)	(-2.7)	(-4.0)	(-3.7)	(-1.6)
SUB-INC:	Perceived change in respondent's position in income hierarchy.					
downward	47.5	25.1	23.0	48.7	12.0	30.7
	(6.4)	(6.6)	(5.3)	(3.4)	(4.4)	(5.4)
no change	34.1	16.9	14.9	43.5	6.8	20.9
	(-4.8)	(-2.0)	(-3.9)	(-.9)	(-2.7)	(-4.5)
upward	30.4	9.9	11.8	34.5	3.5	22.0
	(-3.2)	(-5.5)	(-2.3)	(-3.6)	(-2.9)	(-1.3)
ASCRIP:	Belief about the role of ascriptive mechanisms and informal (political) networks					
bottom quartile	25.9	14.0	15.4	39.7	6.2	21.8
	(-7.7)	(-3.5)	(-1.5)	(-2.3)	(-1.6)	(-2.2)
top quartile	50.2	25.9	21.8	50.5	11.2	32.9
	(4.6)	(6.5)	(3.8)	(2.8)	(2.3)	(4.9)
CPTEVER:	Ever member of the communist party?					
yes	76.5	47.6	48.4	63.7	17.3	51.5
	(15.6)	(19.4)	(14.1)	(6.7)	(5.4)	(14.1)
no	33.4	12.1	13.9	41.7	7.4	19.3
	(-15.6)	(-19.4)	(-14.1)	(-6.7)	(-5.4)	(-14.1)

Notes: See the text for the explanation of categories.
* Adjusted residuals were computed for tables "variable" by LEFTVOTE by COUNTRY.

rather than for other parties, the parameters of four types of models were estimated by logistic regression. Tables 3a and 3b display parameters for all models estimated on the pooled data (all six countries are analyzed together).

Coefficients returned by Model I (Table 3a) show that after controlling for large differences between countries, three variables show significant effect on left-voting: age, income and class.[16] However, compared to age, both income and class show much weaker effects. Regarding class location, this model suggests that in formerly communist countries, the objective criteria of one's position in the system of social stratification and in class structure do not play as strong a role as in relatively stable social systems with well crystallized class structures (see e.g., Heath 1990). Only two classes show significant deviations from the general tendency to vote for the left: self-employed (−.477, factor 0.62) and unskilled workers (.120, factor 1.15). As predicted, professionals do not show any deviation from the general propensity toward left-voting (−0.039, factor 0.96).

After incorporating type of mobility (Model II), the effect of class disappears almost entirely, while mobility itself shows three strong and significant coefficients: the move to entrepreneurship (−.338, factor 0.71), downward mobility (.259, factor 1.30) and unemployment (.229, factor 1.26).

Model III adds all the "subjective" variables: perception of the change in one's position on the social status hierarchy (SUB-SOC), relative income (SUB-INC) and perception of change in the role of ascriptive factors of life-success (ASCRIP). Adding these variables improved both the model fit and its predictive capacity significantly (Model II predicted only 12.5% of left-votes correctly, Model III predicts 20.1% correctly). Parameter estimates from Model III corroborate theoretical assumptions as to the *social* determination of voting preferences for the left in post-communist countries. First of all, the coefficients as well as the levels of their statistical significance support the initial assumption that voting preferences for the left in post-communist countries are strongly grounded in a massive downward shift on the hierarchies of subjective social status and subjective income. Figures 1 and 2 have already confirmed that the extent of the downward shifts on subjectively defined social hierarchies differ significantly from nation to nation. In addition, the parameters of Model III show that the growth in the proportion of individuals who feel that their social position has declined produces a significant increase in the proportion of votes for the left political parties (both variables that measure a subjective change in one's position on the two important hierarchies turned out to predict significantly the analyzed voting preferences). It is also evident that, in general, the feeling of relative social descent has a stronger effect on voting preferences than the feeling of a relative deterioration of income. For example, those who feel that their social status decreased between 1988 and 1993 are 1.62 times more likely to vote for the left than those who feel an improvement in their position in the hierarchy of social status has improved (1.32/0.80 = 1.62). In terms of income

Table 3a. Logistic Regressions of Left-voting Analysis on Pooled Data

		Model I				*Model II*			
	df	*B*	*S.E.*	*Wald*	*Exp(B)*	*B*	*S.E.*	*Wald*	*Exp(B)*
NAT	4			534.8***				522.3***	
BUL	1	.745	.059	157.7***	2.11	.729	.060	148.1***	2.07
CZR	1	-.379	.056	45.5***	.68	-.363	.057	41.2***	.69
HUN	1	-.250	.064	15.4***	.77	-.272	.064	17.8***	.76
POL	1	1.046	.062	286.3***	2.84	1.050	.062	287.1***	2.86
RUS	1	-1.289	.105	151.3***	.28	-1.278	.105	147.9***	.27
SLO	1	.128	.056	5.2**	1.14	.135	.056	5.7*	1.14
AGE	1	.021	.003	66.4***	1.02	.020	.003	46.7***	1.02
EDUC	1	.013	.035	.1	1.01	.054	.035	.0	1.00
QHSHL	1	-.063	.021	9.6**	.94	-.053	.021	6.4*	.94
CLASS	5			21.6***				10.0	
PROF	1	-.039	.063	.4	.96	-.026	.066	.0	1.00
NONM	1	.164	.069	5.6*	1.18	.134	.071	3.5	1.14
SELF	1	-.477	.120	15.7***	.62	-.327	.135	5.5*	.72
SKLD	1	.139	.056	6.0*	1.15	.108	.059	3.3	1.12
UNSK	1	.067	.061	1.2*	1.06	.002	.064	.0	1.00
FARM	1	.147	.086	2.9	1.16	.109	.087	1.6	1.12
MOBILITY	5							.20.3**	
PRIV	1	.	.	.	.	-.338	.130	6.7*	.71
UPWD	1	.	.	.	.	-.115	.102	1.3	.89
STAB	1	.	.	.	.	-.068	.050	1.8	.93
DOWN	1	.	.	.	.	.259	.097	7.1**	1.30
RETR	1	.	.	.	.	.032	.084	.2	1.03
UNMP	1	.	.	.	.	.229	.093	6.1*	1.26
SUB-SOC	2			.				.	
DOWN	1	.	.	.	.	.	.	.	.
STAB	1	.	.	.	.	.	.	.	.
UPWD	1	.	.	.	.	.	.	.	.
SUB-INC	2			.				.	
DOWN	1	.	.	.	.	.	.	.	.
STAB	1	.	.	.	.	.	.	.	.
UPWD	1	.	.	.	.	.	.	.	.
ASCRIP	1	.	.	.	.	.	.	.	.
CPTEVER	1	.	.	.	.	.	.	.	.
Constant	1	-1.914	.164	136.7***		-1.872	.175	114.4***	
%MDIF			7.6				7.8		
%PRED-TOT			73.8				73.9		
%PRED-LFT			11.2				12.5		

Notes: For all categorical variables DEVIATION contrasts were applied.

Significance: * < 0.05, ** < 0.01, *** < 0.001.

%MDIF percentage of change in -2LL between the model with constant only and the current model.

%PRED-TOT percentage of correctly predicted votes by the model - TOTAL.

%PRED-LFT percentage of correctly predicted votes by the model - LEFT.

Table 3b. Logistic Regressions of Left-voting. Analysis on pooled data

		Model I				*Model II*			
	df	*B*	*S.E.*	*Wald*	*Exp(B)*	*B*	*S.E.*	*Wald*	*Exp(B)*
NAT	4			511.9***				535.5***	
BUL	1	.716	.061	135.6***	2.04	.733	.064	134.6***	2.08
CZR	1	-.253	.058	18.9***	.77	-.331	.061	29.3***	.72
HUN	1	-.309	.066	22.0***	.73	-.261	.068	15.0***	.77
POL	1	1.091	.064	294.6***	2.97	1.194	.066	326.2***	3.30
RUS	1	-1.398	.107	170.3***	.25	-1.431	.109	169.8***	.24
SLO	1	.154	.058	7.2**	1.17	.097	.059	2.6	1.10
AGE	1	.019	.003	40.8***	1.02	.009	.003	8.7**	1.01
EDUC	1	.021	.036	.3	1.02	-.127	.037	11.5***	.88
QHSHL	1	-.025	.021	1.3	.97	-.044	.022	3.8*	.96
CLASS	5			8.7				7.8	
PROF	1	-.012	.066	.0	.98	-.061	.068	.8	.94
NONM	1	.138	.072	3.6*	1.14	.173	.072	5.3*	1.18
SELF	1	-.309	.141	4.7*	.73	-.245	.145	2.9	.78
SKLD	1	.098	.060	.0	1.10	.039	.063	.4	1.04
UNSK	1	-.005	.064	.0	.99	.028	.067	.2	1.03
FARM	1	.088	.088	.9	1.09	.066	.090	.5	1.07
MOBILITY	5			10.6				10.2	
PRIV	1	-.207	.132	2.4	.81	-.239	.137	3.1*	.79
UPWD	1	-.079	.104	.6	.92	-.111	.107	1.1	.89
STAB	1	-.054	.051	1.1	.94	-.043	.053	.6	.95
DOWN	1	.259	.098	6.8**	1.29	.203	.103	3.9*	1.22
RETR	1	-.018	.085	.0	.98	.050	.088	.3	1.05
UNMP	1	.099	.095	1.1	1.10	.141	.097	2.1	1.15
SUB-SOC	2			34.5***				17.3***	
DOWN	1	.281	.048	33.9***	1.32	.203	.050	16.4***	1.23
STAB	1	-.068	.047	.3	.94	-.069	.049	2.0	.93
UPWD	1	-.212	.064	10.8***	.81	-.133	.067	4.0*	.88
SUB-INC	2			13.6**				15.9***	
DOWN	1	.183	.050	13.5***	1.20	.201	.052	15.1***	1.22
STAB	1	-.026	.046	.3	.97	-.008	.048	.9	.99
UPWD	1	-.157	.067	5.3*	.85	-.192	.070	7.5**	.82
ASCRIP	1	.254	.027	86.6***	1.29	.233	.028	67.8***	1.26
CPTEVER	1	.	.	.	.	1.521	.070	466.1***	4.57
Constant	1	-2.141	.179	141.7***		-1.599	.187	73.2***	
%MDIF			10.1				15.4		
%PRED-TOT			74.9				76.7		
%PRED-LFT			20.1				29.9		

Notes: For all categorical variables DEVIATION contrasts were applied.
Significance: * < 0.05, ** < 0.01, *** < 0.001.
%MDIF percentage of change in -2LL between the model with constant only and the current model.
%PRED-TOT percentage of correctly predicted votes by the model - TOTAL.
%PRED-LFT percentage of correctly predicted votes by the model - LEFT.

the difference between "losers" and "winners" is smaller: the odds of voting for the left is 1.41 times higher among those who feel a relative deterioration in their income than among those who feel that it has improved. However, the effect of the ASCRIP variable is absolutely dominant (.254, factor 1.29, meaning that one standard deviation in ASCRIP produces a 29% increase in the odds of a vote for the "Left").[17] Thus, the results prove that those who tend to believe that informal networks, political connections, and so on play an even more important role during the transformation than prior to the collapse of the communist regime are much more likely to vote for the left than those who interpret the development in the opposite direction.

The results from the application of Model IV corroborate the hypothesis that Communist Party membership in the past dramatically increases the odds of voting for the left today (factor 4.57), but—as presumed—it does not account for the effects of other relevant variables predicting voting behavior, though, of course, the regression coefficients changed after the inclusion of Communist Party membership in the equation. It is worth noting, however, that the inclusion of party membership weakened the effect of relative decline of *social* status (from 0.281 to 0.203) while, on the contrary, the effect of the relative deterioration of *income* position has slightly increased (from 0.183 to 0.201). We assume that it is because downward social mobility was more likely among former party members than among non-members; at the same time, party members have been able to convert their former political capital into economic assets, securing high or at least above-average income after the collapse of the communist regime (see e.g., Matějů and Řeháková 1993; Matějů 1993). Surprisingly, the inclusion of party membership has not greatly changed the effects of the three variables measuring subjective perceptions of change in factors underlying life-success. Thus, subjective perceptions of the development of factors underlying life-success has a strong effect on voting preferences independent of the respondent's political history and potential ideological bias.

A comparison of logit regression coefficients for the three categories of subjective social mobility (SUB-SOC) between Model III and Model IV suggests that there may be interaction effects between party membership and type of subjective mobility. The results displayed in Table 3c actually testify to this assumption. Two interaction terms have significant effects on left-voting: the interaction between *stability of income* and party membership (strongly *positive* effect on left-voting: 0.338, factor 1.41), and the interaction between *upward income mobility* and party membership (strongly *negative* effect: −0.249, factor 0.77).

Table 3c clearly shows that voting preferences for the left depend on subjective mobility far more among former party members than among non-members. In other words, among former party members, other things being equal, those who experienced downward *social* mobility are 1.65 times more likely to vote for the left than those who believe they have experienced upward social mobility. This gap is much smaller among those who have never been members of the Communist Party (1.31). Similarly, those former party members who experienced downward *income* mobility are almost 1.66 times more likely to vote for the left than those who believe that they experienced upward income mobility. At the same time, among former party members, the feeling of improving *income* prevents left-voting more than the feeling of upward *social* mobility (the odds multiplier for former party members experi encing upward income mobility is 2.77, whereas the odds multiplier for party members experiencing upward social mobility is 3.42). To put it simply, former party members who received little economic gain from the transformation are more likely to vote for the left.

To establish country specific patterns in the determination of voting preferences for the left, Model IV was applied to individual countries. As expected, the estimated parameters (Tables 4a and 4b) have shown interesting differences. Three countries in which the model has a rather weak explanatory power (Hungary, Poland and Slovakia) simultaneously show little effects of relative *social* deprivation but quite strong effects of relative *economic* deprivation. It seems that in these three countries, economic inequality is a key issue in shaping political orientations.

In Bulgaria, where the general tendency to vote for the left is very high, the relatively high explanatory power of the model results from an opposition to the left. This opposition is represented by individuals who feel that their social status has improved (coefficient −0.379, factor 0.68) as well as by individuals with higher education (−0.257, factor 0.77). On the other hand, there is a very strong continuity of political preferences among former members of the Communist Party (2.275—which means that the odds of voting for the left is 9.7 times higher with former party members than with those who have never

Table 3c. Logistic Regressions of Left Voting. Interaction Effects (Pooled Data)

	df	*B*	*S.E.*	*Wald*	*Exp(B)*
		>> *see note* <<			
SUB-SOC	2			7.5*	
DOWN	1	.159	.058	7.6**	1.17
STAB	1	-.038	.055	.4	.96
UPWD	1	-.121	.076	2.69	.89
SUB-INC	2			16.9***	
DOWN	1	.221	.058	13.4***	1.17
STAB	1	-.096	.056	2.9	.96
UPWD	1	-.125	.081	2.3	.88
SUB-SOC by CPTEVER	2			3.9	
DOWN by CP	1	.177	.112	2.5	1.26
STAB by CP	1	-.132	.115	1.3	.87
UPWD by CP	1	-.044	.153	.0	.96
SUB-INC by CPTEVER	2			12.7**	
DOWN by CP	1	-.089	.112	.7	.91
STAB by CP	1	.338	.115	9.7***	1.41
UPWD by CP	1	-.249	.153	2.4**	.77
CPTEVER	1	1.394	.092	230.6***	4.03
Constant	1	-1.559	.186	69.6***	
%MDIF			15.6		
%PRED-TOT			76.8		
%PRED-LFT			31.3		

Notes: This table shows only the effects of variables SUB-SOC and SUB-INC since adding the interaction terms between these two variables and CPTEVER had no significant effect on any other parameter of Model IV except SUB-SOC and SUB-INC.
For all categorical variables DEVIATION contrasts were applied.
Levels of significance: * < 0.05, ** < 0.01, *** < 0.001.
%MDIF percentage of change in -2LL between the model with constant only and the current model.
%PRED-TOT percentage of correctly predicted votes by the model - TOTAL.
%PRED-LFT percentage of correctly predicted votes by the model - LEFT.

been members of the Communist Party). In other words, massive *absolute economic deprivation* in Bulgaria has produced very strong political orientations toward the left, opposed only by the minority of those who have experienced some improvement in their life-chances since the collapse of the communist regime.

The Czech Republic is another special case. The relatively high explanatory power of the model is due to the very strong effect of two variables: (a) relative *social* deprivation (0.498, factor 1.65), which, interestingly enough, is not coupled with a similarly strong effect of relative *economic* deprivation, and (b) the belief that the role of ascription in life-success is growing (0.272, factor 1.32). On the other hand, the potential "left-turn" encounters strong opposition from those who feel that the transformation has brought an improvement in their life-chances (see parameters for categories SUB-SOC/upward, SUB-INC/upward). Relative to the other post-communist countries, this group preventing the "left-turn" is quite large in the Czech Republic. Furthermore, the Czech Republic turns out to be the only country in the analysis in which those who have not reported any change in their social status represent an important social force (−0.231, factor 0.79).

Regarding the effect of "objective class" and mobility, we find that in the Czech Republic particularly, the self-employed constitute a strong opposition against the left-turn (−1.021, factor 0.36). An interesting finding is that in both the Czech Republic and Hungary, higher social classes (namely professionals and non-manuals) show a very high propensity toward left-voting (0.220, factor 1.24 for professionals in the Czech Republic; 0.246, factor 1.27 for professionals in Hungary).

Left political parties in Poland receive massive support from the population, and it is quite difficult to find any strong link in the propensity toward left-voting to major social and economic characteristics of the potential voters. The overall explanatory power of the model is quite low (actually the lowest among the analyzed countries) and, with the exception of education (negative effect) and the perceived increase in the role of ascription (positive effect), there are no other significant coefficients (though the general pattern is quite similar to other countries).

Interpreting the results for Russia is rather difficult. First, the truly left political parties that could have received votes from potential supporters of the Communist Party were banned in Russia at the time of the survey. This partly explains both the very low general tendency to vote for the left and large errors of estimates of the parameters. As a result, the very high values of regression coefficients that would otherwise allow us to draw quite an interesting picture of voting behavior have not reached statistical significance. However, it is evident that in Russia voting preferences are firmly linked to one's perception of life-chances during the transformation—both social and economic deprivation (hitting a majority of the population) dramatically increasing the probability of casting a vote

Table 4a. Logistic Regressions of Left-voting Model IV Applied on Individual Countries

	BULGARIA			*CZECH REPUBLIC*			*HUNGARY*		
	B	*WALD*	*Exp(B)*	*B*	*WALD*	*Exp(B)*	*B*	*WALD*	*Exp(B)*
AGE	.013	2.6	1.01	.014	3.5	1.01	.024	8.2**	1.02
EDUC	-.257	9.1***	.77	-.129	2.1	.88	-.129	1.7	.88
QHSHL	-.106	3.7*	.90	-.070	1.9	.93	.003	0.0	1.00
CLASS		13.2*			8.7			7.5	
PROF	-.374	4.6*	.68	.220	1.6	1.24	.246	1.8	1.27
NONM	.196	1.0	1.22	.493	7.1**	1.63	.392*	4.7	1.48
SELF	.567	2.1	1.76	-1.021	4.3*	.36	-.309	.9	.73
SKLD	-.410	5.9*	.66	.234	2.1	1.26	.027	.0	1.02
UNSK	.132	1.0	1.14	.263	2.5	1.30	-.241	1.8	.79
FARM	-.111	.2	.89	-.190	.5	.82	-.114	.2	.89
MOBILITY		3.3			3.7			1.4	
PRIV	-.407	1.1	.66	-.332	1.2	.72	.066	.0	1.06
UPWD	.196	.3	1.21	-.054	.0	.95	-.262	.9	.76
STAB	.147	.1	1.16	-.018	.0	.98	-.014	.1	.98
DOWN	-.448	2.4	.63	.314	1.9	1.36	.197	.6	1.21
RETR	.231	1.2	1.25	-.152	.6	.86	.054	.1	1.06
UNMP	.280	1.9	1.32	.243	.3	1.28	-.043	.0	.96
SUB-SOC	4.0			23.7***			0.2		
DOWN	.246	2.7	1.27	.498	20.8***	1.65	.029	.1	1.03
STAB	.136	.9	1.14	-.231	4.9*	.79	-.062	.2	.94
UPWD	-.379	3.6	.68	-.267	3.5	.76	.032	.0	1.03
SUB-INC		5.5			3.9			5.7*	
DOWN	.216	2.5	1.25	.130	1.2	1.13	.288	3.5	1.33
STAB	-.269	3.3	.77	.146	2.1	1.16	-.125	.9	.88
UPWD	.053	.0	1.05	-.279	3.7	.75	-.163	.5	.85
ASCRIP	.424	34.4***	1.52	.272	16.1***	1.32	.155	5.4**	1.17
CPTEVER	2.275	127.1***	9.70	1.760	159.5***	5.80	1.390	55.0***	4.02
Constant	-.708	2.3		-2.449	29.8**		-2.541	30.7***	
%MDIF		26.9			16.1			9.1	
%PRED-TOT		72.0			82.3			81.8	
%PRED-LFT		57.9			25.4			17.7	

Notes: For all categorical variables DEVIATION contrasts were applied.
Significance: * < 0.05, ** < 0.01, *** < 0.001.
%MDIF Percentage of change in -2LL between the model with constant only and current model.
%PRED-TOT Percentage of correctly predicted votes - TOTAL.
%PRED-LFT Percentage of correctly predicted votes - LEFT.

for the left. On the other side, those who report a *relative* improvement in their social and economic situation (a very small segment of the population) would strongly oppose a potential left-turn.

Table 4b. Logistic Regressions of Left-voting Model IV Applied on Individual Countries

	POLAND			RUSSIA			SLOVARIA		
	B	WALD	Exp(B)	B	WALD	Exp(B)	B	WALD	Exp(B)
AGE	-.003	.2	.99	.054	16.5***	1.05	-.004	.4	.99
EDUC	-.170	3.4*	.84	.038	.0	1.04	-.076	.8	.93
QHSHL	.017	.0	1.01	.149	2.2	1.16	-.061	1.5	.94
CLASS		2.2			18.7*			2.8	
PROF	-.204	1.6	.81	-.416	.0	.65	.169	.2	1.18
NONM	-.043	.0	.96	.060	.0	1.06	.231	1.7	1.26
SELF	-.262	1.2	.76	-1.710	.0	.18	-.467	1.0	.62
SKLD	.272	3.5	1.31	.605	.1	1.83	.049	.1	1.05
UNSK	-.089	.1	.99	-.047	.0	.95	.112	.5	1.11
FARM	.247	1.3	1.88	1.509	.4	4.52	-.094	.1	.91
MOBILITY		5.4			1.4			12.5**	
PRIV	.056	.0	1.06	-3.967	.2	.02	-.608	3.6**	.54
UPWD	-.262	1.3	.76	1.050	.3	2.85	-.109	.2	.89
STAB	-.089	.5	.91	.705	.1	2.02	-.138	1.4	.87
DOWN	-.085	.1	.92	1.022	.3	2.77	.608	7.1**	1.83
RETR	-.058	.0	.94	.392	.0	1.48	.164	.7	1.18
UNMP	.438	3.7	1.54	.796	.1	1.21	.083	.1	1.08
SUB-SOC		5.1			3.3			1.7	
DOWN	.196	3.4	1.21	.571	3.2	1.77	-.045	.2	.96
STAB	-.172	2.8	.84	.127	.1	1.13	.132	1.5	1.14
UPWD	-.023	.0	.98	-.698	1.6	.49	-.088	.4	.92
SUB-INC		5.5			3.6			6.6*	
DOWN	.081	.3	1.08	.652	3.7	1.91	.219	3.9*	1.24
STAB	.224	4.5*	1.25	.122	.1	1.13	-.164	2.5	.84
UPWD	-.305	4.5*	.74	-.775	1.7	.46	-.053	.1	.95
ASCRIP	.197	8.2**	1.22	.047	.1	1.04	.213	10.7***	1.24
CPTEVER	.991	24.9***	2.69	.592	3.9*	1.81	1.480	110.1***	4.39
Constant	.129	.1		-7.314	5.5**		-.884	4.8*	
%MDIF		4.1			12.2			8.8	
%PRED-TOT		57.2			91.3			74.9	
%PRED-LFT		48.6			0.4			27.9	

Notes: For all categorical variables DEVIATION contrasts were applied.
Levels of significance: * < 0.05, ** < 0.01, *** < 0.001.
%MDIF Percentage of change in -2LL between the model with constant only and current model.
%PRED-TOT Percentage of correctly predicted votes - TOTAL.
%PRED-LFT Percentage of correctly predicted votes - LEFT.

The interaction effects between subjective mobility and party membership in the individual countries (Tables 4c and 4d) give no simple, universal answer. There seem to be two types of systems. All countries except Poland and Hungary show a quite strong common

Table 4c. Logistic Regressions of Left-voting Interaction Effects in Individual Countries

	BULGARIA			CZECH REPUBLIC			HUNGARY		
	B	*WALD*	*Exp(B)*	*B*	*WALD*	*Exp(B)*	*B*	*WALD*	*Exp(B)*
				>> see note <<					
SUB-SOC		3.8			18.1*			0.5	
DOWN	.260	2.5	.1.29	.571	17.5***	1.77	-.063	.1	.94
STAB	.173	1.1	1.19	-.144	1.2	.86	-.095	.4	.91
UPWD	-.434	3.7	.65	-.427	5.5**	.65	.158	.5	1.17
SUB-INC		8.2			1.0			5.9*	
DOWN	.210	1.6	1.22	.138	.9	1.14	.369	4.5*	1.44
STAB	-.429	7.1	.65	-.031	.1	.96	-.097	.5	.90
UPWD	.227	1.1	1.25	-.106	.4	.89	-.271	1.0	.76
SUB-SOC by CPTEVER									
DOWN by CP	.061	.0	1.06	-.183	.6	.83	.456	1.8	1.58
STAB by CP	-.188	.2	.83	-.276	1.5	.76	.187	.4	1.21
UPWD by CP	.127	.1	1.13	.459	2.3*	1.58	-.643	1.8	.53
SUB-INC by CPTEVER									
DOWN by CP	-.069	.1	.93	-.056	.1	.94	-.353	.8	.70
STAB by CP	.748	4.2*	2.11	.515	5.8*	1.67	-.212	.1	.88
UPWD by CP	-.679	2.5	.50	-.459	2.3	.63	.475	.6	1.60
CPTEVER	2.136	62.4***	8.5	1.725	91.7***	5.60	1.276	18.1***	3.58
Constant	-.696	2.2		-2.232	26.6**		-2.527	28.6***	

Notes: This table shows only the effects of variables SUB-SOC and SUB-INC since adding the interaction terms between these two variables and CPTEVER had no significant effect on any other parameter of Model IV except SUB-SOC and SUB-INC.
For all categorical variables DEVIATION contrasts were applied.
Levels of significance: * < 0.05, ** < 0.01, *** < 0.001.

pattern: everything else being equal, former party members whose position in the *income* hierarchy has not changed during the transformation show a much stronger propensity toward left-voting than party members who report upward income mobility: in Bulgaria 4.2 times (2.11/0.50), in the Czech Republic 2.5 times (5.8/2.3) and in Slovakia 2.3 times (1.4/0.61). In these countries, which only started their economic and political reforms in 1989, the *economic* success among former party members contributes to the sudden "metamorphosis" of political affiliations, playing a "compensatory" role for the loss of *social* status. In Hungary and Poland, it is rather subjective *social* status that plays a similar role: again, everything else being equal, former party members who experienced upward mobility in their *social* status are less likely to cast their votes for left political parties than those who remained stable or experienced downward

Table 4d. Logistic Regression of Left-voting Interaction Effects in Individual Countries

	POLAND			*RUSSIA*			*SLOVARIA*		
	B	*WALD*	*Exp(B)*	*B*	*WALD*	*Exp(B)*	*B*	*WALD*	*Exp(B)*
				>> *see note* <<					
SUB-SOC		3.6			4.4			5.8	
DOWN	.087	.5	1.09	2.923	.2	18.59	-.104	.6	.90
STAB	-.208	3.5	.81	2.015	.1	7.50	.282	5.3*	1.33
UPWD	.121	.8	1.13	-4.937	.2	.01	-.178	1.0	.84
SUB-INC		6.3*			3.9			6.2*	
DOWN	.181	2.1	1.20	.052	.0	1.05	.173	1.7	1.18
STAB	.219	3.6	1.24	-.140	.1	.86	-.261	4.6	.77
UPWD	-.399	6.2*	.67	.088	.0	1.09	.087	.2	1.09
SUB-SOC by CPTEVER									
DOWN by CP	.654	4.8**	1.92	-3.512	.3	.02	.264	1.4	1.30
STAB by CP	.239	.7	1.27	-2.261	.1	.10	-.576	5.7**	.56
UPWD by CP	-.894	6.2**	.41	5.773	.2	321.50	.312	1.0	1.36
SUB-INC by CPTEVER									
DOWN by CP	-.550	3.4	.58	3.423	.1	30.66	.127	.3	1.13
STAB by CP	-.049	.0	.95	2.544	2.3	12.73	.363	2.6	1.43
UPWD by CP	.600	2.4	1.82	-5.968	.1	.00	-.490	3.8*	.61
CPTEVER	.979	18.8***	2.66	.577	.0	1.78	1.307	48.9***	3.69
Constant	.201	.2		-9.383	.8		-.789	3.7*	

Notes: This table shows only the effects of variables SUB-SOC and SUB-INC since adding the interaction terms between these two variables and CPTEVER had no significant effect on any other parameter of Model IV except SUB-SOC and SUB-INC.
For all categorical variables DEVIATION contrasts were applied.
Levels of significance: * < 0.05, ** < 0.01, *** < 0.001.
%MDIF Percentage of change in -2LL between the model with constant only and the current model.
%PRED-TOT Percentage of correctly predicted votes by the model - TOTAL.
%PRED-LFT Percentage of correctly predicted votes by the model - LEFT.

subjective status mobility. These results suggest that the two groups of post-communist countries (i.e., countries at the beginning of their reforms and countries that started economic reforms a long time before communism collapsed) differ significantly in terms of the role played by subjective social and income mobility in the determination of voting preferences among former party members.

CONCLUSIONS

As initially stated, this paper intends to provide neither a complete picture nor an exhaustive explanation of the left-turns that have recently occurred in some post-communist countries. Indeed, the major purpose of the analysis is to demonstrate to what extent the voting preferences for the left are grounded in the specific developments of socio-economic inequality and social stratification in the individual countries "escaping from socialism." The main analytical questions were quite simple:

1. to what extent can the voting preferences for the left be explained by those "objective" criteria of class location that play a very significant role in shaping voting behavior in Western democracies;
2. what role is played in changing voting behavior by socio-economic inequality, relative socio-economic deprivation and popular beliefs about the development of factors determining socio-economic success.

Regarding the role of "objective class" in predicting voting preferences for the left, the survey has shown quite clearly that this factor is far weaker than in Western democracies, or—better said—that it is basically insignificant. The type of mobility during the transformation has a modest effect.

Regarding the "subjective" dimensions of social stratification, the results are convincing in three respects. First, we found that there are substantial cross-national differences in the development of distributions of two important measures of relative socio-economic deprivation: that is, the perception of change in one's position in the social status and income hierarchy. Second, it turned out that the level of relative socio-economic deprivation significantly predicts voting preferences for the left. Therefore, other things being equal, the higher the number of people who feel they are "losers" in a given country, the higher the risk of a left-turn. Third, voting preferences for the left are also significantly related to subjective evaluations of changes in the role of ascriptive and meritocratic factors of life-success. The belief that there is now more ascription than before the collapse of the communist regime increases the probability of left-voting. Obviously, these conclusions prompt another sociologically interesting question: To what extent are the subjective evaluations predetermined by one's political history, or—more specifically—by either past or present Communist Party membership. Evidently, if such a political bias is strong then the results of analyses of the social costs of the transformation can only make a minor contribution to understanding the political climates in the post-communist countries.

Logistic regression has shown that Communist Party membership definitely has a strong influence on voting preferences, although it eliminates neither the effects of beliefs grounded in the social costs of the transformation (change in subjective status, change in subjective income), nor the effects of evaluations of changes in factors underlying life-success (ascription, meritocracy, credentialism).

Regarding the question of cross-national differences in the possibility of experiencing a left-turn, the results provide both direct and indirect evidence that there are three different types of determination of voting preferences for the left. First, there are social systems in which the risk of a left-turn develops from absolute socio-economic deprivation. In such a social system, the general tendency to vote for the left is very strong and only a tiny segment of the population that has experienced a relative improvement in their socio-economic status create an opposition to the re-establishment of communist redistributive practices (Bulgaria, Russia).

Second, an entirely different pattern emerges, if the government succeeds in eliminating absolute socio-economic deprivation. Under such conditions, both the political scene and voting preferences are shaped by social forces similar to those in Western democracies. The "losers," in terms of one's position in social stratification and life-prospects, show strong inclinations toward the left, whereas the 'winners' create a very strong force preventing a potential left-turn. Such a political scene is much more predictable and quite stable, especially if the government can influence the proportion of "losers" and "winners." The only country in our analysis that resembles such an "ideal" model of post-communist development is the Czech Republic. Stratification-related variables play a strong role in predicting voting preferences and those who have experienced no dramatic change in their relative socio-economic position represent an important social force preventing the left-turn. Moreover, the political scene seems to be more sensitive to relative *social* deprivation (mobility between positions) than to *economic* deprivation (subjective income mobility). In any case, in such a social system the probability of an unexpected "swing-vote" is quite small.

The third type of determination is based on the rather weak role of social factors that traditionally predict voting behavior and, in particular, voting preferences for the left. In such a social system, voting preferences for the left seem to result predominantly from specific political factors that make the probability of the unpredictable "swing-vote" quite high (nationalist sentiments, separatist movements, racial issues, corruption, etc.). Of course, these factors do not entirely eliminate the political consequences of inequality and social policy issues, but temporarily override them and make them secondary. Three countries show such a tendency: Hungary, Poland and Slovakia.

In Hungary and Poland, historical and political factors can explain such a situation. Communist systems in Hungary and Poland were disintegrated at the time of their ultimate collapse in 1989. This may have caused the less negative attitudes toward the left than in countries where tough communist regimes survived up until the last minute (e.g., in the former Czechoslovakia). It also may explain the more negative popular evaluations of the failures in economic reform, especially in comparison with countries in which transformation started from "scratch." In addition, the Hungarian political scene is traditionally much more sensitive to changes in *economic* inequality than to subjective *social* mobility.

In searching for the specific factors shaping the political scene in Slovakia, we find almost no effect of subjective social mobility but a very strong effect of relative economic deprivation. However, the very weak explanatory power of the model seems to be a result of strong "external" factors, be it either general disappointment or strong nationalist movements, racial issues, and so forth, all of which make the political scene unpredictable.

In conclusion, we can say that the results presented in this paper have shown that despite the vital role played by *specific* historical, political and economic circumstances in shaping political scenes in the post-communist countries, the social costs of the transformation constitute a very important *common* factor that may contribute to an understanding of voting behavior and the political future of the countries escaping socialism. This message goes not only to economists, who have been traditionally averse to the analysis of the *social consequences and conditions* of economic reforms, but also to those politicians, on both the left and the right, who are convinced that the political scene and attitudes can be shaped by political rhetoric, with little attention paid to the underlying social and economic processes.

APPENDIX

A. The list of political parties coded as the "Left":

Bulgaria

Bulgarian Communist Party, Union of Democratic Forces, Bulgarian Social Democratic Party

The Czech Republic and Slovakia

The Communist Party of Bohemia and Moravia, Left Bloc, Party of the Democratic Left, Czechoslovak (Czech, Slovak) Socialist Party, Czechoslovak (Czech, Slovak) Social Democracy.

Hungary

Hungarian Socialist Party, Workers' Party, Social Democratic Party.

Poland

Union of Democratic Left, Polish Peasant Party, Union of Labor ("Unia Pracy").

Russia

"Communist parties"—category created by the research team in Moscow.

Factors of life-success (questions, variables, factor analysis)

Question: *Now I'm going to read a list of things that may be important for getting ahead in our society. Could you please tell me how important each of these was in 1988, and how important each is now, using the categories on this card* [*Show card A*].

Card A: 1 = essential, 2 = very important, 3 = fairly important, 4 = not very important, 5 = not at all important.

RICH88	RICH93	Coming from a wealthy family [in 1988, now]
EDUC88	EDUC93	Having a good education [in 1988, now]
AMBIT88	AMBIT93	Having ambition [in 1988, now]
WORK88	WORK93	Hard work [in 1988, now]
NET88	NET93	Knowing the right people [in 1988, now]
POL88	POL93	Having political connections [in 1988, now]
RISK88	RISK93	Willingness to take a risk [in 1988, now]

For the analysis the scale was reversed: (1=5)(2=4)(3=3)(4=2)(1=5)

New variables were created for factor analysis:

XRICH	=	RICH93	-	RICH88
XEDUC	=	EDUC93	-	EDUC88
XAMBI	=	AMBIT93	-	AMBIT88
XWORK	=	WORK93	-	WORK88
XNETW	=	NET93	-	NET88
XPOLI	=	POL93	-	POL88
XRISK	=	RISK93	-	RISK88

Results of principal component analysis (oblique rotation, pattern matrix):

	MERIT	*ASCRIP*
XRICH	.215	.215
XEDUC	.439	.155
XAMBI	.708	.070
XWORK	.726	−.116
XNETW	.094	.777
XPOLI	−.228	.734
XRISK	.609	−.122
% of variance	25.0	17.6

Regression factor scores were calculated for further analyses.

ACKNOWLEDGMENT

This research received support from several sources. The international research project "Social Stratification in Eastern Europe after 1989" received a grant from the National Science Foundation (NSF). In addition to the funds from NSF, the Czech survey was supported by grants from the Grant Agency of the Czech Academy Sciences, the Grant Agency of the Czech Republic and the Ministry of Labor and Social Affairs of the Czech Republic. This research was made possible by the Grant from the Grant Agency of the Czech Republic (grant number 403/93/0622). I would like to thank Nelson Lim, Donald Treiman, Blanka Řeháková, Jiří Večerník, and Klára Vlachová for their helpful comments on a previous draft of the paper

NOTES

1. The Alliance of the Democratic Left (the successor of the Polish Communist Party) received only 20.4 percent of valid votes and 37.2 percent of the seats in the Lower House of the Polish Parliament. The discrepancy between the proportion of votes and the proportion of the seats in the parliament is due to the fact that over one third of the valid votes yielded no seat in the parliament (see Lipinski 1993 for details and explanations).

2. In Hungary the Hungarian Socialist Party—a pro-reform wing of the former Hungarian Socialist Workers' Party (the Hungarian communist party before 1989)—has received as much as 32.9 percent of the valid votes and 54.1 percent of parliamentary seats. It is worth noting that in March 1990 the same party received only 10.9 percent of the valid votes and secured only 8.6 percent of the parliamentary seats. In Bulgaria the postcommunist "Bulgarian Socialist Party" obtained as many as 43.75 percent of the valid votes and secured the majority of the parliamentary seats.

3. For example, the *Financial Times*—reporting on May 9, 1994 on the Hungarian election—expressed the view that Hungarian voters were punishing the previous government for the 20 percent fall in industrial output over the past four years.

4. Dahrendorf argues that passing through the second stage of the transformation does not necessarily mean that society is no longer at risk. "The third condition of the road to freedom is to provide the social foundations which transform the constitution and the economy from fair-weather into all-weather institutions which can withstand the storms generated within and without" (Dahrendorf 1990, p. 100). Thus, during the third stage, we are primarily dealing with changes in the deepest structures of a social system, including deeply ingrained strategies of life-success and the degree of their compatibility with general social and economic progress, beliefs about distributive justice, habits, patterns of behavior and the value system.

5. See Lipset 1981 for an extensive overview of various theoretical and empirical studies.

6. In his interview for the Bulletin of the East & Central Europe Program (Bulletin 1994) the Hungarian political analyst, János Kis, explicitly stated that the most important factor for the post-communist Hungarian Socialist Party's electoral victory was the general discontent people feel at the quite severe costs imposed on various strata of society by the transition to a market economy. According to Kis, "There are winners, but in the short run there have been far more losers. The overwhelming majority of losers do not see a timetable for restructuring and recovery, thus they are more and more afraid that the whole process of marketization is leading them and their families down an economic blind alley" (Bulletin 1994, p. 1).

7. There were six countries involved in this project: Bulgaria, the Czech Republic, Hungary, Poland, Russia and Slovakia. In each country, both the "General population survey" (about 5,000 randomly selected respondents) and the "Elite study" (a survey of members of the former and current political elites) were

conducted in 1993. The international research project was supported by the National Science Foundation (USA), the Dutch Social and Environmental Research Foundation (SRO/NWO), and the Dutch Social and Cultural Sciences Foundation (SSCW/NWO). In addition to international funds, all national surveys were also supported by national foundations. The Czech research team was supported by the Grant Agency of the Academy of Sciences of the Czech Republic, the Grant Agency of the Czech Republic and the Ministry of Labor and Social Affairs.

8. In the first step, regional units were selected randomly, in which, in the second step, individuals or households were also drawn by random. If the second step was a random selection of household instead of an individual, the respondent was chosen randomly from the household members and data were weighted to eliminate the effect of the household size.

9. See Appendix 1 for the list of political parties classified as left. Respondents who did not answer the question (due to a refusal or because they did not know what party they would vote for) were excluded from the analysis. There were both substantial and technical reasons behind the decision to analyze only potential voters. Among the substantial reasons the most important was that the decision not to participate in the elections may have quite different social bases, from apathy stemming from strong disappointment, confusion due to the extremely large number of parties with loosely defined political programs, to satisfaction with a given order. Furthermore, due to some problems in coding various missing codes in a standard form in all participating countries ("don't know," "refused," "no answer," etc.) it was technically impossible to make clear distinctions between the various reasons for not having any code for the preferred political party. The analysis of potential no-voters would require a specific approach, both theoretical and analytical.

10. Coefficient GAMMA reached the value of 0.80 in the Czech Republic and Slovakia (pooled data). A simple crosstabulation has shown that of those who expressed extreme left political orientation (point 1 or 2 on a 10 point scale of the left-right political orientation), as many as 81 percent would vote for some of the political parties classified as belonging to the "Left." On the contrary, only 2 percent of those who expressed a strong "right" political orientation (points 9 or 10) would vote for any of the "left" political parties. Those who identified themselves with the political center (point 5) would only rarely vote for left political parties (17 percent). Since in other countries the question as to the respondent's position on the left-right political continuum was not posed we could not carry out similar control analyses for the remaining countries, though we believe that the results would show a similar consistency.

11. In order to avoid empty cells in the analyses, we collapsed higher and lower professionals, self-employed with and without employees, and created one category for all farm occupations (both private and employed).

12. The exact wording of the questions is provided in the Appendix.

13. The International Social Justice Project, a collaborative international survey research effort, was supported in whole or in part by each of the following organizations: The National Council for Soviet and East European Research (USA); the National Science Foundation (USA); the Institute for Social Research, University of Michigan; OTKA (National Scientific Research Fund, Hungary); the Economic and Social Research Council (UK); the Deutsche Forschungsgemein-

schaft (German Research Council); Institute of Social Science, Chuo University (Japan); the Dutch Ministry of Social Affairs; the Bulgarian Academy of Sciences; the Grant Agency of the Czechoslovak Academy of Sciences; Saar Poll, Limited (Estonia); the Ministry of Science and Technology of the Republic of Slovenia; the State Committee for Scientific Research (Komitet Badan Naukowych, Poland); and the Russian Federation Ministry of Labor. The following principal investigators were involved in this project and the development and analysis of the data: Galin Gornev and Pepka Boyadjieva (Bulgaria); Petr Mateju (Czechoslovakia); Andrus Saar (Estonia); Bernd Wegener (Germany); Gordon Marshall, Adam Swift and Carole Burgoyne (United Kingdom); Gyorgy Csepeli, Antal Orkeny, Tamas Kolosi and Maria Nemenyi (Hungary); Masaru Miyano and Akihiro Ishikawa (Japan); Wil Arts and Piet Hermkens (the Netherlands); Bogdan Cichomski and Witold Morawski (Poland); Ludmila Khakhulina and Svetlana Sydorenko (Russia); Vojko Antoncic (Slovenia); and Duane Alwin, James Kluegel and David Mason (United States of America).

14. Deviation contrast compares the effect for each category of the independent variable on the overall effect.

15. Table 1 shows some additional figures regarding the extent of relative deprivation in the individual countries. The relative deterioration of social status between 1988 and 1993 was reported by 64 percent of Bulgarians, 56 percent of Hungarians, 51 percent of Russians, 49 percent of Slovaks, 46 percent of Poles, but only 36 percent of Czechs. Figures regarding subjective income show a similar story: 59 percent of respondents in Bulgaria reported relative deterioration, 56 percent in Russia, 50 percent in Poland, 42 percent in Hungary, 41 percent in Slovakia and 32 percent in the Czech Republic.

16. To evaluate the strength of the effect (factor), we use both the level of statistical significance and the WALD statistic (defined as a square of the ratio between the regression coefficient and its standard error).

17. See also the values of the WALD statistics that are very high for all the three variables, but especially for ASCRIP.

REFERENCES

Bulletin of the East & Central Europe Program. 1994. 5/2(17, December).

Dahrendorf, R. 1990. *Reflections on the Revolutions in Europe*. New York: Times Books.

Della Fave, L.R. 1980. "The Meek Shall Not Inherit the Earth." *American Sociological Review* 45:955-971.

________. 1986a. "The Dialectics of Legitimation and Counternorms." *Sociological Perspectives* 29: 435-460.

________. 1986b. "Toward an Explication of the Legitimation Process." *Social Forces* 65: 476-500.

Habermas, J. 1975. *Legitimation Crisis*. Boston: Beacon Press.

Heath, A. 1990. "Class and Political Partisanship." Pp. 161-170 in *John H. Goldthorpe. Consensus and Controversy*, edited by J. Clark, C. Modgil, and S. Modgil. London: The Falmer Press.

Huber, J. and W.H. Form. 1973. *Income and Ideology*. New York: Free Press.

Janos, A.C. 1994. "Continuity and Change in Eastern Europe: Strategies of Post-Communist Politics." *East European Politics and Societies* 8(1): 1-31.

Kluegel, J.R., and P. Matějů. 1995. "Principles of Distributive Justice in Comparative Perspective." In *Social Justice and Political Change: Public Opinion in Capitalist and Post-Communist States*, edited by J.R. Kluegel, D.S. Mason, and B. Wegener. Hawthorne, NY: Aldine de Gruyter.

Kluegel, J.R., and E.R. Smith. 1981. "Beliefs about Stratification." *Annual Review of Sociology* 7: 29-56.

————. 1986. *Beliefs about Inequality*. Hawthorne, New York: Aldine de Gruyter.

Lenski, G. 1976. "History and Social Change." *American Journal of Sociology* 72: 548-564.

Lipset, S.M. 1981. *Political Man. The Social Bases of Politics*. Baltimore: The Johns Hopkins University Press.

Marshall, T.H. 1964. *Class Citizenship and Social Development*. New York: Doubleday.

Matějů, P. 1993a. "From Equality to Equity? The Czech Republic Between Two Ideologies of Distributive Justice." *Czech Sociological Review* 1(2): 251-276.

————. 1993b. "Determinanty Ekonomickeho Uspechu v Prvni Fazi Postkomunisticke Transformace. Ceska Republika 1989-1992" (Determinants of Economic Success in the First Stage of the Post-Communist Transformation. Czech Republic 1989-1992). *Sociologicky Casopis* 29(3): 34-366.

Matějů, P., and B. Řeháková. 1993. "Revolution for Whom? Analysis of Selected Patterns of Intragenerational Mobility 1989-1992." *Czech Sociological Review* 1(1): 73-90.

Offe, C. 1991. "Capitalism by Democratic Design? Democratic Theory Facing the Triple Transition in East Central Europe." *Social Research* 58(4): 865-892.

Parkin, F. 1971. *Class, Inequality and Political Order*. New York: Praeger.

Polanyi, K. 1944. *The Great Transformation. The Political and Economic Origins of Our Time*. Boston: Beacon.

Ritzman, R.L., and D. Tomaskovic-Devey. 1992. "Life Chances and Support for Equality and Equity As Normative and Counternormative Distribution Rules." *Social Forces* 70: 745-763.

Shepelak, N. 1987. "The Role of Self-explanation and Self-evaluation in Legitimating Inequality." *American Sociological Review* 52: 495-503.

Shepelak, N. and D. Alwin. 1986. "Beliefs about Inequality and Perceptions of Distributive Justice." *American Sociological Review* 51: 30-46.

Staniszkis, J. 1991. *The Dynamics of the Breakthrough in Eastern Europe: The Polish Experiment*. Berkeley: University of California Press.

Stark, D. 1992a. "Path Dependence and Privatization Strategies in East Central Europe." *East European Politics and Societies* 6:17-51.

————. 1992b. "From System Identity to Organisational Diversity: Analyzing Social Change in Eastern Europe." *Contemporary Sociology* 21(3).

Sztompka, P. 1992. "Dilemmas of the Great Transition." *Sisyphus* 8: 9-27.

Wesolowski, W., and E. Wnuk-Lipinski. 1992. "Transformation of Social Order and Legitimization of Inequalities." Pp. 83-95 in *Escape from Socialism. The Polish Route*, edited by W. Connor and P. Ploszajski. Warsaw: Fis Publishers.

Wnuk-Lipinski, E. 1992. "Freedom or Equality: An Old Dilemma in a New Context." Pp. 179-190 in *Social Policy, Social Justice and Citizenship in Eastern Europe*, edited by B. Deacon. Leeds: Faculty of Health, Sciences and Social Studies.

_______. 1993. *Left Turn in Poland.* A Sociological and Political Analysis. Warsaw: Institute of Political Studies, Polish Academy of Sciences.

_______. 1994. "The Vicissitudes of the Market Principles." *The International Social Science Journal* 140(May).

STATISM, EGALITARIANISM AND TRANSITION:

THE CASE OF SLOVAKIA

Iveta Radičová

In contrast to the Czech Republic the economic situation in Slovakia prior to 1989 was unusual. While under communism the Czech Republic experienced stagnation or even a decrease in the standard of living, socialist industrialization in Slovakia improved the economic position of households. As a consequence, Slovak citizens were not aware of the need for fundamental economic changes. Prior to the beginning of the economic reform in 1990, the attitudes of the Slovak population to such changes were less favorable than they were in the Czech Republic. In 1992, two thirds of the Slovak population thought that the principles of radical economic reform should be modified.

The results of the elections held in June 1992 and the consequent split of the Czech and Slovak Federal Republic caused a diversion in Slovakia from radical economic reform. (Under the government

International Review of Comparative Public Policy,
Volume 7, pages 83-100.

ISBN: 0-7623-0153-8

that was in office from March to September 1994, the original concept of reform was revitalized.) The September 1994 election was the third one in a sequence (1990, 1992, 1994), and after each election the government was substantially modified.

It is not a coincidence that people in Slovakia make a distinction between radical and gradual reform rather than between the ways in which the relationship between the state and the market will be re-established. How much state regulation should there be? Which powers should be given to the state bureaucracy? What is the desirable extent of privatization? These are the real questions. The two conceptions of the reform—the radical and the gradual one—are not heading toward the same target.

SOCIO-CULTURAL PARAMETERS OF THE SLOVAK SOCIETY

High Expectations of State Interference

"Generally states have been considered to be responsible for (1) setting collective goals, (2) gathering resources (taxes, draftees, and so on), (3) arbitrating relationships among the parts of society, (4) maintaining relationships with other societies. The days are long gone, however, when these were the only tasks of the state. A recent poll indicates that the majority of Americans also think the government is responsible for such things as taking care of the elderly, providing health care for the sick, keeping prices under control, providing industry with the help it needs to grow and providing a decent standard of living for the unemployed. One-third of Americans expect the government to be responsible for reducing income differences between the rich and poor and providing a job for everyone who wants one. As a consequence of these changing expectations, the jurisdiction of the state is growing" (Brinkerhoff and White, p. 392).

Zbigniew Brzezinski defined totalitarianism as a new kind of authoritarianism, one in which the state tries to pulverize all existing associations in society in order to remake that society and subsequently even man himself, according to certain ideal conceptions. The Soviet system after World War II was not merely authoritarian but totalitarian.

The common denominator of contrasting processes that are going on in "the Eastern" and "the Western" world is a redefinition of the role of the state. In many countries of the former Eastern bloc this process means the reduction of state functions.

In Slovakia, the opinions of the role of the state have been stable for a long period. In the eyes of the public, the state still preserves important functions; the demand for strong state intervention prevails. 80 percent of the population claims that the state should provide employment for everyone who wants to work. 75 percent of the population claims that the state should regulate prices more strictly, provide housing for every family that fails to acquire it, and order entrepreneurs to reduce the prices of some products. In 1993/94 the proportion of people who preferred state ownership slightly increased (48% in May 1994). Thus, in contrast to the early 1990s, it is not the opponents of state ownership but their advocates who now prevail. At the same time, the opinions supporting free market decreased. This shift corresponds to a slight decrease in confidence in the International Monetary Fund (the proportion of confidence/doubt in October 1993 was 48:36, and in May 1994 it was 40:39).

Strengthening Egalitarianism

The influence of the Communist ideology of egalitarianism is still manifested in an increased sensitivity to the perception of social inequality. Two thirds of the adult population would welcome a decrease in income differences. In 1994, the number of those who considered it appropriate for people to have much money, even millions of Crowns, has decreased (a drop from 60% in October 1993 to 53% in May 1994). At the same time, the prevalent opinion (83%) in Slovakia is that people only become rich through illegal business practices.

Cognitive Incompetence

Ambivalence and discrepancy of economic opinions are due not only to the conflicting experiences of the Communist period and of the new reality after 1989, but also to the projection of economic disorientation or even ignorance.

For example, 22 percent of the population claim that there should be unrestricted free private business and, at the same time, they think that state ownership should be predominant.

17 percent of the population think that the majority of enterprises should be privatized but, at the same time, state ownership of enterprises should prevail.

16 percent of the population think that foreign companies should enjoy maximal freedom in Slovakia and, at the same time, state ownership of enterprises should prevail.

40 percent of the population think that private business should enjoy maximal freedom and, at the same time, they claim that the state should officially set the prices of goods.

Approximately one third of the population express inconsistent or unclear opinions of different kinds. Part of them can be characterized as having discrepant or conflicting attitudes.

Passive Life Strategies

Afrustrated society represents defensive and passive life strategies. Because people lack experience in a market economy, economic pressure activates them to a much lesser degree than in Western societies. On the contrary, traditional adaptive strategies are activated. The Slovaks compensate for their worsening financial situation after 1989 by choosing a modest way of life, using "do-it-yourself strategies," or by spending their savings. Less frequently, they apply more innovative techniques, for example, starting their own business, finding a new job or producing for the market. Prior to 1989, a shadow economy developed in Slovakia. Very likely, it is still in existence.

Nostalgia

As the time passes, the positive rating of the past regime increases. This phenomenon is present in all post-communist countries, but to a different degree. The strength of nostalgia correlates differently with the economic situation and the threat to social safety in each country.

ECONOMIC ORIENTATION

Poor awareness of the need for systemic changes and ignorance of the depth of economic crisis (growth of unemployment, devaluation of the Slovak currency, increase of cost of living, financial problems in education, health care, and culture) and political instability is manifested in opinions on the preferred models of economy.

Referring to 16 indicators used in the May 1994 survey (Appendix), three types of economic orientation of Slovak citizens can be identified. They range from state-paternalism to individualism.

Socialist or state-paternalistic orientation is represented by 43 percent. Those of this opinion have great expectations of the state, its role and responsibility. They have little confidence in privatization, private business in general and quick transformation. They prefer strong state intervention in the economy.

Liberal orientation is represented by 19 percent. This is the counterpart of the previous attitude. Its followers expect that the state will intervene in the economy to a minimal degree. It is the individual who takes responsibility, and the transformation should be fast.

Social-market economy orientation is represented by 38 percent. This is an intermediary position between the two orientations described above. It shows a moderate or an unclear preference for radical transformation, or a clear preference for cautious change.

Businessmen have distinctly different opinions on the role of the state. 53 percent of them prefer a liberal state, 36 percent prefer a social-market state and only 11 percent prefer the socialist type of state.

CURRENT SOCIAL POLICY

Attitudes to Social Policy

The emphasis on the role of the state also applies to social policy. On the whole, inclinations to three basic social policy models can be identified: the institutional redistributive model, the corporatist model and the liberal-conservative model.

The three social policy positions were identified (March 1993) by means of negative or affirmative replies to the following five statements:

1. "If parents want their children to receive a better quality education at private elementary or secondary schools, they should pay for it themselves."
2. "Unemployment benefit should be low enough to motivate the unemployed to search for a job."

3. "People should have only as many children as they can bring up themselves."
4. "If people want better health care, they should pay for it."
5. "If people do not have enough money to afford the rent or to buy an apartment, they should move to a cheaper place.

The institutional redistributive model of welfare involves a universal, state-financed social policy. This is expected by 40 percent of respondents who expressed their agreement with a maximum of one of the above statements.

At the opposite end of the scale there is the liberal-conservative, residual type of social policy whose main actors are the individual, the family and private agencies. Social policy aims specifically at those members of the society who are in a situation of threat, unable to take care of themselves. The propensity for the residual model of social policy is found among 18% of respondents who expressed their agreement with at least four of the five possible statements on social policy.

The corporatist model of social policy has a pluralist character; its actors include—in addition to the state—also the employers. This is a model in which the state, the individuals, the family and the social agencies all play their role in social policy. This model is supported by 42 percent of the respondents who expressed their agreement with two or three of the above statements.

Social policy in prewar Czechoslovakia was based on a corporatist model. That model was modified by the communist system. It can be characterized as a mix of universalist elements of the redistributive system and the corporatist model. The residual model does not have a strong tradition in Slovakia. Past experience is also reflected in the present-day preferences of the population in favor of the redistributive and corporatist welfare model.

Any preference for a social policy model is interconnected with ideas concerning the role of the state. Individuals who support the redistributive model include 46 percent of those of socialist orientation, 39 percent of those of social market orientation, and 23 percent of those of liberal-conservative orientation.

In contrast to the 90 percent of individuals of socialist orientation and 79 percent of individuals of social market orientation who stress the combination of redistributive and corporatist models, 79 percent of individuals of liberal-conservative orientation prefer the combination of corporatist and residual models.

Conception of Social Policy

"The issue of social welfare reform and implementation of adequate social policy is becoming more and more urgent. It can affect the implementation of transformation as a whole. This is even more important because of the fact that citizens perceive the level of social rights provided by the former communist "social state" as natural, and they are very sensitive to any reductions of these rights. With this characteristics the transformation of post-communist countries of Eastern Europe differs from modern Western countries that proceeded first from civil rights to political rights, and only then to social rights. It is therefore obvious that no political party in the elections of 1990, 1992 or 1994 claimed to change the deeply rooted system of social benefits and social care... The basic strategic task of the transformation is to decrease the subjective importance of social benefits and pensions by increasing dynamism of incomes" (Faltăn 1994, pp. 30-31).

In the social policy of the Slovak government after the 1992 elections the main components were employment policy and the transformation of the system of social benefits, that is, its separation from the state budget. Governmental measures, sometimes chaotic, were rooted in the government's inclination to preserve the redistributive model of social policy. However, the necessity of implementing a restrictive economic policy pushed the government toward the residual or the mixed model. The government was not ripe for the implementation of this conception, in particular because social policy reductions bring a decline of public support.

Social Welfare

Current political and economic development in Slovakia affected the transformation of the former state welfare system to a system of public insurance. Both its organization and financing and its legal status were transformed. In 1993, an act on the establishment of National Insurance and on financing health, medical and pension plans was passed. At the same time, the Act on Health Insurance Fund, Pension Insurance Fund and Medical Insurance Fund was passed as well.

The National Insurance Act contained a number of formal, financial and legislative inadequacies. During 1993, a so-called "small amendment" to this act was passed. It concerned self-employed persons, and included a number of additional provisions.

From a legislation point of view, the terms "insured person" and "insurance payer" were not defined clearly. Under the present act, the employer is required to pay insurance twice—once for himself and once for his employees. After one year, the government decided to change the organization of National Insurance. The three divisions—health, medical and pension—now constitute separate bodies.

The completion of the insurance system requires two other insurance plans: an accident plan and an additional pension plan. The National Insurance Act, however, caused, at least theoretically, a transformation of social-security relations to social-insurance relations. These compel the individual to be more active, socially independent and responsible for his/her social situation. The state, however, offers a necessary social provision for those who need it.

Employment Policy

A factor that makes the National Insurance Act problematic is the insufficient linkage between individual governmental measures. This factor—together with others such as hasty decisions, overestimation of the absorption capacity of the economy, overestimation of managers' abilities, concentration on macroeconomic questions—caused a crisis in the company sector. The number of companies that suffered losses and indebtedness increased, sales decreased, and this, in turn, caused a loss of jobs. This situation in the business sector affected the overall decline of the economy. As compared to 1990, in the period from 1991 to 1993 the GNP decreased by 23.7 percent. This decline has not as yet stopped. Compared to 1990, industrial production in 1993 was reduced by about 40 percent.

In Slovakia, unemployment is defined as the number of applicants for jobs who are filed with employment offices. An internationally recognized measure of unemployment is, however, the duration of

Table 1. The Rate of Unemployment in Slovakia

1990	*1991*	*1992*	*1993*	*1994*
1.5%	11.5%	10.38%	14.4%	14.88%

being without job. This determines the intensity of effects of unemployment and thus also the amount of costs.

Long-term unemployed constitute one third of the overall number of unemployed. Among the long-term unemployed there are groups which find it difficult to be placed in the labor market. Specifically, these are people with no education or with basic education only. In other words, the lower the qualifications, the smaller the opportunities in the labor market, and vice versa.

So far, employment policy in Slovakia has consisted of partial measures that were used in a sporadic way (e.g., support of some preferred group of citizens, such as small businessmen, school graduates, handicapped persons, or creation of new jobs through public works). An urgent task is to shift the emphasis from a "social treatment" policy to an active employment policy using well-defined employment programs. The success of employment programs, however, depend on the efficiency of the work of the employment offices and on the strategic policy of the government. Governmental activities should include, first of all, legislative changes, especially changes in tax laws, support of entrepreneurship, creation of jobs, improving conditions for the entry of foreign capital, and so forth.

Educational Policy

One of the preconditions for the successful transformation of Slovak society is raising the educational level of the population. In contrast to the developed countries of Europe, education in the Slovak Republic is over-represented by lower educational categories, while university graduates are under-represented. This is demonstrated in Table 2.

Table 2. Educational Structure of Population in Slovakia

Year	*1970*	*1980*	*1991*
Completion of the level of education of the Slovak population, expressed as a percentage of the population			
primary	61%	52%	39%
lower secondary	21%	23%	29%
secondary	13%	18%	25%
university	3%	5%	8%

Table 3. Number of Schools in Slovakia by Type and Level of Education in 1993-1994

	Type		
Level	*State*	*Private*	*Church*
primary (8-9 yrs. of instr.)	2,577	4	83
secondary (3-5 yrs. of instr.)	885	16	32

In 1990 the Educational System Transformation Program was developed. This made it possible to establish new church and private elementary, lower secondary and secondary schools. Additionally, secondary vocational schools for household economics and bilingual grammar schools were established, and religious instruction was introduced at elementary schools.

In higher education, academic liberty and self-administration were strengthened. New academic fields, faculties and universities were established. The existing University Act has, however, many inadequacies. Issues such as doctoral studies, students' participation in university self-government, self-management of universities and faculties are all unresolved. In 1993 an amendment to the University Act was prepared as well as a new version of the act, but they were not passed by the parliament.

The educational sector is funded by the government but the deficit in the budget is large. There are plans to diversify education so that its costs would be covered, not only by the state, but also by tuition, individual sponsors, foundations or other sources. Under the current financial situation of families, however, tuition would discriminate against a large portion of the population. Even without tuition, the current cost of schooling (housing, meals, fees, transportation) causes severe financial problems for half of the families. Three fourths of the population claim that the cost of education should be paid by the state.

In Slovakia, the non-profit sector is weak. The country lacks a law on non-profit institutions. Profit-making companies are overloaded with high taxes, loans, and so forth.

Housing Policy

Before 1990, the state covered most of the costs of housing construction. It provided funds by means of subsidies, to fully cover the construction of communal houses, technological infrastructure and public services, and to partly cover the construction of cooperative flats and individual houses through cheap loans and credits. It also covered losses of housing management, and, in part, rent, heating, energy, water supply and other services related to housing. These benefits were provided to every citizen regardless of the person's income. By the end of 1993, most of these benefits were gradually removed. Since 1990, due to these changes, housing costs for the families have increased by five times.

Most citizens (52.6%) live in their own houses. The remaining 47 percent live in flats. 3 percent of these flats are owned by their users. Due to this fact 90 percent of house owners are satisfied with their housing conditions. Houses have a larger overall area if compared with flats in apartment houses (83.6 m^2 : 61.9 m^2), more rooms (3.2 : 2.5), fewer inhabitants per flat (1.07 : 1.22), more space for one person (16.2 m^2 : 12.8 m^2) (Slovak Census data, 1991).

Typically, Slovak citizens are strongly linked to their own houses or flats. Only 20 percent of citizens consider changing their flats. This immobility is not caused by external pressure only (i.e., by the difficulties of changing a flat, lack of flats, etc.), but also by a high degree of satisfaction with housing (80% of citizens are very satisfied or more or less satisfied with their housing conditions). In the turbulent and unstable life after communism the flat became an important "fixed star." This fact is reflected in the life strategies, for example, an unwillingness to change residence when having a new job, and so forth.

The year 1992 brought serious changes for 44 percent of Slovak citizens residing in state and cooperative houses, and also for those who decided to construct their own houses in spite of the termination of the above-mentioned state subsidies. For 27 percent of the Slovak population, increased costs for housing did not cause serious problems, for 48 percent they caused some problems and 20 percent claim the new situation caused great problems.

Currently, a law enabling the purchase of state-owned houses by individuals is being discussed. Two thirds of the tenants are inclined to purchase their flats and half of them have firmly decided to do so. Their decision is due to the fact that they expect purchase prices to be lower than the cumulated rent. The law makes it possible to purchase a flat for a price that is much lower than its market value, and provides loans without interest.

SOCIAL SITUATION

Social Differences Prior to 1989

Until 1989, many of the favorable indicators of the standard of living in Slovakia had been reached at the expense of an enormous amount of work and energy. They were the result of a high level of employment, double employment in families, exceptionally long working times in international comparison, a great deal of casual work in the shadow economy, time losses in queues and traveling to the workplace.

In the officially homogeneous society there were three basic types of families: the family as a self-supplier, the family as an entrepreneur, the family as a consumer. Their common feature was that the individual members of the family were originally employed in the state sector.

The distribution of the family types was the following: family-entrepreneur—one-tenth of the population, family-self-supplier—six-tenths and family-consumer—three-tenths of the population. This means that 70 percent of the population was engaged in domestic production, 11% of them on the basis of market principles (Database "Investigation of the Class and Social Structure of Slovak Population," microcensus 1984).

Slovak people traditionally relied more on themselves and on their family to satisfy their basic needs. Even after the changes in 1989, part of the families' consumer expenditure is covered by household production.

In 1991, 8.5 percent of the citizens in Slovakia (21% in the Czech Republic) tried to improve their standard of living by becoming entrepreneurs. One third of these were only second-job entrepreneurs. They used entrepreneurship as an additional source of income.

Types of Consumer Behavior

Regarding income distribution, 62 percent of the Slovak population has a net income per member of the household under the average. Businessmen report their situation to be good; the income of three fourths of them is above the average level.

According to our findings, 6 percent of the population live under the minimum income level. This, however, does not automatically mean that this social group is poor in terms of property. There is a difference between income minimum or social minimum income or the state of material need.

The financial situation of the family is reflected by its consumer behavior. We have created a typology of consumer behavior based on a survey on the consumption of meat, other grocery goods, alcohol, clothes and shoes, expenditure for visiting cultural events, for durables, and holidays and housing. The typology is as follows: Type 1—unrestricted consumer behavior (restriction in one or in none of the above categories of items), Type 2—slightly restricted consumption (in 2 to 4 categories), Type 3—strong restriction in consumption (in 5-7 categories), Type 4—radical restriction (in all, or at least in 8 out of 9 possible categories).

Businessmen differ from others by their consumption behavior. Half of them have no problems with household expenditures. At the same time, one quarter of the businessmen strongly or radically restricted their consumption.

The highest rate of restriction in consumption is reported by people in their middle ages (25 to 44 years). Expenditures of this group are naturally higher than those of younger and older age groups. The extent of restrictions depend on the level of education—2/3 of lower education respondents report strong or radical restriction of consumption, while 2/3 of university graduate respondents restricted their consumption only slightly or not at all. Of course, this corresponds to the traditional consumption behavior of people with different educational levels.

The largest restrictions were reported by persons who are economically inactive: unemployed, housewives, those on maternity leave, and retired. Similar rates of restriction were reported by workers, manual employees in services, and cooperative farmers (65-75% of respondents in these social groups claim that they had to restrict expenditures for consumption strongly or radically).

Table 4. Typology of Consumer Behavior

	Total	*Businessmen*
Unrestricted Consumption	16%	52%
Slightly Restricted Consumption	27%	24%
Strongly Restricted Consumption	41%	19%
Radically Restricted Consumption	17%	6%

The least affected group were students, businessmen and private farmers. Only 1/4 of them had to restrict expenditure on consumption strongly or radically.

Officials, technicians and intellectuals are spread in the center of continuum between economically inactive people and businessmen. The proportion of those who have to "tighten their belts" substantially in comparison to those who do not restrict themselves much was one to one.

Social Differences and the Transformation

Those respondents who experience a "tightening of belts" are substantially less persuaded to accept that the economy needed deep changes. Twice as few respondents in this category are persuaded about the need for deep changes in the economy as in the opposite category (39% versus 62%).

The stricter the restrictions, the higher the preference of the individual for a socialist or social market oriented economy with strong state intervention. Also, a positive relationship between the subjective evaluation of one's standard of living and self-rating on the left-right political continuum is manifested. The lower the standard of living, the stronger the leftist inclinations, and vice versa.

The view of a better economic situation is linked with a stronger emphasis on individualism. 60 percent of respondents of the first type of consumption behavior claim that individuals should take more responsibility for their living, while 20 percent think that the state should take more responsibility and ensure fair living for everyone. At the other end, those with radically restricted consumption represent a different ratio between individualism and paternalism (35%:41%).

Typical statements of the well-to-do are: people are responsible for their own poverty; it is correct that skillful people earn a lot of money, even millions; private business should be restricted as little as possible; as many companies as possible should be privatized. On the other hand, respondents who restricted their consumption expenditure radically claim that the state should regulate prices; differences in incomes should be reduced; the state should provide employment for everyone who wants to work; people get rich by being involved in illegal business. The results of discriminant analysis confirmed that from differences in the above attitudes the standard of living of the individual could be inferred. As many as 73 percent of respondents could be correctly categorized in this way.

In Slovakia, a trend toward the crystallization of attitudes and the creation of coherent interpretation schemes of macro and micro level relationships of social phenomena can be detected. There is an obvious connection between the level of consumption of households and macroeconomic attitudes, values, and political orientation. A broader support of systemic changes is possible only if the positive impacts of these changes occur in the everyday life of the individual and if the well-to-do social group is strengthened and increased.

APPENDIX

The Role of the State

In Slovakia, attitudes toward the role of the state in the period from 1991 to 1994 were stabilized. This can be illustrated by the following findings:

Role of the Individual and the State

A. Individuals should take more responsibility in caring for their own living.
B. The state should take more responsibility in caring for everyone.

(5-point scale with a central point; strongly agree and agree with A = individualism, strongly agree and agree with B = paternalism) Businessmen differ considerably from this trend. The score of individualism versus paternalism in this group is 71% : 15%.

State Ownership of Companies Should Prevail

(4-point scale without a central point; strongly agree and agree versus strongly disagree and disagree)

Table 5.

	1990	Sept. 1992	Oct. 1993	May 1994
Individualism	34%	41%	60%	44%
Paternalism	40%	28%	15%	32%

Table 6.

	Slovak Republic	Czech Republic
May 1991	42.2 : 45.9	
January 1992	43.2 : 47.7	27.3 : 65.0
April 1992	44.2 : 40.9	
March 1993	43.2 : 45.2	
October 1993	45.0 : 46.1	
May 1994	48.1 : 43.4	

"Should the role of the state in setting the prices of goods be more extensive?"

Real Economic Orientations—Indicators

Do you think that our economy prior to 1989: did not need changes/only small changes/deep changes.

Foreign companies should act freely in this country.

It is correct that skillful people earn a lot of money, even millions.

Private businessmen's activities should be restricted as little as possible.

Economic changes should be slow in order to prevent unemployment.

People are responsible for their own poverty.

People in this country get rich predominantly by being involved in illegal business.

Most of the unemployed are people who no not want to work.

Changes in the economy should be as quick as possible, even if they cause a temporary decrease of the standard of living.

State ownership of companies should prevail.

The state should provide employment for everyone who wants to work.

Table 7.

	March 1993	October 1993	May 1994
Strongly Agree	43%	49%	43%
Rather Agree than Disagree	32%	31%	32%
Rather Disagree than Agree	16%	14%	14%
Strongly Disagree	5%	5%	7%
I do not know	5%	2%	3%

The role of the state in setting the prices of goods should be more extensive.

Differences in incomes should be reduced.

(A) The individuals should take more responsibility in caring for themselves, (B) The state should take more responsibility in caring for everyone.

Which economy do you prefer?

What is your opinion on the establishment of private elementary and secondary schools?

REFERENCES

Aaron H.J., T.E. Mann, and T. Taylor. 1994. *Values and Public Policy*. Washington: The Brookings Institution.

Aktuálne problémy Slovenska - Máj 1994. Správa zo sociologického výskumu

V. Krivý, and I. Radičová. 1994. *Aktuálne Problémy Slovenska - Máj 1994, Správa zo Sociologického Výskumu* (Topical Problems of Slovakia. Sociological Research Paper). Bratislava: FOCUS, SPACE.

Radiçová, I. 1993. *Aktuálne Problémy Slovenska po Rozpade ÇSFR–Október 1993, Správa zo Sociologického Výskumu* (Topical Problems of Slovakia after the split of Czechoslovakia. Sociological Research Paper). Bratislava: FOCUS.

———. 1993. *Aktuálne Problémy Slovenska po Rozpade ČSFR - Marec 1993, Správa zo Sociologického výskumu* (Topical Problems of Slovakia After the Split of Czechoslovakia. Sociological Research Paper). Bratislava: CSA.

Brinkerhoff D.B., and L.K. White. 1988. *Sociology* (2nd edition). St. Louis, MO: West Publishing Company.

Daneková Z. 1994. *Bývanie a Komunálne Byty* (Housing and Communal Flats). Bratislava: SPACE.

Faltăn, S. et al. 1994. *Slovensko a Jeho Premeny na Začiatku 90. Rokov. Spoločnost–Ekonomika–Veda a Technika* (Slovakia and its Transformation in the Early 90s). Bratislava: Socologický ústav SAV, Komisia DGXII Európskeho spoloçenstva.

Eliášová D. 1994. *Sociálne Poistenie* (Social Insurance). Bratislava: SPACE.

Koşta J. et al. 1994. *Vývoj dlhodobej nezamestnanosti v SR* (Development of Long-term Unemployment in Slovakia). Bratislava: SPACE.

Letková T. 1994. *Dokumentačná štúdia za oblast školstva a Kultúry* (Documentational Study of Education and Culture). Bratislava: SPACE.

Radičová, I. 1993. "Privatization: The Case of Slovakia." *History of European Ideas* 17(6).

———. 1994. "Attitudes to the Present Economic Situation in Slovakia." *Acta Oeconomica* 446(1-2).

———. 1989. "O zemitosti Nášho Vol'ného času (On Earthiness of our Free Time). *Sociológia* 4.

Sharp A.M., C.A. Register, and R.H. Leftwich. 1990. *Economics of Social Issues*. Boston.

Sullivan, T.J., and K.S. Thomson. 1988. *Introduction to Social Problems*. New York: Macmillan Publishing Company.

Štatistická Ročenka Slovenska (Statistical Yearbook of Slovakia). 1991. Bratislava: Slovenský Štatistický úrad.

TWO SOCIETIES?

POLAND IN AND BEYOND TRANSFORMATION

Andrzej Rychard

INTRODUCTION

In my paper, I would like to focus on certain hypotheses concerning the shape of society in Poland. Each social policy must, in fact, be based on a diagnosis defining the state of the society. It should use such a diagnosis as a starting point and, at the same time, develop a vision of the future condition of society.

In Poland, we are dealing with at least two conceptions of the present state of the society.

According to one of them, the phenomena of poverty and unemployment are becoming increasingly lasting and profound. This stems, among other things, from a steady increase in long-term unemployment. It may lead to a durable structural division of the society, and the marginalization of a group of people unable to take

International Review of Comparative Public Policy,
Volume 7, pages 101-107.

ISBN: 0-7623-0153-8

advantage of the economic growth. This may lead to a destabilization of the political and social system. According to some experts, the economic growth alone, even if sustained, would not solve this structural problem and the question should be asked whether a social policy can serve as a remedy here.

I shall start with what I find unquestionable. It is certain that economic growth alone does not solve the problem of uneven distribution of poverty and marginalization of several social groups. This is where active social policy should come into action. However—to touch upon more questionable issues—the size of these groups and the proportion of society affected by marginalization are debatable.

Various hypotheses might be put forward here. On the one hand, on the basis of available data, including regional statistics, an upward trend has been observed. On the other hand, dichotomy can be expected to spring up as a result of such differentiation. Those who take advantage of the transformation process, and those who are "beyond the transformation"[1] forming an important part of the community affected by marginalization.

The fundamental question is, in my view, whether, as a consequence of the transformation process, a dual form of society with impenetrable boundaries, or rather a more gradual social structure is likely to arise.

Parenthetically, I would like to mention that such a dispute about the nature of society is not a specifically Polish phenomenon. In addition, as in Poland, the choice of one of these approaches depends not only on empirical data but also on the adopted ideology. Generally, partisans of ideologies leaning toward the left tend to see societies as dychotomic entities marked with a deep fundamental conflict, whereas, among followers of rightist orientations, the conception of a gradationed social structure is more common.

TOWARD THE GRADUAL STRUCTURE

I believe that the decreasing probability of a dichotomy is one of the features specific to the Polish transformation process. For the time being, the conception of a bipolar society does not reflect the reality of the situation.

First, with the end of the initial stage of the transformation process, the phase of mass support for the new order came to an end. This also means that mass rejection, mass rebellion is no longer possible, or at least less feasible. Nowadays, it is difficult to mobilize long-term support, but also eminently hard to mobilize a protest (the ambiguous course and outcome of the strikes in 1993/94 might be a good example here). The present phase is characterized by differentiation of conflicts, by their local nature, as well as by their increasingly pragmatic course.

What we are witnessing in Poland is not a conflict between the interests of the poor groups of society and liberal reforms. Frequently, it is a series of heterogeneous, local, sometimes vague disagreements, which are often related to the definition of the reform rather than directly and decisively oriented against it. Similarly, the left swing at the last elections should not, in my view, be interpreted as an expression of a mass "no" to the policy of reforms, but rather as a result of the fact that an important segment of society—including people who are actually or potentially partisans of the reform—lives "outside politics," having lost interest in it and consequently abstaining from voting. Within this segment, there are people who, in their everyday life, "make the transformation" by getting on within the "gray" zone between the supporters and the opponents of liberal reforms, but who do not vote because they do not see any link between the act of voting and their own future situation.

Secondly, division between the winners and the losers is not clear or bipolar. A considerable fluctuation in the criteria for success and failure can be observed. These criteria are more multi-dimensional than ever. I suppose, instead of total success or total failure we see a growing number of cases of relative deprivation.

The notion of deprivation is becoming relative in three different ways:

1. People compare themselves with other people—that is, with various groups of other people.
2. People compare themselves with others on various planes; not only in respect of their welfare, but also in terms of prestige and freedom—and these planes are hardly connected with one another. In some respects you are above others, in some you are beneath them; what is more, some planes are losing significance, while others are becoming more valued.
3. Finally, people make comparisons according to various expectations or various points of reference. For some of them,

> the past is the point of reference, others are already making comparisons with the Western world. In this context, it is not surprising that even some groups which are very high in the hierarchy of affluence may feel quite bad—having reached a point, where they are already able to compare themselves with their counterparts in the West.

Combined, this results in an increasing differentiation, the sources, advancement and degradation mechanisms of which remain unclear. The borderline of the existing division is not drawn between the poor and the rich. It is rather a "cognitive" division, which varies according to the degree of familiarity with the rules of advancement and ability to assess one's own qualifications. This is where active social policy should enter the scene in order to explain that even those who are relatively poor often have some kind of capital (knowledge, leisure, etc.). It is specific to such new divisions that they run across the social structure portrayed in a conventional way. Therefore, sociologically, they are still difficult to discover.

I do not want to avoid the question of whether there is really no risk of developing two societies[2] with impenetrable boundaries: a society of victory and a society of social defeat, a society under transformation and a society beyond the transformation. The obstacles to the mobility processes and the high degree of centralization in the country's government structure are, in my view, the main factors increasing the chances for developing a dual structure. Local governments and various self-organizing institutions may lower the risk of creating a "Poland with two societies." Social policy is, in fact, a mechanism serving to construct passages between these two worlds. I believe that social differentiation, in particular its multi-dimensional nature, facilitates the construction of such passages. The more equal the chances and the more recognizable and attainable the advancement mechanisms are, the easier the transformation of a "two worlds" society into "a ladder society" becomes. In Poland, there are many ladders—some are dead-end, others are yet unknown.

In our times of confusion, certain signs of order begin to appear, even though, for the time being, they are of a local character. Education is more and more appreciated in the society. In addition, the links between education and income are growing stronger. For instance, according to Henryk Domanski's studies, Polish society is now undergoing a process of "re-composition:" various aspects of the social status are linked in a more transparent way than before. Linking outlays with outcomes in a meritocratic manner, aided by social policy, is precisely what serves to build these passages.

There are also other factors which reduce the risk of a social closure and help build an open society. People, although withdrawn from politics, are active outside it. It is a sort of evolution from passive politicization toward active depoliticization. From normative support during the first stage of transformation toward local activity and strategies of "getting on" and "coping." Many initiatives are being born, social movements are evolving and becoming institutional. The number of households with more than one source of revenue is growing (from 40% in 1986 to 55% in 1992, see Beskid 1993). People do feel increasingly threatened with poverty, nevertheless, in 1991/92 there was, for instance, a considerable rise in the number of people declaring that they would manage to cope with it (from 29% to 49%) (ibid). Thus, people's activity outside politics, in the social and economic fields, is becoming more intense and visible.

Whether the dichotomy will or will not develop depends on the degree of impenetrability of both worlds—"the world of success" and "the world of failure." Alone the existence of the world of winners and the world of losers does not create a dichotomous social structure. If people see a passage between the two worlds, they are better motivated for active strategies. If the system is open and permits social mobility, then the transformation is a process of revealing opportunities. Sociological tests indicate that over longer periods, social structure tends to remain rigid and it is only during dramatic transformations that mobility gains momentum. In so-called normal times, social structure tends toward self-reproduction. This finding shattered one of the liberal myths according to which mobility would increase with growing industrialization (see Allardt 1994; Pontinen 1994). In other words, transformation gives us a chance which, however, does not have to be long-lasting. It is impossible to make the most of it unless the openness of the social structure is beyond any doubt and the rules of success are clear.

At some point in the future, the groups which are active outside politics may decide to use political instruments to attain their objectives. Hence, whether or not the political system will be open to their aspirations seems to be a fundamental question in this context. If it is not, there will be a risk of destabilization. That is where social policies can help: they can institutionalize activities already carried out by the people. This is also where a "political policy" should come into action—in other words, a policy that creates mechanisms which facilitate the functioning of active social policies.

POLITICS AND SOCIAL POLICY: CONCLUSIONS

The basic problem is not the lack of activity on the part of society, but the fact that this activity is seldom connected with people's participation in politics. Thus, while we have a society coping with the transformation "outside politics," there are nevertheless essential imperfections in the institutional structure to be observed in Poland. Jadwiga Staniszkis (1994) points out that truly important institutions in Polish society are born outside politics and beyond any democratic control. What she has in mind is the emergence of major economic projects with unclear structures of ownership. A. Kaminski and J. Kurczewska (1994) observe that a sort of "political nomadism" characterizes the construction of new institutions by the political elite. It means that certain groups of the elite gain control over a given institution in order to assert their group interests and then, having made the most of these institutions, leave them without attempting to create a strategic vision of the new order as a whole.

Thus where the society is living "outside politics," important institutions, or elements of the developing institutional order, are also beyond politics or, being part of it, they are created according to rules which do not necessarily have anything to do with democratic control. All in all, taking a pessimistic approach, we can say that politics and its democratic rules lose significance, as a large part of what is important takes place beyond them. There is a question to be asked here: Is it not possible that the society and the institutions remaining outside the democratic discourse find a way to communicate outside the framework of this discourse? Could this not result in some kind of attempt to create an order combining autocratic elements with elements of social consent? This is one of the possible scenarios for the future.

However, another scenario exists; a scenario of hoping that the present social activity outside politics will give birth to a true civic society, one which will find a new political structure. Such a structure, remaining within the framework of the democratic order, would not be legitimated by its genesis or its origins, but by its strategic program for the future. The trend toward the institutionalization of such a political system is essential to social policy.

NOTES

1. The term "beyond the transformation" is used here as shorthand, to designate those who are beyond the reach of positive effects of the transformation.
2. Compare the conception of two and three worlds presented by J. Wertenstein-Zulawski (1993).

REFERENCES

Beskid, L. 1993. "Social Feelings about the Change of Welfare (Nastroje spoleczne wobec zmian sytuacji materialnej)." In *Society Under Transformation. Experts' Reports and Studies* [*Spoleczenstwo w transformacji. Ekspertyzy i studia*), edited by M. Federowicz. Warsaw: IFiS PAN.

Allardt, E. 1994. "Major Trends in Society and Sociology (Główne tendencje w spoleczenstwie i w socjologii). In *The Transformation of Europe* [*Transformacja Europy*], edited by Alestalo, Allardt, Rychard, Wesolowski. IFiS Publishers (under printing).

Kaminski, A., and J. Kurczewska. 1994. "The Constancy of Social Mobility in Fluctuating Class Structures" (Stalosc mobilnosci spolecznej w plynnych strukturach klasowych). In *The Transformation of Europe* (*Transformacja Europy*], edited by Alestalo, Allardt, Rychard, Wesolowski. IFiS Publishers.

Wóycicka, I. 1994. Paper presented to the 3rd Central European Forum (Wystapienie nt. polityki spolecznej na II European Forum), Vienna: Institute for Human Sciences (Instytut Nauk Spolecznych).

Staniszkis, J. 1994. *Searching for a Transformation Paradigm: Introduction* (W poszukiwaniu paradygmatu transformacji: wprowadzenie) (mimeo).

Westenstein-Zulawski, J. 1993. *Between Hope and Distress* (*Miedzy nadzieja i rozpacza*). Warsaw: Institute of Culture (Instytut Kultury).

PART II

ECONOMIC POLICY, REGULATIONS AND SOCIAL CHANGE: SOCIAL (IN)EQUALITY

SOCIAL DIFFERENCES IN POLAND

Michal Boni

SOCIAL PERCEPTION AND AWARENESS

During the 1980s, the Polish intelligentsia was characterized by the domination of non-egalitarian, pro-capitalist ideas. At the same time, the non-skilled workers and some of the skilled workers opted for the values of the socialist system, while rejecting the manner in which those values were implemented. The support for non-egalitarian slogans in the latter groups was a form of political protest against communist power rather than a conscious acceptance of free-market rules.

Since 1989, the process of systemic transformation has crystallized mass opinion and significantly increased differences in material standing. The past six years have brought an increase in income differences between blue-collar workers, white-collar workers and managers. Income per capita in blue-collar families (in relation to the national average) was lower in 1993 than in 1987, while white-collar incomes increased 1.5 times, and managers' incomes 2.5 times.

International Review of Comparative Public Policy,
Volume 7, pages 111-123.

ISBN: 0-7623-0153-8

Education became an important element, facilitating adaptation to the new economic and living conditions. Persons with a university education in Poland have about a three times better chance of finding a job than persons with only an elementary education: their quarterly rate of leaving the group of unemployed is 22 percent, compared to 8 percent for the second group.

Current research on income hierarchy confirms an overall tendency toward egalitarianism. According to research conducted by the Center for Public Opinion Research (CBOS), of the social income ladder in Poland is as follows: president of the republic, private entrepreneur, prime minister, minister, manager of a state-owned company, member of parliament, priest, politician, university professor, army officer, medical doctor, engineer, miner, policeman, worker in a private company, individual farmer, clerk, teacher, worker in a state-owned company, cleaner (CBOS, Warsaw, March 1994). The income of a cleaner is estimated to be 15 times lower than that of the president, and twelve times lower than that of a private businessman. However, people claim that the gap between the highest and the lowest earners should be smaller, ranging from 1:10 to 1:7. Those at the top of the list should have lower salaries, while the salaries of those professions which fall under the national average should be increased. This latter category includes the workers in both private and state-owned companies, clerks, teachers, farmers and cleaners. There was also some support for increasing the earnings of university professors, doctors and miners. Opinions seem fairly unified as to which groups have lost and which have gained in the course of the transformation (see Table 1).

At first glance it seems that according to Poles, the highest price for the introduction of a market economy is being paid by non-skilled workers, skilled workers and farmers. White collar workers, managers and priests are viewed, along with the owners of private companies, as beneficiaries of the transformation. However as the economic reform develops, the number of social groups which gain due to this process is increasing. Following an initially hard period, doctors, engineers employed in state industry, and even teachers entered a better phase.

But how are the various factors contributing to social differences viewed? Clearly, the role of material factors in determining social status is increasing. In 1994, wealth was listed as the criterion of social difference by 72 percent of CBOS respondents. Social awareness

Table 1.

How do the following persons fare in comparison to the situation five years ago?	1994 better	1994 worse	1993 better	1993 worse	1991 better	1991 worse
owners of private companies	82	7	75	9	76	9
priests	73	5	—	—	—	—
dissidents from the 1980s	55	6	53	29	52	8
employees of private companies	53	22	54	17	—	—
directors/managers in state enterprises	51	14	49	15	41	20
Solidarity activists	48	9	48	8	47	12
employees of government administration	46	5	59	7	43	11
doctors	46	17	40	21	30	33
employees of the former PUWP*	29	16	23	22	28	23
craftsmen	29	34	26	38	32	36
activists of the PCTU**	28	8	18	13	13	18
engineers in state-owned industries	24	26	21	27	15	34
skilled workers	18	53	14	60	13	63
teachers	17	45	18	49	5	78
farmers	9	70	5	81	3	86
non-skilled workers	2	87	2	81	3	81

Source: "Old and New Conflicts," Center for Public Opinion Research, (1994).

Notes: * Polish United Workers' Party (the Communist Party).
** Polish Convention of Trade Unions (the Communist trade unions).

appears to be completely dominated by economic divisions, which are understood either as a dualism of rich versus the poor or as a gradation which includes median groups and mobility between groups.

Two important issues are related to these differences. The first concerns chances for economic mobility and social promotion. In the opinion of those groups endangered by the loss of employment and falling incomes, promotion is only possible for those who are on the top levels of the social ladder. Thus the dominant tendency is not the split into rich and poor, but rather a "cognitive split" due to the unclear sources of social differences and mechanisms of promotion and degradation.

The second issue is related to the risk of Poland splitting into "two societies" (see Rychard's paper in this volume). To avoid this threat, I believe Poles should support the self-organization of society and the decentralization of state power. Providing the conditions for individual mobility and dynamic social structures should result in the conversion of a closed, static society into an open "ladder" society.

Do social differences translate into conflicts? Sociological research confirms that it is not the economic split among groups that constitutes the axis of conflicts. Political conflicts dominate, as they did in the 1980s.

The clear division into "us" and "them"—society versus the communist authorities—completely disappeared in 1989, giving way to conflicts inside the structures of power—that is, inside Solidarity. In 1992 the original division awoke with a vengeance. In 1990 social conflict was explained in economic terms by 4 percent of respondents, in 1994 by 21 percent. The government is blamed for all troubles (successes are rarely remembered), including all social differences. Almost 60 percent of the Poles think that the condition of the economy depends on the political situation, and 63 percent believe that the decisions of politicians have a strong influence on the personal fate of the citizens. This means that opinions concerning the government are not related to any evaluation of Poland's economic position but to the respondent's perception of his or her own situation.

The acceleration of privatization can de-politicize many conflicts, including economic conflicts. At the same time, it is very important to avoid creating a dualistic and confrontational society based on economic differences. For this reason gradual privatization may be preferable, in which mechanisms for promotion and prospects of personal development are protected and created.

THE SCALE OF SOCIAL DIFFERENCES

Employment in the private sector is steadily growing, and so is the number of persons who have experienced working for themselves as owners, employers, or family workers (over 30% of the workforce or about 4.4 million people). Self-employment undoubtedly affects their approach to life and leads to greater social ambition. Unfortunately Poland is still dominated by people with a very elementary and narrow professional education. This is a result of under-investment in education under communism. The consequence is a correspondingly low level of social mobility and of the capability to master changing life situations. A fundamental problem of the economic transformation is the threat faced by many people of marginalization, poverty, passivity and social pathology.

Given ongoing methodological disputes, it is not possible to rely on the calculations of the social minimum when defining the level and extent of poverty. Using the current basket of goods which constitute the minimum, we could point out many groups which are situated below the level of the social minimum but still are not poor.

The best way to define poverty is to consider as poor all members of a household in which expenses for an adult lie below the level of the lowest retirement pension (children are considered "halves" of adults). The level of the lowest retirement pension in Poland is the factor which defines the right to apply for welfare. The poverty borderline calculated in such a manner is three times higher than the absolute poverty borderline defined by the World Bank.

In this way, 14.4 percent of Poles could be defined as poor (about 5.5 million). In the 1980s, this figure ranged from 5 percent to 10 percent. A significant number of people oscillate near the borderline. If the borderline for measuring poverty were increased by 25 percent, the number of poor would grow by 26.2 percent. Within the possible poverty borderlines, from the lowest pension to the social minimum, any increment of 10 percent will increase the number of poor people by about 2.5 million. Since the average monthly expenses of the poor are only 12-15 percent less than the lowest pension (which is the poverty borderline), the definition of poverty is "shallow" and an increase in incomes resulting from economic development may move persons out of poverty. An increase in GDP of one percentage point, without changes in income distribution, causes a decrease in poverty of 0.5 to 0.7 percent. A 5 percent increase in GDP this year would cause a decrease in poverty from 14.4 percent to 11-12 percent, income distribution remaining constant. Steady growth could limit poverty by the end of the century to 5 percent.

More than one third of the poor are poor because one of the members of the household is unemployed. Households whose members are unemployed fall into poverty twice as often as the average household (28% versus 14.4%). If an unemployed family member remains jobless for longer than one year, this number grows to 45 percent, and if this person is the head of the family, it rises to 57 percent.

Poverty especially daunts those persons who remain unemployed for a long time (those seeking work for over 12 months), are less mobile, and have low or very low qualifications. This group constitutes 41.7 percent of the total unemployed population (1,136, calculated not according to registered unemployment but by an analysis of the economic activity of the population).

About 60 percent of the poor live in poverty even though there is no unemployed person living in the household. Only 5 percent of the poor are old people. About 60 percent of the poor live in the countryside, 27 percent in towns with less than 100,000 inhabitants, and only 13 percent live in large cities. Families of workers constitute 40 percent of the whole poor population. Large families (those with three or more children) provide 30 percent of the overall number of poor people. Over 40 percent of the poor come from multi-generation families. In fact, one third of the poor are children above 14 years of age. In Poland, one in five children lives in poverty.

A significant element in defining the scale of social differences is the changing structure of personal incomes:
(A) Basic changes in personal income have been as follows:

- Following a 15 percent drop in 1990, between 1991 and 1993 real personal incomes increased by 5.9 percent, 3.5 percent and 3.6 percent annually. The forecast for the period from 1994 to 1997 estimates an average increase in salaries of 11 percent, and a tangible growth in the purchasing power of retirement and health pensions, coming on top of a real increase of 7 percent in 1994.
- There was a significant decrease in incomes from employment, about 30 percent in 1992 as compared to 46 percent in 1989. The forecast does not assume a further decrease in those

incomes, and indeed it speaks of an increase of a few percentage points.

- The share of incomes from employment in the private, non-agrarian sector grew significantly, from 6.9 percent in 1989 to 16.5 percent in 1992. A further increase is projected.
- Between 1989 and 1991, the share of incomes from welfare money transfers increased from 15.9 percent to 20.7 percent, and stabilized at around 20 percent in 1992 and 1993.

The growing share of incomes from welfare, together with the existence of equal numbers of the employed and the professionally passive and unemployed, demonstrate a serious threat to the state budget. This is due to an excess of inflexible, mandatory social expenses.

(B) The allocation structure of nominal personal incomes for Poland in 1992 was as follows:

- personal consumption of goods and services: 75.6 percent
- other expenses (including housing construction): 12.8 percent
- savings: 11.6 percent (this is slightly less than the figure in 1990).
- Comparing 1992 to 1991, the dynamics of real personal incomes for the consumption of goods and services was 105.2 percent, for other expenses (including housing construction) 83.1 percent, and for savings 125.3 percent.

(C) It is worth adding that among full-time workers in 1993, about 64 percent received gross salaries below the national average, the group receiving average to double the average salary included 31.4 percent, and the group earning over double the average salary comprised 4.6 percent of the total workforce.

Significant changes occurred also in household income.

(A) In 1990, all types of households experienced a reduction in real incomes much greater than the reduction in personal incomes. The decrease ranged from 36 percent in farmer households to about 16 percent in retired persons' families.

- In rural families a further reduction of real incomes occurred in 1991, which stopped only in 1992.
- In the families of retired persons and people on health pensions, there were no constant tendencies. A relatively small decrease

in real incomes was noted in 1990, and a slight growth in 1991. 1992 again brought a decrease by 7.3 percent, and 1993 another increase.

- The households of workers and employees experienced a slight increase in average real incomes between 1991 and 1993.

(B) Income relations differed among types of households. The standing of rural families was worse than that of full-time workers and employees, while the situation of retired persons' families significantly improved. In 1989, retired families' incomes amounted to 73 percent of those of workers and employees, in 1991 to 97 percent, and in 1992 to 89 percent.
(C) As for the structure of incomes within particular types of households, the following tendencies appeared:

- The differences among rural households grew smaller. For example, 20 percent of the richest rural households in 1992 had average incomes only 5 times higher than 20 percent of the poorest families, while 5 years earlier this difference was sixfold.
- In the case of the families of workers and employees as well as of retired persons the income gap increased, although it was still smaller than in rural families. In 1992, 20 percent of the best-off households had incomes higher by 3.75 times than 20 percent of the poorest ones. In 1985 this proportion was 3.25.
- Workers' and employees' households experienced a drop in the number of highest-income families, while their share of lowest-income families increased. The opposite was true for the families of retired persons.

(D) The comparison of monthly expenses for food per capita with other expenses for various types of households proves very interesting. The share of food expenses is falling among the self-employed and city dwellers. These households spend more on non-food consumption and services, and save more money. The share of expenses for food in 1993 was as follows:

- households of self-employed workers (urban): 745.4 thousand—35.3 percent
- workers' and employees' households: 656.5 thousand—40.2 percent

- households of retired people: 818.7 thousand—43.4 percent
- households of rural employees: 667.6 thousand—49.6 percent
- households with non-salary sources of income: 522.3 thousand—50 percent
- rural households: 739.8 thousand—50.5 percent.

(E) The comparative analysis of households regarding purchase of durable consumer goods in 1993 shows the following:

- Color TV sets are most common in households of self-employed workers (96.4%) and employees (91.3%), and the least prevalent among farmers (55.8%).
- Satellite TV receivers are most often found in self-employed households (41.9%) and in employees' households (31.3%). For retired persons the figure is 12.5 percent, for farmers 4.5 percent.
- VCRs: self-employed households 75.4 percent, employees 63 percent, retired households 19.7 percent and farmers 25.3 percent.
- Personal computers are owned by 19.9 percent of self-employed workers, 10.9 percent of employees, and 2 percent of other households.
- 83.6 percent of self-employed households possess cars, 51.3 percent of rural employees, 48 percent of farmers, 43.9 percent of urban employees, and about 18 percent of retired persons and those with non-salary sources of income. The CRPO survey of March 1994 states that cars are owned by about 40 percent of Polish households, and 4 percent possess more than one car (about 500 thousand households). Therefore the car as such is no longer a symbol of wealth. Differences in incomes define the type and make of the vehicle owned. Poles drive mainly Polish cars (61%). Skoda and Lada also have a strong position (19%) and Western European and Japanese cars amount to 19 percent. The market is dominated by old cars, with an average age of about 10 years.

The size of personal and family incomes and their purchasing power in relation to consumer goods, services and saving possibilities decide the scale of social differentiation. Important factors are the availability of goods and a wide range of social services, particularly education and health. That the Polish society of the transformation period does not experience a feeling of degradation and excessive differentiation could be a result of the availability of such services.

Almost 80 percent of Poles questioned by CBOS in January 1994 were convinced of the importance of higher education. Two thirds of respondents said they would like their children to complete a university education. Preferences varied according to gender. The main choices were polytechnic studies, the medical academy, economy/trade school, and law and administration. Even if some social groups are not satisfied with their educational choices, the discomfort stems from the possibility of making a mistake in choosing a specific field of education, and not with the quality of high-level education as such. The high opinion of education is accompanied by the conviction that salary should correspond to the level of education. People express a high opinion of the quality of non-state schools, regardless of their accessibility.

The situation is similar in the case of health services. It is considered obvious that many of those services should require a fee, whether on the private or social security model. Only older people consider the health protection system created under the old regime relatively safe and secure. The general dislike for the current health system comes from the fact that it is disorderly and offers limited solutions, rather than from a sense of losing something which used to be guaranteed.

Certainly the most important factor affecting social differentiation among families is housing. A shortage of over 1.6 million apartments in Poland in conjunction with the coming demographic high will only increase this factor's importance and might cause conflicts of an unprecedented strength. The frustration of new generations will cumulate as beginning an adult life becomes more difficult. The housing shortage might delay the commencement of grown-up, independent lives, and increase illegitimacy with all the legal and other consequences following upon these facts. Lack of housing might become a reason for emigration.

It is interesting to compare the actual data regarding the scope of social differentiation with the public perception of it.

(A) 60 percent of CBOS respondents declared incomes lower than average (compared with about 64 percent of workers and employees, according to data from the Main Bureau of Statistics), 84 percent considered their incomes too low in relation to needs, and 52 percent of respondents assessed the standard of living of their family as poor or moderate (CBOS, April 1994). 75 percent of all persons questioned spent all their money for day-to-day needs. Only 15 percent of Poles stated that they saved some money, and a further 7 percent said that they invested part of their income.

(B) In the opinion of CBOS respondents (May 1994) an average 4-person family would need about 9.5 million PLZ a month to cover the fundamental necessities, about 15 million to live moderately, and 23 million to feel prosperous.

(C) 92 percent of households in a bad financial situation and 25 percent of those who assess their financial standing as good only spend money for their current needs. 86 percent of respondents with the lowest incomes (below 750.000 PLZ per household member) do not save or invest, and neither do over half of those who have the highest income (2.250.000 PLZ per person and above). Private entrepreneurs are most likely to save and invest. One farmer in five invests money, and among managers and white-collar workers 45 percent claim that they saved or invested money in the last 6 months. At the same time, 44 percent of respondents say that they have to save to meet current needs. The awareness and will to save is present, but not the capacity to do so, which leads to quite a strong feeling of discomfort not only among those in poverty, but also among those who should have clearer development perspectives.

Table 2. (in %)

Do you save money in any form?	*YES*	*NO*
Savings account	21	79
Term deposit in Zloty	6	94
Deposit on demand in Zloty	6	94
Savings bonds	2	98
Foreign currency term deposit	6	94
Foreign currency deposit on demand	6	94
Stocks	4	96
State bonds	2	98
Shares in a trust fund	2	98
Life insurance policy	23	77
Valuables (gold, jewelry)	9	91
Cash kept at home	16	84
Foreign currency in cash, kept at home	3	97
Other forms of savings	2	98

At the same time over 50 percent of respondents declare that they have no savings which would allow them to live without income in a crisis situation (CBOS, May 1994). 14 percent of those questioned, have savings which would allow them to live without changing their lifestyle for one week only, 21 percent have sufficient savings for a month, 5 percent for 4 to 5 months, 4 percent for about half a year, and 2 percent have savings which would support them for longer than 6 months.

Among Poles, fears regarding the financial security of their families dominate the fear of unemployment or even the fear of health problems. The most acceptable form of saving is a life insurance policy. Preferences in this area are presented in Table 2. It is worth noticing the traditional approach of Poles to savings. Decreasing incomes and feelings of degradation and danger direct savings to non-development areas such as the traditional savings booklet, insurance policies and cash kept at home.

(D) Only a small group of respondents (7%) declared an improvement in their material standing in the course of 1993/94. The reaction to this improvement was as follows:

- The respondents designated the additional funds first of all for improving their housing conditions (58%) and equipping their households with durables (50%), and then for health protection (50%), hygiene (52%) and food (50%).
- A small group increased their expenses for cultural needs (22%) and for social life and amusements (25%). Farmers, private entrepreneurs, the unemployed and housewives did not spend any money on culture.
- 35 percent of those who declared an improvement in their living conditions increased savings, and 30 percent of them increased investments.

(E) Expenditures according to social and professional categories are presented in Table 3. When incomes decrease, the first reaction is to undertake additional jobs, especially with people of a certain level of education and skills.

As Poland continues to develop, the scale of visible social differentiation will increase. But so should the social acceptance of these differences and the readiness to start investing or saving in order to improve one's standard of life.

Table 3. What Did Your Household Spend Money On During the Last Six Months? (in percent)

1. current needs of the family
2. part on current needs, part was saved
3. part on current needs, and part invested in something that should bring a profit (starting or developing own business, purchase of stocks, etc.)
4. part on current needs, part saved, part invested

Actively employed	*1*	*2*	*3*	*4*
managers, intelligentsia	55	33	7	4
lower level white-collar workers	74	17	2	5
white and blue collar workers	77	7	11	5
skilled workers	83	12	4	1
non-skilled workers	85	10	0	1
farmers	69	9	18	2
private entrepreneurs	24	34	35	7
Professionally passive retired and on health pension	81	14	3	1
students, college and university	63	15	14	5
unemployed	81	9	6	4
housewives and others	70	20	4	4

THE ROLE OF WELFARE PROGRAMS IN ALLEVIATING POVERTY IN HUNGARY, 1992-1993

István György Tóth

INTRODUCTION

Poverty has increased and become more visible in Hungary as an inevitable consequence of the "transformational recession" (Kornai 1993). According to the latest data from the Hungarian Central Statistical Office the number of people living under the poverty line in 1992 was approximately 50 percent higher than the relatively stable 10 percent poverty rate of the 1980s (KSH 1993). According to data from the Hungarian Household Panel poverty grew to 22-25 percent in size by 1993 (Kolosi, Szívós and Bedekovics 1993).

The social policy programs of the government have certainly kept poverty from growing to an even greater degree, thereby reducing the social costs of the economic transformation. However, concern

International Review of Comparative Public Policy,
Volume 7, pages 125-145.

ISBN: 0-7623-0153-8

about the efficiency and equity of the social welfare system are well based. This study attempts to contribute to the debate about the effectiveness of in-cash social programs in Hungary.

The first part of this paper summarizes the results of some previous analyses of the type and extent of poverty in Hungary. Next follows an investigation into the role welfare programs such as social insurance, family aid and financial support play in reducing poverty. Two basic considerations guide our work here. First the patterns of incidence of social programs are examined. Then an attempt is made to learn if any groups are neglected by the welfare system (that is, whether there are any gaps in the social redistribution of wealth). In the final part we look at the role social policy plays in the reduction of poverty.

The following analysis relies solely on the database of the 1993 wave of the Hungarian Household Panel (HHP), a longitudinal study of incomes, wealth and the labor market positions of Hungarian households in 1992, using a 2000 starting sample. The HHP annual data collection is completed by TÁRKI (Social Research Informatics Center). The whole project is a joint exercise of TÁRKI, the Department of Sociology at the Budapest University of Economic Sciences and the Central Statistical Office. The first wave of data collection occurred in spring 1992, while the second wave of data (used here) was collected in April and May 1993.[1]

In what follows the poverty-related variables are composed from answers to question blocks mapping incomes of persons and households. Poverty, of course, could also be measured with other variables than income. In this period of transition from communism in Hungary an approach to poverty analyzing consumption and belongings might help to sift out uncertainties arising from a simple measurement of poor family incomes. However consumption data would also be of limited value because while income reflects the possibility to consume, the actual consumption style is determined by personal spending preferences. This might render the categories used in analysis arbitrary.

Household incomes can be compared in several ways. At one extreme we do not distinguish between households on the basis of size. This method ignores the fact that family size determines both earning capacity and consumption needs. The underlying assumption here is that household expenses do not change with family size. At the other extreme, when per capita incomes are compared, the assumption is that the cost of living rises in direct proportion to family size. Both methods are used in the literature on income inequalities, though a method which lies between these two extremes would better reflect reality. The assumption behind using equivalent incomes is that a growth in family size means a non-linear growth in the cost of living. Thus equivalence scales assign a weight to individual household members taking economies of scale into account. To put it more formally: a family's income is equivalent to that of a single-person household if $J = h/N$, where J = the income of a single-person household, h = the total income of the household in question, and N = a co-efficient indicating differing needs depending on family size. It is shown in the literature that the co-efficient expressing family needs can be expressed by the formula $N = S^e$, where S equals the family (household) size, while e represents the elasticity of needs to unit size (Buchman et al. 1988; Förster 1994).

In this study weighted household incomes are used. In the calculation of equivalent incomes the following consumption weights are assigned to the respective household members:

Household	*Consumption Unit*
first person	1
second person	0.7
third and subsequent persons	0.5

These weights were estimated with the value $e = 0.73$.

WHO ARE THE POOR?

The charting of the composition of absolute poverty based on data from the Hungarian Household Panel was carried out by Tamás Kolosi (1992), while the charting of the composition of relative poverty was initially carried out by Rudolf Andorka (Andorka 1992; Andorka-Spéder 1993a, 1993b). A more recent analysis took a detailed look at the composition of poverty using three different equivalence scales and four definitions of poverty (Tóth, Andorka, Förster, and Spéder 1994). Here we do not intend to carry out a detailed analysis of poverty characteristics. Since the topic of this study is the distribution of welfare and the role welfare programs play

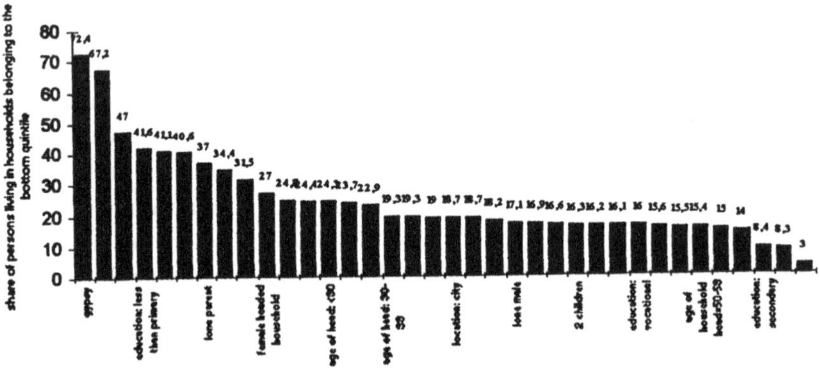

Figure 1. Person-specific Poverty Rates by Household Characteristics in Various Population Groups

in easing poverty, only a short overview of the social groups most at risk of poverty will be given.

Figure 1 displays the risks of falling into poverty run by households and individuals according to the ethnic affiliation of the household head, his/her occupational status, level of education, age, size of the household, location of the home, and number of children under the age of 18. The figure contains the cell frequencies of nine cross-tables in decreasing order. This compact presentation allows for a direct comparison of poverty risks shared by people of differing household categories.

In summarizing the data and earlier results of our research into poverty the following theses hold:

1. Gypsy families are seriously affected by poverty. Their poverty rate is very high—69 percent of all gypsy households are poor and 72 percent of those living in families in which the family head is a Gypsy are poor. A more refined analysis shows that the more restrictive the definition of poverty used, the higher the percentage of Gypsies will be poor. Longitudinal analysis proves also that these people seldom escape from poverty.
2. Clear demographic determinants of poverty are also visible. Poverty rates are higher among households with at least three children if the household head is under 40 years of age, or if he/she is raising the children alone. Differences between various household types are smaller for age categories between

40 and 60 years, but here also single-parent families and families with three or more children are more likely to be poor. Finally, households headed by a person above 60 years of age are greatly at risk of being poor if the elderly person lives alone. The lower we descend in the income hierarchy, the greater the number of families with four or more children and of single-child families, and (partially in consequence) the greater the number of people from three-person households and five-or-more person households. Regarding age, younger heads of households are over-represented in the lower poverty strata.

3. Home location and education have a great influence on poverty. People with a lower-level education, and those living in the lower segments of the settlement hierarchy (mostly rural areas) are especially vulnerable to poverty. Those living in isolated farmhouses, or in homes where the family head is poorly educated (e.g., he/she has completed less than 8 primary school grades) are twice as likely to be poor as the average. The lower the level of income used as the poverty threshold, the more at risk these groups are compared to the general population.
4. The labor market also plays an important role in determining poverty. Those living in households with an unemployed head run twice the risk of being poor as the average. It should be added, however, that it is not primarily the temporarily unemployed who are threatened by permanent or long-term impoverishment. Rather those who have been permanently driven out of the labor market and who are not yet eligible for pensions or other social-security benefits are the ones who are truly in trouble.
5. The magnitude of poverty risks run by various social groups, however, is only one aspect of the poverty profile. From a social policy point of view, the actual size of the groups concerned determines the potential clientele for welfare programs (and of course a potential voter base). As Figure 2 clearly shows, the number of poor persons living in households where the head is employed, not a gypsy, and not a woman is higher than the number of persons living in households with unemployed, gypsy or female heads. Thus one should not draw the conclusion that only those who are at greater risk of being poor will be impoverished. They may be

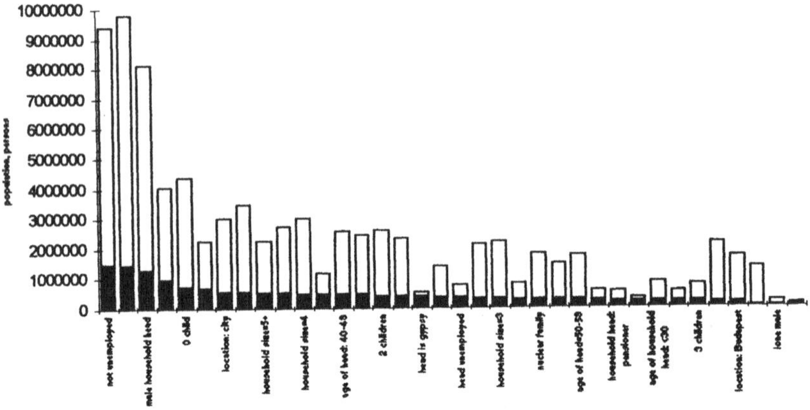

Figure 2. The Size of the Poor Population Within the Reference Population Various Population Groups

more likely to be poor, but other categories may include a greater number of poor. For instance: although a great number of Gypsies are poor, the majority of the poor are not Gypsies. Similarly, although a great number of the unemployed are poor, the majority of the poor live in households with employed heads.

THE FORMS OF SOCIAL SUPPORT PROGRAMS

In-cash redistribution programs in Hungary fall into three groups. The first group replaces earnings with benefits related to earnings. The eligibility criteria of these programs are tied to employment status. That is to say, one of the conditions attached to the payment of benefits is that the recipient has a prior employment record and pays or paid social security contributions. Contributions and benefits are also tied to previous wages through a formula. Pensions, sick-pay, unemployment benefits and maternity fees are the major types of benefits in this category. The second group of benefits includes the so-called "basic incomes." Here eligibility criteria are not attached to income or employment status and the amount of the benefit is not tied to income or prior earnings. The applicants need only meet a demographic criterion to be eligible for benefits.

The best examples of this are the family allowance and the maternity allowance (a fixed monthly payment to mothers on child-care leave). The third group consists of benefits solely granted to those with low incomes. Assistance payments in this category have been designed specifically to alleviate poverty and are generally granted on the basis of a means test.

This paper shows how these macro expenditures trickle down to individual households: how macro data look from the worm's eye view of individual families. What sort of social differences are found behind the diversity of income structures? How well are individual cash programs targeted, and do these programs find those whom they were designed to serve?

Incomes are divided into five major groups for further analysis. The first group (following the literature) is called "market income." Earnings and cash property incomes belong to this group. Personal incomes from primary jobs (wages, overtime payments, benefits in kind, cost allowances), personal income from secondary jobs, and household income arising from small-scale agricultural production also fit into this income category. Profits and dividend incomes make up the "cash property" income category. In this case the returns gained from capital investment contribute to the total income of individual households.[2] Earnings-related social security benefits (pensions, sick-leave benefits, unemployment benefits, and maternity allowances—with the exception of the child-care allowance) belong to this second income group. Non-insurance type public social transfers make up the third category. Some of these (the family allowance, for example) are independent of the recipients' incomes, while others are means-tested and dependent on income (such as regular and occasional social assistance benefits. The fourth category includes inter-household transfers like alimony and cash help between families.[3] The fifth type of income includes other earnings which do not fit into any of the previous categories.

THE DISTRIBUTIONAL PATTERNS OF WELFARE PAYMENTS

The growth of social expenditures was profound in the last decade. At the start of the eighties, Hungary's social expenditure as a share of GDP ranked with the less developed OECD countries (Gacs 1987).

Due to political decisions and the transformational recession, the social expenditure share has grown to a level which puts Hungary on a par with the highest spenders in the OECD (Andorka, Kondratas, and Tóth 1994; Tóth 1994). Among social expenditures cash transfers especially increased their share.

The Incidence Study ordered by the World Bank provided insight into the incidence of social transfers at the end of the eighties (CSO 1990). It raised both adequacy and equity concerns and showed the need for reforms. Data from the HHP, despite all of its limitations, increases our understanding of these issues.

The Incidence of Cash Transfers

The distributional effects of various types of incomes and social benefits strongly depend on how household incomes are measured. For Hungary, it has been shown elsewhere that variations in poverty rates are very sensitive to the income measurement concept used (Förster and Tóth 1993, 1994; Tóth, Andorka, Förster, and Spéder 1994). In what follows we will use an equivalence scale of 0.73 elasticity to examine the composition of incomes.

In general, there has occurred significant growth in the share of social incomes and a decrease in the share of social incomes in the composition of household budgets due to the transition process in the last few years. The proportion of households with no market incomes at all is fairly high—just over 20 percent of the total sample. 75 percent of these households are headed by someone over 60 years of age, 25 percent of them are headed by an individual of active working age, and more than 50 percent of them contain more than two people. About 94 percent of households with no market income receive some sort of social insurance, about 20 percent receive some form of public social transfers, and within this 20 percent a very low percentage—9.4 percent—receives social assistance.

The proportion of households that receive earnings-related social insurance benefits is almost as high as the ratio of market income recipients (74.8%). This is because more than half of such households receive some sort of pension (old age pension, disability pension, widow's pension). About 13 percent of all households received unemployment benefits in 1992-93. This represented an increase over the past years as the unemployment rate has risen in the meantime (10% of households received unemployment benefits in 1991-92). Another

Table 1. Decile Shares of Various Types of Incomes

	deciles										
	1	2	3	4	5	6	7	8	9	10	*Total*
Market incomes total	1,5	2,5	3,1	4,8	6,1	8,1	11,0	13,7	18,3	30,9	100,0
earnings	1,5	2,5	3,2	4,9	6,2	8,2	11,1	13,8	18,5	30,0	100,0
cash property incomes	0,9	0,1	0,3	0,9	1,2	4,3	5,2	6,7	6,3	74,1	100,0
Social Insurance benefits	6,9	9,0	10,3	11,4	12,3	11,5	10,6	10,9	8,8	8,3	100,0
pensions	5,6	8,7	10,4	11,7	13,1	11,9	10,2	11,1	8,5	8,9	100,0
unemployment benefits	18,5	13,2	10,1	10,3	8,9	10,4	11,4	9,3	4,7	3,1	100,0
maternity support	9,5	7,9	13,2	11,8	9,8	11,4	11,9	11,3	10,4	2,8	100,0
Public social transfers	10,5	9,2	10,2	8,9	9,1	12,2	10,4	11,2	9,4	9,0	100,0
social assistance	16,8	13,5	7,4	8,4	6,9	12,7	15,3	7,5	8,1	3,5	100,0
family allowance	9,3	7,7	9,6	9,6	9,5	12,9	11,1	12,3	9,8	8,1	100,0
Inter-household transfers	7,6	13,3	9,0	9,9	7,6	7,4	14,6	8,4	10,7	11,5	100,0
Other household incomes	1,6	1,7	2,2	2,7	2,4	5,0	5,7	3,7	15,0	59,8	100,0
Total household incomes	3,7	4,9	5,7	7,0	8,0	9,3	10,7	12,3	14,8	23,6	100,0

Source: Hungarian Household Panel (HHP), 1992/93.

Note: ranking for the deciles is based on total equivalent household incomes. Meaning of a cell: received income/benefit of the given type in the given decile as a percent of the total benefit/income of that type in the sample.

fairly large group of households (about 10%) received maternity fees or maternity allowances. Approximately one third of all households received family allowances for at least one child, whereas only about 10 percent of the households received social assistance.

Table 1 displays the shares the individual deciles (based on total, adjusted household income) received of total income and of various income types. Overall it is clear that the wide inequalities of primary earnings (earnings in the top decile are twenty times as high as earnings in the bottom decile) are significantly reduced by social incomes (the ratio between the total household incomes of the upper and lower deciles is 6.3). Nonetheless the distribution of various social incomes between deciles shows various patterns. In general, a larger proportion of social insurance benefits payments reaches the middle deciles than the lower deciles. The lowest decile enjoys 5.6 percent of pensions, while the 5th decile receives 13 percent of pensions. Similarly but less strikingly, maternity benefits tend to benefit the middle deciles. Unemployment benefits, however, seem to be targeted.

The distribution of social incomes would be well-targeted if the lowest deciles enjoyed the highest benefits. The data show this is not the case. Family allowances are granted to the 6th and 8th deciles to a higher degree than to any other decile. The distribution of social assistance is also thought provoking. The lowest decile enjoyed 17 percent of all social assistance, but a rather high proportion of aid was also granted to the 6th and 7th deciles.

The preceding table shows decile distributions where the household ranking is based on total household income (including in-cash social benefits). However, this ranking might not always be appropriate. An examination of what happens when the population ranking is made on the basis of incomes supplemented by social transfers is needed. In what follows it is assumed that the original, or primary, income inequalities are determined by income differences generated by market forces. Social redistribution programs modify this original inequality in one way or another.

The blocks in Table 2 were designed with this in mind. Block one represents the distribution of various types of pensions among the household quintiles that were defined on the basis of adjusted market incomes. Here it seems clear that the lower a household's market income, the greater the likelihood that it will receive a pension. 68 percent of households from the lowest market income quintile and 16 percent of households from the highest quintile receive some sort

Table 2. Incidence of Social Transfers: The Share and Distribution of Benefit Recipient Households

Form of support	percentage of household receiving the form of given support	Quintiles 1	2	3	4	5	Total pop.	pop.	income
	Note: method used to form the quintiles								
Block 1.									
Old age pension	... in percent of households in the quintile	68,1	56,3	36,6	22,7	15,9	40,0	a	c
	... in percent of households receiving pensions	34,1	28,2	18,3	11,4	8,0	100,0		
Disability pension	... in percent of households in the quintile	11,9	17,4	13,5	9,9	5,6	11,6	a	c
	... in percent of households receiving disability pensions	20,4	29,8	23,2	17,0	9,6	100,0		
Other pensions	... in percent of households in the quintile	13,4	8,8	7,2	4,6	3,3	7,5	a	c
	other pensions	35,9	23,6	19,3	12,3	8,8	100,0		
Block 2.									
unemployment benefits	... in percent of households in the quintile	35,2	23,7	19,6	12,8	6,0	19,5	b	
	... in percent of households receiving unemployment benefits	36,2	24,4	20,1	13,2	6,2	100,0		
maternity fee	... in percent of households in the quintile	13,6	15,6	9,6	5,3	0,0	8,8	b	c
	... in percent of households receiving maternity fee	30,8	35,4	21,8	12,0	0,0	100,0		
maternity allowance	... in percent of households in the quintile	10,0	21,2	10,8	3,6	0,8	9,3	b	c
	... in percent of households receiving maternity allowance	21,6	45,7	23,3	7,8	1,7	100,0		
family allowance	... in percent of households in the quintile	46,5	61,4	64,6	48,3	27,7	49,7	b	
	... in percent of households receiving family allowance	18,7	24,7	26	19,4	11,1	100,0		
Block 3.									
social assistance	... in percent of households in the quintile	24,5	10,2	6,5	4,6	5,4	10,2	a	d
	... in percent of households receiving social assistance	47,9	19,9	12,7	9	10,5	100		

Source: HHP 92/93.

Notes: a: total households. b: active households. c: equivalent market income. d: total equivalent household income support.

of pension. Within this distribution the incidence of retirement, disability and other pensions (e.g., widow's pensions) differs. The proportion of people receiving old age pensions is highest in the second quintile. 34% of households receiving old age pensions, 20 percent of those receiving disability pensions and 36 percent of those receiving some other form of pension belong to the lowest quintile. The function of pensions is to replace former market incomes. Consequently, a result of ordering households by market incomes is that relatively more retired people fall into the lowest quintile, despite the fact that based on their total incomes (which include pensions) they do not rank among the poor.

Family allowances are designed to fulfill a different function. The aim of these allowances is essentially to support active households (raising children). People in the active-age group generally have market incomes and receive various types of social support which supplement these incomes. Therefore in the second block of Table 2, the distributional patterns of family allowances displayed according to quintiles of households with active-age heads, are ranked on the basis of their equivalent market incomes. Almost half of all the active-aged households enjoy a family allowance. Most households which receive a family allowance are found in the middle (third) quintile. It can easily be seen that the distributional pattern of family allowances takes a reversed U shape, though it is a bit skewed toward the lower incomes. The maternity fee and the maternity allowance seem better directed toward those with lower incomes.

For unemployment benefits as for family allowances, a ranking of active-age households based on market income seems appropriate. Here it appears that unemployment benefits are relatively well targeted toward the poor: the proportion of households receiving this type of benefit significantly decreases with increases in adjusted market income. Approximately 60 percent of all households receiving unemployment benefits belong to the lowest two quintiles.

The main function of social assistance is to supplement total household income if it is not sufficient to provide a family's subsistence, irrespective of age, number of people living in the household, or the householder's job status. Therefore, a ranking of all households according to pre-assistance adjusted household income seems appropriate (Table 2, block 3). All in all, some 10 percent of households receive means-tested assistance. However, our data show that even this modest level of assistance does not primarily reach those with the lowest incomes. About 24 percent of the lowest quintile receive some sort of aid, and approximately 10 percent of the second quintile. More than half of all households receiving such assistance payments cannot be classified as poor if the poverty threshold is defined as an income equaling the upper boundary for the lowest quintile.

The Income Composition of Various Social Policy Target Groups

Benefits arising from social redistribution (social insurance programs and other aid) account for nearly 40 percent of annual total household incomes in Hungary. Market incomes, however, barely exceed half of all household incomes (56%). Since the income composition of social policy target groups might be quite different from the overall average, it is worth examining them separately.[4]

The set of social groups to be targeted by social policies is, of course, a matter for debate. In what follows, the income composition of four vulnerable social groups is outlined. "Old" households were those in which the family head was above retirement age. This population does not exactly match the pensioner population since there are a number of old people who receive no retirement benefits, and very large numbers of pensioners are under the age limit. "Unemployed" households were defined as those in which the household head was unemployed according to the ILO definition of unemployment. "Large" families were defined as families with three or more children under the age of 18. Finally, "poor" households were defined as all those belonging to the lowest quintile.

A main determinant of the incomes of the average "old" household proved to be pensions, which provide 73 percent of all income to this group. Of course, this average includes people whose sole source of income is their retirement benefit, and others for whom their pension forms an insignificant part of their income. For "unemployed" households the proportion of earnings to total income is relatively high (45%). On average this proportion is significantly higher than with "poor" and "old" families, but lower than with "big" families where it reaches 53.6 percent. The income structure of "poor" households is surprising. In their case, welfare payments (namely allowances that are specifically designed to help the poor) account for only 8 percent of total income (Table 3).

Table 3. The Income Composition of Social Policy Target Groups

	"elderly" households	*"unemployed" households*	*"large" households*	*"poor" households*
Market incomes	20,1	45,5	53,6	22,9
Earnings	19,2	45,4	49,9	22,8
Cash property incomes	0,9	0,1	3,7	0,1
Social insurance benefits	*73,1*	*33,7*	*14,8*	*61,6*
Pensions	71,8	12,3	3,8	51,2
Unemployment benefits	0,6	16,4	4,4	6,5
Maternity support	0,2	2,7	5,2	2,5
Public social transfers	*1,2*	*15,8*	*26,7*	*13,1*
Family allowance	0,5	8,3	23,7	2,4
Social assistance	0,5	1,4	2,0	7,8
Private transfers	*0,4*	*1,0*	*0,9*	*0,9*
Other household incomes	*5,2*	*4,0*	*4,0*	*1,5*
Total	100,0	100,0	100,0	100,0
N=	728	145	97	432

Source: Förster - Tóth, 1993, data from HHP 1992/93.
Definitions:
"older household": households where the household head is above the retirement age (women 55, men 60).
"unemployed household": households where the household head is unemployed (according to ILO's definition).
"large household": where there are three or more children under the age of 18.
"poor household": where the household, on the basis of its total (equivalent) income, belongs to the bottom quintile.
The types here are not mutually exclusive.

The Role Social Support Plays in the Reduction of Poverty

Table 4 shows the distribution of households among quintiles based on adjusted market incomes. If there were no non-market redistribution, the households would be arranged along the diagonal of the matrix. As we can see, the existence of non-market incomes shifts the cell frequencies from the diagonal. From the point of view of this study the first row of the table is the most significant. About 43 percent of those who belong to the lowest quintile according to their market incomes belong to the category of the poor (the lowest quintile, based on all types of household income). Others with non-market incomes are aided to such a degree that they belong to quintiles 2-5. Pensions unambiguously play the greatest role in this.

Table 4. Distribution of Households in Various Adjusted Market Income Quintiles by their Position in Total Adjusted Household Income Quintiles

		Quintiles based on total adjusted household incomes					
		1	*2*	*3*	*4*	*5*	*Total*
Quintiles based	1	43,1	27,9	16,8	8,9	3,3	100,0
on market	2	37,6	31,9	21,1	6,3	3,2	100,0
incomes	3	14,6	28,4	32,4	20,1	4,4	100,0
92/93	4	3,0	9,1	24,2	44,9	18,8	100,0
	5	1,9	2,6	5,8	19,4	70,2	100,0

Let us now move to the social composition of two separately defined lowest income groups. "Post-transfer" poverty rates are defined by the proportion of those from a given population group who belong to the lowest quintile based on total adjusted household incomes. "Pre-transfer" poverty rates are defined with reference to the lowest quintile of adjusted market incomes. The differences between these rates reflect changes in the ranking of households as a result of non-market incomes.

If only market incomes existed, then the relative risk of falling into poverty would significantly increase for the following social groups (Table 5).

- homes where the household head is above 60 years of age.
- childless households.
- homes in which the household head is employed.
- singles.
- those with higher education levels.
- households in Budapest and other cities.

It appears that non-market redistribution decreases the risk of falling into poverty for these groups to a greater extent than for others. However, it must also be stressed that the above statements only refer to the relative alteration of positions. All in all, the introduction of non-market incomes helps the whole range of households. To put it differently, complete elimination of non-market sources of income would result in a dramatic fall in the position of almost all households.

Table 5. Ratio of Households Belonging to the Bottom Quintile Based on Market Incomes /"Pre-transfer Poverty Rates"/ and Households Belonging to the Bottom Quintiles Based on Total Household Incomes /"Post-transfer Poverty Rates"/

	Household Size				
	1	*2*	*3*	*4*	*5 and more*
"pre-transfer" poverty rates	47,1	25,9	10	2,8	6,1
"post-transfer" poverty rates	34,4	15,5	14,0	16,9	24,4

	Age of Head-of-Household				
	under 30	*30-40*	*40-50*	*50-60*	*60+*
"pre-transfer" poverty rates	7	7,4	5,5	12,6	42,3
"post-transfer" poverty rates	24,3	19,3	19,0	15,4	19,3

	Number of Children				
	0	*1*	*2*	*3*	*more than 4*
"pre-transfer" poverty rates	30	5,8	2,8	10	27
"post-transfer" poverty rates	16,6	18,2	16,3	24,8	67,2

	Occupational Status of Head	
	employed head	*unemployed head*
"pre-transfer" poverty rates	19,7	24,1
"post-transfer" poverty rates	16,2	47,0

	Household Types						
	single male	*single female*	*male headed household*	*female headed household*	*single pensioner*	*lone parent*	*nucle-ar family*
"pre-transfer" poverty rates	37,1	50,8	12,1	19,1	59,1	11,6	3
"post-transfer" poverty rates	17,1	40,6	16,1	27,0	41,1	37,0	15,6

	Education of the Head				
	less than primary	*primary*	*vocational school*	*high school*	*university*
"pre-transfer" poverty rates	39,4	25,5	12,7	14,8	13,1
"post-transfer" poverty rates	41,6	31,5	16,0	8,4	3,0

(continued)

Table 5. (Continued)

	Type of Settlement				
	detached house	village	city	county capital	Budapest
"pre-transfer" poverty rates	23,7	14,9	20,4	23,3	27,2
"post-transfer" poverty rates	22,9	23,7	18,7	18,7	8,3

Source: HHP 92/93.

Note: "pre-transfer" poverty rates: the percentage of households in the lowest quintile as defined by market incomes.
"post-transfer" poverty rates: the percentage of households in the lowest quintile as defined by the household's total equivalent incomes.
In both cases the household income is weighted by the number of household members, e = 0.73.

Let us now examine this with the help of a counterfactual experiment! We fix the poverty threshold at the level of the upper breakpoint of the lowest quintile of all equivalent household incomes. Then, we examine how the poverty rates of various groups targeted by social policies would be affected if social policy benefits designed for them were eliminated (Table 6).

Without pensions the risk of falling into poverty run by families where the household head is above the retirement age would increase to 88 percent, compared with the present 24 percent. Moreover, 81 percent of these people would fall under the quintile limit, and also under the 50 percent level of median incomes. A loss of pensions would also significantly increase the poverty risk run by households where the family head is under retirement age (from 18% to 27%). These results can be variously explained. The share of pensions in total household incomes is above 70 percent in old-age households, as we saw earlier. This proportion is even higher in the case of single pensioners and retired couples. Therefore, the reduction or, *ad absurdum*, the cessation of pensions would immediately push many of these people into absolute poverty. On the other hand, this would not be true of all retirees. It is quite clear that the risk of falling into poverty would be smaller for pensioners who earn market incomes, and for those who live in households with at least one active wage earner. These sorts of incomes would buffer them from the crash brought along by a reduction in pensions. From this one can certainly draw the conclusion that the vulnerability of pensioners' households could be significantly decreased if their income structure were diversified.

Table 6. Household Specific Poverty Rates Based on Total Adjusted Household Incomes and on Total Incomes Minus Benefits, for Various Social Policy Target Groups

	Household Head Above Retirement Age		*Household Head Below Retirement Age*	
poverty rate, total income	24,2		17,6	
poverty rate, total incomes-pensions	87,9		26,9	
	Number of Children Under 18 Years of Age in the Household			
	1	2	3	4+
poverty rate, total income	19.,3	16,4	25,6	65,2
poverty rate, total incomes-pensions	27,5	29,5	51,6	86,9
	Occupational Status of the Household Head			
	not unemployed			unemployed
poverty rate, total income	18,2			41
poverty rate, total incomes-pensions	19,9			50,7
		Income Position of the Household Bottom Quintile		
poverty rate, total income			20	
poverty rate, total incomes-pensions			20,6	

The poverty risk run by families with children would also significantly increase if (ad absurdum) there were absolutely no form of family allowance, but this risk would be shared differently by households with differing numbers of children. The poverty rate of households with one child would increase from 19 percent to 27 percent, while the poverty rates of households with two children would grow from 16 percent to 26 percent. The poverty rate of families with three children would increase more, doubling from 26 percent to 52 percent. The already high poverty rate of families with four or more children would increase to an even greater degree. A lesson from these figures can be summarized as follows. Although the family allowance tends to benefit middle income groups, an erosion of the family allowance would have a greater effect on those whose income status is lower. Consequently, the effectiveness of the family allowance as an income support program could be increased by making it more dependent on the number of children, and by making it dependent on income (more exactly, by using taxation to make the net family allowance depend on income).

Among the four groups targeted for analysis here the repeal of unemployment benefits and social assistance benefits would have the least dramatic effects. That is, these are the types of social support programs that contribute the least to alleviating poverty among these social groups. The poverty risk run by households where the household head is unemployed would increase by approximately 25 percent (from 40% to 51%), if these benefits and supports were eliminated. Thus half of all households headed by an unemployed individual would not sink into destitution even if unemployment benefits were completely eliminated.

The repeal of social assistance benefits would not significantly increase the poverty risk run by the population as a whole. This, of course, does not mean that the discontinuation of these allowances would not cause a grave problem for the poorest of the poor. On the contrary, the cessation of these allowances would significantly harm those who are already impoverished, as well as decreasing the income of poor households living above the absolute poverty level.

SUMMARY

Poverty in Hungary is determined by a number of social factors. Ethnic affiliation, old age, adverse labor market position, low levels of education, low occupational status and geographic location all contribute to impoverishment. Social transfers play an important role in decreasing poverty, and are consequently badly needed. At the same time, however, significant parts of welfare programs do not favor poor people, but instead leave those groups most in need and unprotected.

NOTES

1. The initial sample was a four-stage stratified sample taken from the 1990 census. 2,059 households were questioned in the first wave, while 1,931 were questioned in the second wave—a very low drop-out rate in comparison to other panels. However, since the drop-out was not entirely random, it was necessary to weight data from the second wave. 2,157 weighted cases are included in the workfile used here.
2. In theory incomes from the sale of property or possessions should fit into this category, but since selling an asset in one year may be followed by buying another one in the next, huge uncertainties may arise for the amount of net income. So, these types of incomes are excluded from the present analysis. In future studies, however, these forms of income will be examinable with more certainty.
3. The Hungarian Household Panel questionnaire asks about net incomes—the wage actually taken home by a head-of-household. Exceptions are incomes brought in by the whole family (for example, income from the sale of agricultural products). This form of income does not cause a great distortion in data: incomes from small-scale agricultural production, for example, enjoy such large tax allowances that the overwhelming majority of them can be regarded as net income.
4. For more about the structure of Hungarian household incomes and the methodology applied (see Förster, and Tóth 1993, 1994).

REFERENCES

Andorka, R. 1992. "Szegénység" *Sik-Tóth.*

Andorka, R., and Z. Spéder. 1993a. "Szegénység." *Sik-Tóth.*

________. 1993b. *Poverty in Hungary. Some results of the First Two Waves of the Hungarian Household Panel Survey in 1992 and 1993.* Mimeo: Berlin.

Andorka, R., and I. György Tóth 1992. "A szociális kiadások és a szociálpolitika Magyarországon. Pp. 396-508 in *Társadalmi Riport 1992,* edited by R. Andorka, T. Kolosi, and G. Vukovich. ÅRKI.

Andorka, R., A. Kondratas, and I.G. Tóth 1994. "The Hungarian Welfare State in Transition: Structure, Developments and First Steps Towards Reform." *The Joint Hungarian International Blue Ribbon Commission Policy Study* No. 3. Washington, DC: Hudson Institute.

Buchman, B., L. Rainwater, G. Schmaus, and T. Smeeding. 1988. "Equivalence scales, Well-being, Inequality and Poverty: Sensitivity Estimates Across Ten Countries using the LIS Database." *Review of Income and Wealth*, pp. 115-142.

Förster, M., and I.G. Tóth 1994. *Income Poverty and Households' Income Composition in Hungary*. Paper prepared for the Third Prague International Workshop on Social Responses to Transformations in East-Central Europe, May 6-8, Prague.

———. 1993. "A háztartások jövedelmi helyzete és a szociális újraelosztás, In *Sik-Tóth.*

Förster, M.F. 1993. *Comparing Poverty in 13 OECD Countries: Traditional and Synthetic Approaches*. Luxemburg Income Study Working Paper No. 100.

Kessides, C., K. Davey, J. Micklewright, A. Smith, and C. Hinayon. 1991. *Hungary: Reform of the Social Policy and Distribution System*. The World Bank, Draft, (February).

Kolosi, T. and E. Sik 1992. "Munkaeropiac és Jövedelmek." *Sik-Tóth.*

Kolosi, T. 1993. "A népesség Követése." In *Sik-Tóth.*

Kolosi, T., P. Szívós, and I. Bedekovics. 1993. "Munkaerôpiac és Jövedelmek." In *Sik-Tóth.*

Kopits, G., R. Holzmann, G. Schieber, and E. Sidgwick. 1990. *Social Security Reform in Hungary*. Washington, IMF.

Kornai, J. 1993b. "Transzformációs Visszaesés Egy Általános Jelenség Vizsgálata a Magyar Fejlôdés Példáján." *Közgazdasági Szemle 1993*, 7-8, pp. 569-599.

KSH. 1990a. *Incidence Study, '90. The Hungarian Social Policy Systems and Distribution of Incomes of Households*. Paper Prepared by an expert team of the Ministry of Finance and of Central Statistical Office, Budapest, Kézirat.

———. 1990b. *A természetbeni társadalmi jövedelmek és a dotációk rétegeloszlása 1989-ben.* Budapest.

Sik, E., and I.G. Tóth, eds. 1992. *Jelentés a Magyar Háztartás Panel I. Hullámának Eredményeirôl Magyar Háztartás Panel Mühelytanulmányok* 1. szám BKE Szociológia Tanszék-Társadalomkutatási Informatikai Egyesülés Budapest, (December).

Sik, E., and I.G. Tóth, eds. 1993. *Egy év után ... Jelentés a Magyar Háztartás Panel II. hullámának eredményei alapján Magyar Háztartás Panel Mühelytanulmányok* 3. szám BKE Szociológia Tanszék- Társadalomkutatási Informatikai Egyesülés Budapest, (December).

Tóth, I.G. 1992. "A szociális újraelosztás és a helyzete jövedelmi edezete." In *Sik-Tóth.*

———. 1994a. "A jóléti rendszer az átmenet idôszakában." *Közgazdasági." Szemle* (Április).

Tóth, I.G., R. Andorka, M. Förster, and S. Zsolt. 1994. *Poverty, Inequalities and the Incidence of Social Transfers in Hungary*. Paper prepared for the Budapest World Bank Office, Budapest, June, Kézirat.

OLD AND NEW ECONOMIC INEQUALITIES:

THE CZECH CASE

Jiří Večerník

In post-communist societies, economic inequalities are phenomena where the past shakes hands with the future over uncertain ground. The process of total societal reconstruction certainly entails more than a mere shift from equal to unequal distribution of economic resources, or from a system based on political privileges to one based on economic rewards or, for that matter, a shift from social to market principles of welfare allocation and wealth. The process is far more complex. In fact, we face an unpredictable blend of remnants of the old (socialist) system, the newly introduced (market) system and incidental features. All sub-systems of inequality are not only coexistent but actively interacting components of the current social system.

International Review of Comparative Public Policy,
Volume 7, pages 147-175.

ISBN: 0-7623-0153-8

The question of economic inequality is always pertinent. During the transformation period, however, it assumes new salience. First, with the introduction of the market, more goods and services are monetarized than before, more political power passes through economic channels and the manifest economic position of individuals becomes more important. Second, under the newly acquired political liberty, the question of inequality can be discussed publicly, including being used and misused for the interest of individual parties. Third, economic reform brings considerable financial hardship or even poverty for many, which makes inequality a sensitive issue and social transfers necessary. Finally, privatization, restitution and private entrepreneurship generate greater wealth, which challenges the previous system of what we called "maybe equality" and prompts the question of legitimacy.

Below we will first discuss the still fairly widespread illusion that a communist society is a basically egalitarian system. The second illusion we will deal with is that the new market order is a basically homogeneous system, simply replacing unfair equality with fair inequality. The third issue will be the new sources of wealth and causes of poverty and their acceptance by the public. The final issue in the paper juxtaposes changes in economic inequality with people's perception of these changes. We will conclude with an assessment of the specific position of the Czech Republic among the former communist countries.

We have been confronted by numerous difficulties in this research. Analyzing economic inequality under the communist regime is difficult because it was for the most part hidden. Discovering it, moreover, was also forbidden. Explaining economic inequality under the transformation is difficult because societies are in rapid motion and inequality patterns are only now crystallizing. Nevertheless, since the collapse of the old monitoring system, new statistical and sociological tools are being utilized and comprehension of financial institutions is growing. This improvement in the tools of analysis applies to public opinion and sociological surveys as well: people are more ready to respond and less confused when confronted with questions of inequality.

THE COMMUNIST REGIME: CONTRAST BETWEEN IDEOLOGY AND REALITY

Communist revolutions were heralded by the introduction of equality among people. They promised to liquidate private property, make wealth accessible to all and attenuate social disparities. Somewhat more pragmatic, Marx posited equality of rewards according to the person's contribution to the common well-being, which he formulated as "each according to his abilities, to each according to his work" (Marx 1966).

Reality, however, proved far more prosaic and followed a different rational than that of distributive justice. Global political (and military) goals have always dominated ideological and economic ones, and the needs of the command economy suppressed social aims.

Paradoxically, the actual distribution system under communism can be explained by Marx's theory of exploitation under "classic capitalism" as explained in *Capital.* The owner of the means of production does not reward the holder of the labor power according to his work, but only according to the costs of his (and his family's) basic needs (Marx 1965). This mechanism is actually the case with "real socialism," where the state pays workers according to their reproduction costs, rather than according to their contribution to the national product. Consequently, differences in earnings between manual and non-manual labor do not occur; indeed, non-manual labor is sometimes rewarded less than manual as a result of the greater difficulty and nutritional requirements of the latter. Earnings differences between the various educational degrees barely cover study costs or the income forgone during schooling, as there is no need to distinguish by rewarding the greater productivity of better qualified personnel. Additional evidence of this phenomenon is the extremely low share of wage costs in the gross national product.

Once the communist system was established, the new egalitarian reward system operated without substantial change. In former Czechoslovakia, the end of the 1950s marked the beginning of a period of remarkable and perhaps unique stability in overall earnings disparities (Figure 1). Although there was immense inertia in most other European communist countries, periodic pressure was applied in some countries both to increase differentials (during the periods of socialist market reform in Hungary and Poland, for example) or, on the contrary, to reduce the earnings range (through a periodic increase of minimum wages in the USSR and Bulgaria). In communist Czechoslovakia by contrast, no such steps were taken, although the efforts of the Prague Spring economic reform of 1968-1969 led to a slightly more rapid wage rise for qualified people and a mild increase in earnings differentials.

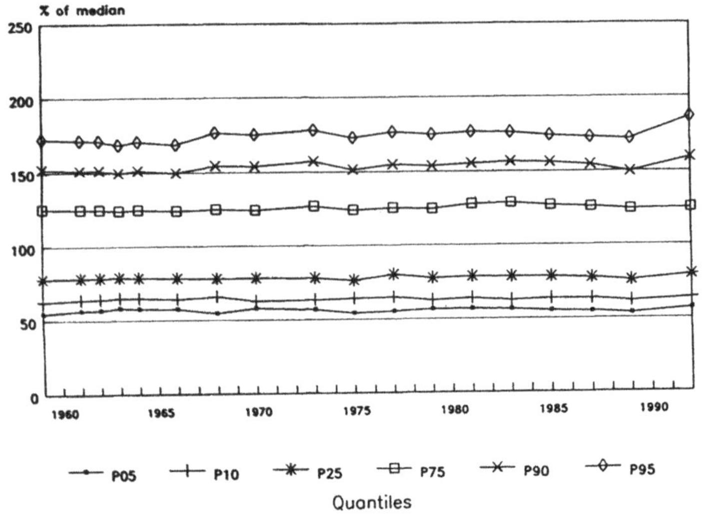

Figure 1. Relative Earnings in 1959-1992

Nevertheless, behind the stability in the overall earnings distribution, important changes occurred in the relative positions of different groups (Večerník 1991a, 1991b). In the analysis of earnings variance based on the data from statistical income surveys and social stratification surveys, three major developments in wage inequality were identified.

First, the peak of the age curve gradually shifted in favor of older employees. The generation to benefit from the communist slogan "youth forward" in 1948 maintained its advantages over its lifetime. Second, the relative wages of those in the "productive sector" (manufacturing, construction and transport) improved continuously, while the position of the service branches (commerce, education, banking and other services) deteriorated. Third, the relative position of university-educated people declined, and differences between various levels of education gradually narrowed. Educational differentials in former Czechoslovakia were kept low, even in relation to the other communist countries.

All the above changes in earnings inequality were prompted by political needs. With its administration of labor and rigid production patterns, the command economy did not require incentives for more qualified and inventive work, labor engagement or risk-taking.

Unlike the distribution of earnings, the period of equalizing household income took slightly longer, that is, it was not completed

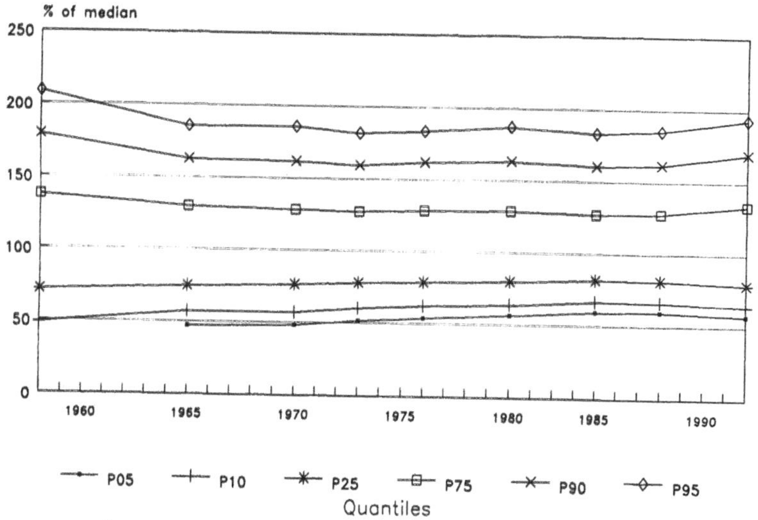

Figure 2. Relative Income Per Capita in 1958-1992

until the 1960s. But then there were very modest changes in the relative distribution (Figure 2). All women were employed and the obligatory double-earnings model replaced the formerly prevailing single-earnings model. A higher than average household income was reached by additional active members (especially in farmers' families) and dispersion of per capita income depended on the number of children. An increase of the lowest pensions (by law, not by valorization or indexation) caused a slight increment of the bottom of the distribution, while the top remained relatively the same for three decades.

What has been described thus far is, however, only one part—the transparent (statistical) part—of the story. The hidden part included only several segments of the population, but produced much greater disparities than the official system itself. As the communist system developed, at least four sources of additional inequalities were established:

1. *"In kind" incomes.* Due to very low real incomes, food expenditures were a substantial drain on household budgets (decreasing only from about 45% to 30% in the period 1948-1988). Any opportunity to economize in this area constituted a special advantage and considerably increased a family's general welfare. After the "class of cooperative peasants" was formed by forced collectivization, its members were privileged by being permitted to

retain pieces of land where food could be produced, either for private consumption or for the market. Simultaneously, in most agricultural cooperatives, in-kind income was provided as a partial payment replacing money.

2. The informal economy. A huge reduction in the service sector provoked a demand for craftsmen work while a scarcity of consumer goods gave rise to private salesmen, who could then charge higher prices. The black market encompassed a wide range of services, including those in the social sector, be it in health care, education, the allocation of apartments, and so on. With each successive "triumph" of communism, the list of informal activities became longer; if scarcity had not occurred "spontaneously," it would simply have been provoked deliberately in order to parasite on it at a later stage.[1]

3. Party privileges. Special rewards were necessary for the "special kind of people" (as the communists once called themselves). Party officials enjoyed privileges such as free or very cheap goods and/or goods unavailable to the ordinary citizen (including special stores, health services and recreation areas). These increased their purchasing power much more than any regular rise in earnings.

4. Hidden "ownership rights." Although large-scale private ownership did not officially exist under the communist regime, actual owners did. Managers, administrators, directors and party officials had extensive opportunities and incentives to transform the ownership status of many goods from state to private, as well as enjoy greater benefits from public services.[2]

Extreme inequalities in housing, for instance, can be explained by all the above mentioned sources. In the countryside, materials, machines and working hours of the cooperative were used for the construction of individual houses. Informal economy networks were also often mobilized to build the family house or buy an apartment. The politically privileged groups were given first option to state apartments which were distributed free of charge. A frequent form of ownership transfer was the purchase of a house for an "official" (often symbolic) price by a manager or party bureaucrat after it had been completely modernized either by the firm or local government. The same was true of the free appropriation of apartments or houses left behind by political prisoners or emigrants.

The system of distribution under communism can be described by various concepts and classifications, in a mix of statistical and anecdotical evidence.[3] Any approach yields the same result, namely that equality under communism is an illusion. This illusion can be supported by the manifest earnings distribution, which was kept narrow for several decades. But within this narrow zone, some important distributive preferences were established and strengthened, resulting in differences which served the "working class in power" (managers, party officials, top and local governors) or the "useful parasites" of the informal economy.

THE REVOLVING MARKET: THE "CORE" AND "PERIPHERY" OF ECONOMIC INEQUALITIES

By the end of 1989, a true revolution was expected by many: in terms of earnings distribution, rewards were supposed to be a response to individual work performance and business success. In terms of household income distribution, a family's standard of living was expected to be determined first and foremost by personal effort instead of the demographic status of households and the needs principle. Although these expectations have become widespread in recent years, they have not as yet been entirely fulfilled.

In order to provide a systematic explanation, we will map out first the earnings distribution and second the distribution of household incomes. With both of these tools, we first reveal the prevailing "core" and then the "periphery" of the inequality system. Finally, we will mention also the problem of property.

The target reward model is expressed by the "meritocratic triad" of education, occupation and income. An individual's qualifications should be convertible into an appropriate occupational position and this position should again be provided with a corresponding income (Kreckel 1992, p. 97). The achievement ideology legitimates income inequality that supports economic efficiency and growth. It creates a vertical stratification whereby people are distinguished by their human capital, occupational prestige and income rewards. In this approach, the "status attainment" perspective (Sewell and Hauser 1975; Featherman and Hauser 1984) is closely interconnected with the theory of human capital (Mincer 1974) and meritocratic ideology (Matějů 1993). This pattern should create a fair base for the new socio-economic order. Consequently, household incomes should be derived from the economic position of family members, with only necessary redistributive corrections.

What we call a "core" system of economic inequalities is easily measurable statistically and presumably vertically ordered. The rest are "peripheral" systems of economic inequalities, which can complete or bias the core system. Peripheral inequalities are distributed mostly horizontally and are not easily measurable statistically.

The primary problem of the "core" system concerns how earning inequalities are emulated by the characteristics of work. After 1989 some important changes in earnings distribution occurred which followed the above-mentioned interrelation between occupation, education and earnings. First, the distribution range has widened and reached a similar level to some Western European countries. Second, the economic reform undermined the importance of employees' demographic characteristics, reducing the gender gap somewhat and producing a much flatter age distribution. Third, the market value of human capital significantly increased: returns to one year of education among men have risen from 4 percent to 5.5 percent of the average earnings in 1988-1992 and continue to rise slowly (Večerník 1995). And fourth, in branch disparities, former privileges in the "production sector" disappeared and a certain improvement in services occurred. We can assume that a systematic shift toward the "western model" is taking place. This shift is, however, more rapid in the private sector and firms with foreign capital and management.

All in all, there has been a tendency to dismantle the previous "labor reproduction costs" model in favor of the "human capital reward" model, replace demographic variables by socio-economic ones and stress correlation between education, occupational rank and earnings.

At the same time, inverse changes are taking place at the "periphery" of the distribution system. The best example is that of Czech guest-workers in Germany or Austria. Due to the Czech currency's low exchange rate, upon their return these people in fact get two or three times more money than they would earn in similar positions in the Czech Republic. Commuting workers are usually not highly qualified professionals but relatively skilled craftsmen or low qualified people willing to perform unattractive or seasonal jobs. They distort the "core" tendency because they are located in the bottom or middle levels of the occupational hierarchy but in the upper level of earnings distribution.

From the opposite side, the "core" model is being challenged by an expanding private business sector. There are many people with university education who start private ventures to compensate for their deficient earnings. University graduates are not only opening law firms, surgeries, ambulances and consulting firms, but also shops and kiosks, restaurants and exchange bureaus. While in the first case there is a consistency between education, occupation and reward, in the second case the occupational prestige is somewhat inconsistent with the educational level, although it is compensated by the higher-than-average income.

In addition, the "core" model is being challenged by various forms of the informal economy. The ability to illegally sell goods, services, finance and information is not necessarily derived from human capital investment and the return is usually beyond the limits of the "normal" wage distribution. The informal economy widens both income inequality and regional disparities considerably. Although the secondary economic activities of Czech households were never so extensive as in Hungary or Poland, their importance seems to have grown in response both to the wider field of opportunities and increasing financial hardship. In the transformation period, when the labor market has not yet stabilized, the two-job model is frequent, the second job being legal or semi-legal, either full-time or part-time and complementary or even more lucrative than the first one. At least 15 percent of the active population combine first and second jobs, increasing their income by 50 percent (Economic Expectations and Attitudes, November 1994).

The second problem concerns household incomes: to what extent are they a product of family member characteristics on the one hand and household size and demographic composition on the other? Important changes occurred also in household incomes regarding not only the range of inequality but also the way of income packaging. In the communist past, the range of distribution of household income was larger but that of per capita income was even narrower than the distribution of earnings. The main factors of household income were of demographic character, that is, the number of active earners and the number of dependent children (Večerník 1991a).

This "demographic model" seems to have been gradually transformed into the "economic model" typical of Western developed countries. In this model, the more favorable placement of a person in the earnings hierarchy can—and actually does—outweigh incomes brought in by additional active earners and social transfers. Whatever the importance of the number of dependent children for family welfare in this model, it is far from being the decisive factor.

This "core" model is also challenged by various segments of income distribution. The obvious corrective factor is the welfare state, which redistributes income from the rich to the poor, from childless people to families with children and from the active to the inactive population. Thus, prominent welfare groups are pensioners, the elderly as well as the disabled. In the communist period, disabled status, far to be always fairly won, provided exemption from work and guaranteed a minimum income. Gypsies constitute a typical category that relies upon pensions or family allowances as the sole regular source of income, supplemented on an irregular basis by market income or illegal activities.

The opening of the market legalized some household-related activities as well as developed others, thus biasing the relationship between the market reward for the individual and the household standard of living. Families with some facilities are able to increase their market income by renting out rooms and apartments.[4]

With regard to both earnings and household income inequalities, the "core" and "vertical" systems are complemented and contested by "peripheral" and "horizontal" systems, the latter being both remnants of the communist past and new products of the transformation period. In any case, recent shifts represent deep changes as the distribution system gradually adjusts to the standards of the advanced capitalist countries.

The third, additional problem concerns family wealth: to what degree is it related to personal earnings and other incomes? Because of the gap between extremely low wages and extremely high prices of durable goods, family wealth under communism was very weakly or not at all correlated with current incomes. In principle, wealth should be a product of long-term saving. However, it was produced by quite other channels than work (both official and informal). This feature was especially the case with housing.

Housing costs represent an extremely important axis of economic inequality, which cuts across family dependence on market income. During the transformation period, discrepancies between the housing statuses of families have persisted as a result of both the problems of ownership change and the extremely slow establishment of the housing market. In state (municipal) apartments, rents are still strictly controlled, and this category of the population is still privileged by the extremely low housing costs (37% of dwellings). In cooperative apartments, people are expected to cover all construction and maintenance costs, with a certain state contribution (17% of dwellings). Families living in their own houses or apartments who have to meet the entire or major part of the real housing costs remain the most burdened (46% of dwellings). Under the communist regime, housing costs were inversely proportional to incomes (the higher the income, the cheaper the housing costs on the average). This remains the case today, with many exceptions and some adjustments.

NOUVEAUX RICHES, NEW POVERTY

In economic terms, the re-introduction of the capitalist system aims to increase the standard of living of the population as a whole. One element of the story is that both "old" poverty and wealth become more visible. Also, markets open channels for producing "new" wealth and poverty for some categories of people.

In communist Czechoslovakia, the discussion of wealth was a taboo. Officially, ownership of capital was eliminated and the ownership of personal goods considerably limited.[5] But once party and state administrators, blackmarketeers and many cooperative farmers enriched themselves, restrained and confidential attempts to detect their wealth were undertaken—by party secretariats and the economic police.

The restoration of private ownership and the emergence of markets provide numerous opportunities both to manifest the old and create new wealth. In this context, it is possible to distinguish five main roads leading to large private property.

- Transformation of the former property (communist, blackmarket, large families) in the privatization process or speculation.
- Conversion of the communist "political capital" by transferring former state firms to private ownership, either directly (whereby managers become legal owners) or indirectly (through the control of share-holding companies or other organizations).[6]
- Restitution of former family property and continuation of family business, which primarily concerns retail trade, services and real estate.[7]

- Exploitation of the failures in justice, lack of control and a virgin market consciousness of ordinary people for speculation, smuggling and cheating against the state, the business partners and consumers.[8]
- Last, but not least: discovering markets through hard work, risk-taking and inventive entrepreneurship; one can become rich without any (communist or pre-communist) roots and by legal and honest means.[9]

Important changes occurred also at the other pole of economic inequality, poverty. In the communist regime, there was officially no poverty thanks to full employment and a comprehensive social security system which, from the late 1960s, covered the whole population. In relative terms, the narrow range of income distribution created a situation in which the bottom sector of the population was not too far from the average. By impoverishing the population as a whole (in absolute terms), the communist regime succeeded in mitigating individual poverty (in relative terms).

However, this does not mean that poverty in absolute terms was entirely eliminated or camouflaged. Extremely low pension benefits for members of the former "bourgeoisie" were used as a weapon of the communist party in the class war. Due to the absence of any valorization or indexing of social benefits, the purchasing power of the pensions for the oldest eligible group dropped far below the average pension and the average pension dropped far below the average wage. The financial situation of single women with children was also acute. In addition, the living conditions of Gypsies concentrated in some East Slovak regions could be characterized as those of an underclass—with the absence of elementary facilities of civilization (e.g., running water, sewerage and heating).

Since the collapse of the communist regime in November 1989, new economic and social developments have manifestly exposed the problem of poverty. In addition to the "old" poverty, mostly demographically defined (elderly, families with more children, single parent households), a "new" poverty began to appear. There are at least three sources of this new poverty:

- A free labor market that transformed overemployment and labor shortage in unemployment.[10]

- The removal of price subsidies (which started in July 1990) and the introduction of market prices (which commenced in January 1991), which increased prices and the costs of living considerably;[11] currently, only rents and prices of energy remain under state control.
- The opening of borders and uncontrolled migration (mostly from the former USSR and the Balkan countries), which resulted in the emergence of a formerly unknown group of homeless refugees, not covered by social benefits.

In order to restrict poverty as much as possible, two important measures were taken. A formerly non-existent minimum wage was introduced in 1991 and increased soon thereafter (2200 CRK = $80 gross monthly). A new Law on the Subsistence Minimum was accepted by the Czechoslovak Parliament in the Fall of 1991 in order to replace the former, rather vague regulation of state assistance for low income households.[12] Since the new subsistence line was established, the poverty rate surprisingly decreased from 4.5 percent to 3 percent of households in 1988-1992. And, because the pension benefits were more rapidly valorized than family allowances, more families with children fell into poverty, replacing part of pensioners.

For displaying poverty trends in the recent period, we can use the data of Economic Attitudes and Expectations survey where several concepts of poverty were applied (Table 1):

- The first concept is that of the abovementioned legal poverty as defined by the Subsistence Minimum Income and covered by means-tested benefits. This indicator gives a poverty incidence for households of about 2-3 percent, the main determining factor for which is the number of dependent children (POOR1).
- The second concept is poverty as usually measured in the European Union. This indicator gives a poverty incidence for households of about 3-4 percent, the main determining factor for which is the number of dependent children and age of the head of the household.
- The third concept is represented by subjective poverty, which results in a poverty rate of about 30 percent and is far more affected by the number of adults in the household and, additionally, predicted by certain social characteristics.[13]

- The fourth concept is a simple declaration of poverty by respondents which provides a poverty rate of about 8-10 percent and which is less affected by the demographic and social characteristics and more by the housing and wealth status of households.[14]

In addition, poverty dynamics differ by indicator. According to the indicator of feeling poor, there is only very little fluctuation over time. According to the concept of legal poverty, there is a certain rise produced by the adjustment of the threshold on rising costs of living.

Table 1. Percentages of Poor According to Various Measurements in 1991-1994

	Households	Persons	Children
June 1991			
POOR1	2.4	3.1	3.8
POOR2	3.7	3.1	3.3
POOR3	22.2	19.8	19.7
POOR4	10.8	10.0	10.6
June 1992			
POOR1	2.7	4.1	6.1
POOR2	2.7	3.5	4.5
POOR3	24.9	20.9	21.0
POOR4	8.1	7.4	8.4
January 1993:			
POOR1	2.0	2.6	4.1
POOR1a	3.8	4.5	6.8
POOR2	2.8	3.0	3.9
POOR3	28.0	22.1	18.5
POOR4	9.7	8.6	7.9
November 1994:			
POOR1a	1.9	2.4	3.4
POOR2	3.0	3.4	4.4
POOR3	32.8	27.0	24.2
POOR4	7.3	6.3	6.5

Source: Economic Expectations and Attitudes 1991-1994.

Notes: *Measurements of poverty:*

POOR1. Households with incomes below the line as established by the Law on the Subsistence Minimum from November 1991.

POOR1a. Households with incomes below the line as established by the update of the Law on the Subsistence Minimum beginning in March 1993.

POOR2. Households with incomes below 50% of the median of income per equivalent adult (European Union measure).

POOR3. Households with incomes below the Subjective Poverty Line (see note 13).

POOR4. Respondents' households who answered "definitely yes" to the question "Do you consider your household to be poor?"

And, according to the subjective definition, we ascertain a much faster increase. Not only do people see the "subsistence income" as much higher than the level established by the state but they also perceive it as growing faster than inflation. This perception is quite understandable given the enrichment of a small part of the population. People would accept modesty and the tightening of belts if these were parts of universal behavior.

With economic transformation, the poles of wealth and poverty apparently become more distant. Extreme need is, however, rare among the population. In this respect, the new system continues in the traditions of the prewar Czechoslovak welfare state, which was one of the most successful in Europe. After 1989 concentrated attention was paid to income minima, social assistance as well as valorizing pensions and social benefits. However, the policy is still challenged by two problems. The first is the continuing rent control, which lowers the costs of living considerably for the tenants of state apartments, while burdening the new private house owners and, consequently, destroying the housing market. The second is the unbalanced system of social benefits which favors pensioners and disregards children and, especially, young couples. Falling natality is a logical consequence.

PEOPLE'S ATTITUDES AND EXPECTATIONS

Current changes in economic inequalities are critically perceived and transformed into expectations and claims. This metamorphosis is not straightforward but filtered by individual situations, social status and political inclinations. The strongest influence comes both from institutions playing a protective role and the ideology of the recent past. The communist society appeared extremely equalized in terms of wages, income and consumer market. Furthermore, people were drilled in and indoctrinated by the ideology of equality in a way that higher incomes and wealths were always considered to be unfairly won. This indoctrination started as early as World War II (when the Nazis corrupted the workers in military industries with higher earnings) and continued without interruption for the next 45 years.

When searching for the evidence of people's attitudes toward inequality, we can use two empirical sources. The first is anecdotical evidence as reflected by the press and other media, which focus on certain themes. The second are sociological and public opinion surveys describing the topic in more general terms. The problem of economic inequality, as handled by the media, deals mostly with three topics:

- the salaries and business activities of top state functionaries and members of Parliament (their tax declarations, earnings appointments, possible misuse of their positions);[15]
- "dirty money," its source and channels of legalization, legislation on and the search for it;[16]
- financial (especially banking) transactions, insurance of savings, stock exchange operations with newly distributed shares, and so forth.[17]

These sources are very telling about people's sensitivity toward high earnings, their envy toward dirty money, and their interest in (but still not readiness to) participate in financial markets with a short-term outlook only for profit. This evidence also makes clear that neither the press and public opinion, nor the government and the politicians are used to treating problems of economic inequalities in more general terms and observing the boundaries between "functional" efficiency and "social" burden. Anecdotal evidence makes it difficult to say whether the population's sensitivity to economic inequality is increasing or decreasing, what could be yet tolerated and what not.

In fact, the increase in criticism against income inequality was higher than the rise of inequalities themselves. Already in 1991, 40 percent of respondents answered that inequality among people is "extensive" and a further 50 percent it is "rather extensive." In comparison with 1989, 45 percent perceived social inequality as definitely "larger" while 50 percent of respondents saw it as "possibly larger." The same percentage also expect increasing inequalities in the very near future. On the other hand, 55 percent of respondents evaluated the current changes as bringing more justice by transforming the social structure. The perception of economic and social inequalities is obviously part of the general social climate that has seen certain fluctuations since 1989.

During the mid-1992 election period the gradual rise of "rightist" attitudes culminated and has since been decreasing. The recent left shift is manifested, among others, by the fact that more people

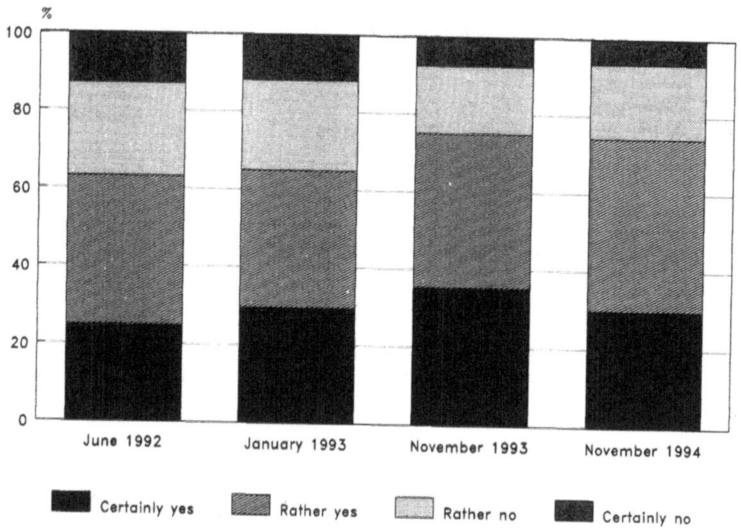

Figure 3. State Should Guarantee Jobs

expect the state to protect jobs (Figure 3), rents and prices. More peopleare also attracted by the "social market" model which, at the end of 1993, appeared to be the most desirable solution, unlike the previous period, when the majority of the population voted for the

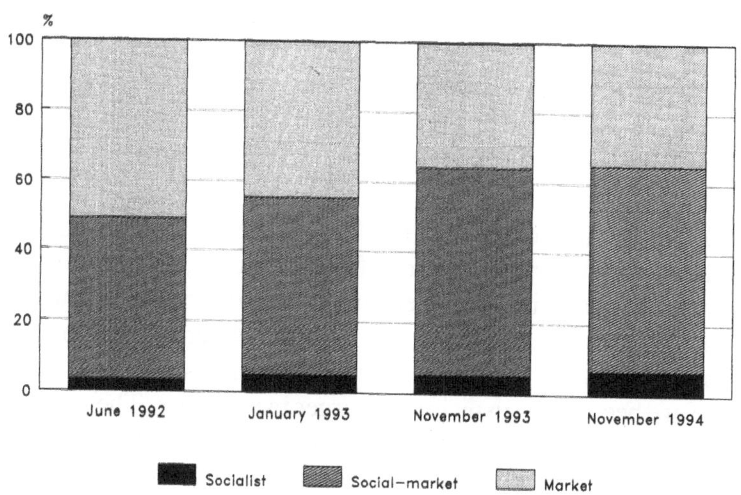

Figure 4. Preference of the Economic Order

Table 2. Opinions on Private Ownership, the Role of the State and Earnings Inequality

First line = % answers "definitely yes".
Second line = % answers "definitely yes" plus "rather yes."

	May 1990	*Decem. 1990*	*June 1991*	*Decem. 1991*	*June 1992*	*Jan. 1993*	*Novem. 1993*	*Novem. 1994*
A. "Private entrepreneurship should be given complete freedom."								
	49.7	45.8	40.0	28.3	33.6	25.8	24.9	21.2
	86.8	79.0	75.6	63.1	67.8	63.3	58.6	59.3
B. "There should be an absolutely open space for foreign firms in our country."								
	17.1	22.5	19.3	15.9	16.6	10.0		7.1
	47.3	54.2	48.2	41.5	48.2	36.7		29.1
C. "Even in the new conditions the economy should be under the control of the state."								
	52.0	39.7	39.0	37.3	229.2	28.6	31.6	27.6
	87.5	77.6	81.6	81.9	72.7	75.2	79.5	78.7
D. "All big firms in state ownership should be transformed into joint-stock or private firms."								
	17.1	23.9	22.2	22.4	23.7	17.3		
	56.9	59.6	56.2	56.8	57.2	51.8		
E. "It is right that capable and competent people have a lot of money, even millions."								
	40.3	47.3	49.5	45.0	47.4	41.8	37.4	33.6
	66.3	74.8	76.9	75.2	78.4	76.7	75.3	75.6
F. "Differences in wages and salaries should increase."								
	57.8	55.5		46.9	43.4	35.2	24.8	18.9
	88.6	87.7		82.6	80.2	72.9	66.0	59.4
G. "Everybody is responsible for his/her own poverty."								
					16.2	10.9		6.8
					46.7	39.1		34.8
H. "People get rich mostly by unfair means."								
						34.3		38.5
					33.6	79.9		80.5

Source: Economic Expectations and Attitudes, 1990-1994.

"market without adjectives" model (Figure 4).[18] Although fewer people agree with state control of the economy, the percentage of respondents accepting complete freedom for private ventures and foreign firms is continuously diminishing. After a short period of enthusiasm about the widening range of earnings distribution, most people are becoming suspicious of larger inequalities. The percentage of people who believe that differences in salaries should grow is decreasing, less people share the attitude that poverty is a question of individual responsibility, and more people consider that wealth is mostly acquired by unfair practices (Table 2).

Such a continuous change in attitudes is partly explained by direct experience, which provides numerous pitiful examples. On the one hand, the communist nomenclature has not only survived but is successfully converting its political and capital into business capital; black marketeers are able to enrich themselves without difficulty, speculators triumph over honest entrepreneurs, and the creation of new firms is burdened by complicated procedures and huge taxation. On the other hand, the costs of living have increased and households without extra incomes are being forced to dramatically limit their habitual expenditures. It should come as no surprise that such changes have brought about the return of the former equality claims and social envy toward the new rich.

There could also be several other explanations for such a shift. First, liberal attitudes were a "fashionable deviation" at the beginning of the transformation but now people are looking for easier solutions. Second, the last years have been a lesson in restraint, with fears of a further rise in living costs, which are generating demands for increased state protection. Third, the pendulum of history has reached the extreme right and is returning to the left, as recent shifts in Poland and Hungary have demonstrated. Fourth, Czechs are traditional levelers and social democrats and have resisted extreme disparities since the loss of their gentry following the battle on the White Mountain in 1620.

However, the most probable and reasonable explanation originates in the ongoing crystallization and differentiation of people's minds, following their experience. Right after the Velvet Revolution, people actually asked for both market freedom and state guarantees at the same time. A new commitment to liberal values was simply added to continuing expectations of state engagement in the economy, job and wage security, price controls, and the like. Such ambiguous attitudes are being dismantled and replaced by less commonly shared but logically more consistent opinions that are inclined either to free market play or to state job and price guarantees. Not only do fewer people accept complete freedom for private entrepreneurship but also fewer people demand state control of the economy. Instead of vague opinion blends, more consistent profiles are being created. However, the common background of those tendencies is a turn to more "social" attitudes, accompanied by people's outflow from the political right to the middle and slightly to the left.[19]

Table 3. Correlations Between Opinions About Private Ownership, the Role of the State and Inequality of Earnings
Spearman Correlation Coefficients

	A.	*C.*	*E.*	*F.*	*LEFT*	*JOB*
May 1990						
A.	1.00	−.10*	18**	.14**	.27**	
C.		1.00	−.20**	−.04	.13**	
E.			1.00	20**	−.15**	
F.				1.00	−.09*	
June 1991						
A.	1.00	−.21**	.43**		−.31**	.05
C.		1.00	−.20**		.22**	−.08
E.			1.00		−.32**	.14**
LEFT					1.00	−.17**
June 1992						
A.	1.00	−.26**	.41**	.14**	−.29**	.02
C.		1.00	−.23**	−.17**	.24**	−.03
E.			1.00	.36**	−.38**	.16**
F.				1.00	−.31**	.12**
LEFT					1.00	−.09*
November 1993						
A	1.00	−.38**	..39**	.21**	−.33**	.12*
C		1.00	−.20**	−.19**	.30**	−.12**
E			1.00	.34**	−.33**	.26**
F				1.00	−.25**	.23**
LEFT					1.00	.27**
November 1994						
A.	1.00	−.40**	.41**	.26**	−.27**	.19**
C.		1.00	−.32**	−.25**	.31**	−.20**
E.			1.00	.47**	−.34**	.26**
F.				1.00	−.31**	.29**
LEFT					1.00	−.18**

Source: Economic Expectations and Attitudes, 1990-1994.

Notes: *A. C. E. F. see questions in Table 2:*

A. "Private entrepreneurship should be given complete freedom."
C. "Even in the new conditions the economy should be under the control of the state."
E. "It is right that capable and competent people have a lot of money, even millions."
F. "Differences in wages and salaries should increase."

LEFT: "In politics, concepts "right" and "left" are often used.
How would you characterize yourself considering opinions you have?" 1. clear left, 2. rather left, 3. middle, 4. rather right, 5. clear right.

JOB: "Do you think your job has good prospects in ongoing changes?" 1. Certainly yes, 2. rather yes, 3. rather no, 4. certainly no.

Statistical significance:
** < 0.001.
* < 0.01.

This crystallization process is documented in Table 3, where several opinions are correlated. The first two (freedom for private entrepreneurshp and state control over the economy) have conflicting meanings. Both were championed at the beginning, but as the transformation progresses, they are conceived of as less compatible. The other two (substantial sums of money for competent people and increasing earnings disparities) are rather similar. Initially considered not to be necessarily interlinked, they are more and more jointly manifested in recent observations. The same is true of those other correlations that testify to the emergence of much clearer opinion patterns. Statistically speaking, opinions proceeded from the multifactorial to the monofactorial solution.

An increasing consistency can also be seen when associating the free market/social protection attitudes with the general political inclination (left/right spectrum) on the one hand and job prospects on the other. In both cases, the increase in the significance of correlation coefficients is considerable. Respondents locate themselves on the general political spectrum according to their individual attitudes toward private ownership, the role of the state and market incentives in a more coherent manner. An even more significant progression is to be seen when the attitudes are correlated to the respondent's expectations of favorable prospects for his or her occupation and job. However, the association of economic attitudes with political inclination remains significantly higher.

Until now, the emerging system of economic inequalities was not legitimate in people's minds. It is surprising that a great majority of respondents (80%) do not accept new wealth as fairly acquired or are suspicious about the procedure. The percentage of people saying that "privatization should be continued regardless that the property could fall into improper hands" dropped from 30% to 19% between mid-1992 and the end of 1993 (Economic Expectations and Attitudes). Both small-scale and large-scale privatization are suspected to attract dirty money and produce corruption.

Thoughts about legitimacy are not so categorical regarding poverty. According to surveys, 35 percent of people still think that it is the individual rather than society who is responsible for his or her poverty (Table 2). However, there has been a change of attitudes over time. Now more people expect greater involvement of the state, especially for older and less educated people. Also on this point, consistency of attitudes is increasing: people contesting the legitimacy of acquired property are the same as those who blame the state for neglecting poverty and who feel poor.

CONCLUSION

We cannot separate changes in the range of economic inequalities from modifications in their character. Moreover, we cannot focus on quantitative shifts and neglect qualitative adjustments. In particular, modifications in the character of inequalities include:

- a growing transparency of inequalities: many of the formerly hidden or officially non-existent disparities and most of the new inequalities have become manifest or at least detectable; with the growing transparency, the legitimacy of economic disparities can be challenged and contested;
- economic inequalities cease to derive from political preferences and privileges to such a high degree as before, and start to be produced by markets to a much higher degree;
- distributions of earnings, household incomes and family wealth, formerly almost separated, start to be linked together with a perspective to form a more or less compact system;
- by liberating the economy and releasing it from the state budget, income distribution can be distinguished from re-distribution and the social sphere can be financed as such, directly and transparently.

Although inequalities are larger and more manifest, it does not mean that they are dysfunctional or harmful to the economic system and society. Unfortunately, we can hardly distinguish between the necessary and excessive "costs" of the economic transformation in this sense. The adjustment of the economic system to "normal," "functional" or "efficient" conditions requires the abolition of overemployment and the production of some reasonable unemployment in order to foster flexibility in the labor force. Hence, the old system of social guarantees should be dismantled because it was actually based on compulsory work. The same is true of earnings disparities which, instead of reflecting costs of the labor force reproduction, have to motivate the acquisition and use of human capital as well as to support business commitment. There are, however, reasonable thresholds of both the unemployment rate and earnings inequality above which costs become excessive and harm the economic system itself.

So far, the Czech Republic has been one of the leaders among East-Central European countries with regard to the efficiency of the economic transformation and the level of macroeconomic stability. Earnings and income inequality revealed by statistics is still rather moderate. In terms of attitudes, Czechs show the highest commitment to the market and "hard work" values and the lowest level of required state protection. They still demand equality and a greater state involvement in individual welfare to a much lesser degree than Poles, Slovaks and Hungarians. Furthermore, commitment to the liberal values remains the highest as does the acceptance of greater inequalities.[20] We can assume that those value preferences manifest the collective memory of Czech capitalism's good performance in the past and present century.[21]

When considering the scope of the core system in rewarding work (the meritocratic triad of education, occupation and income) and packaging household incomes (the market income outweighing influence of the demographic status of the family), we should stress another feature of the Czech transformation. Unlike Poland and Hungary, the Czech economy was more centralized, the social structure of the country more repressed and social life frozen after the 1968 Soviet occupation until the last days of the communist rule. No private sector was allowed, no weakening of centralized power occurred, no privatization attempts before 1990 were possible, no autonomous social actors such as the peasantry or trade unions in Poland emerged, no dual economy as in Hungary ("morning in communism, afternoon in capitalism") prevailed. The negative turned into a positive: an easier administration of the transformation process became possible and the privatization bore less spontaneous or wild forms. Due to this, we can presume that the proportion of the core forms and ways of distribution is higher than elsewhere.

But it is not only economic interests that are important when considering problems of economic inequality, unemployment and poverty. Of equal importance at least are the social and sociological perspectives: society's integration, the protection and development of the moral and cultural level and, last but not least, the re-establishment of a middle class society, similar to prewar

Czechoslovakia.[22] On the one hand, the emergence of the middle classes has been impeded by the fact that the current (presumably conservative) government does not greatly support small entrepreneurs or promote the status of such categories as doctors, teachers or other intellectuals—on the contrary, it is more generous to large capital and monopolistic structures. Nevertheless, Czech society has maintained a relatively good welfare system which thus prevents the formation of an underclass.[23]

In fact, neither economic inequality nor withdrawal from universal social protection have been not issues within the political and academic debates. By keeping unemployment and the officially acknowledged poverty low, and as yet not having produced extreme concentrations of either poverty or wealth, the Czech Republic appears to be an island of social peace. This does not mean that there are no big problems, but they seem to be limited either to certain regions (in the case of unemployment) or to certain categories within the population (in the case of Gypsies). However, left shifts in attitudes and increasing indignation toward inequalities signal the sensitive nature of this topic.

APPENDIX

Surveys Used

"Economic Expectations and Attitudes"

A biannual survey organized by the socio-economics team of the Institute of Sociology of the Academy of Sciences headed by the author. The sample includes adults from 18 to 60 years of age. The sampling procedure is two-step quota sampling, whereby the region and size of the locality were defined in the first step and gender, age and education in the second. Surveys are financed partly by grants from the Academy of Sciences and partly by the Ministry of Labor and Social Affairs of the Czech Republic, and conducted by the Center for Empirical Surveys.

Periods and samples:

	Czech	Slovak
I. May 1990	1107	544
II. December 1990	1160	584
III. June 1991	1092	597
IV. December 1991	1126	583
V. July 1992	1104	980
VI. January 1993	1142	829
VII. November 1993	1113	853
VIII. November 1994	1307	850

"The Transformation of Social Structure"

A survey conducted in September-October 1991 on a sample of 2850 adult respondents by the Institute of Sociology of the Academy of Sciences and the Institute of Socio-Political Sciences of Charles University in Prague.

"The Dismantling of the Safety Net and its Political Consequences"

A survey conducted in October 1991. Coordinated and financed by the Institute of East West Security Studies, New York. The international file includes: the Czech Republic (1187), Slovakia (817), Hungary (1500) and Poland (1491).

"Social Inequality—1992"

A regular module of the ISSP (International Social Science Programme) series, realized in October 1992. Four national files were used here: the Czech Republic (687), Slovakia (423), Hungary (1250) and Poland (1647).

Social Stratification 1992

The national part of the international comparative research project "Social Stratification in Eastern Europe after 1989" coordinated by the Institute for Social Science Research of the University of California in Los Angeles. The principal investigators were Donald J. Treiman and Ivan Szelenyi. Six former communist countries participated in the project: the Czech Republic, the Slovak Republic, Hungary, Poland, Russia and Bulgaria.

ACKNOWLEDGMENT

This study was mostly written during my stay in the Institute for Human Sciences in Vienna and I thank Krzysztof Michalski, Director, for making possible this stay. The research was also supported by the NATO Grant "New poverty, political attitudes and welfare state institutions in former Czechoslovakia: possible impacts on a developing democracy."

NOTES

1. On this point we disagree with Sik (1994, p. 48), who asserts that the second economy under the communist regime caused an insignificant increase in income inequality. Taking into account agricultural plots, moonlighting, bribery, robbery of state property and other forms of enrichment, the widening economic inequality is an undisputable fact.

2. Not only the top politicians but also regional or district "rulers" (directors of big enterprises and cooperatives and party secretaries) used their earnings almost only for savings because they got everything else free of charge, according to the unwritten rules. The list began with meat (a scarce item at the time) and ended with housing.

3. Kornai distinguishes three "other manifestations" of the distribution of material welfare outside financial income: (1) turnover taxes and price subsidies, (2) free goods and services and (3) access to goods in short supply (Kornai 1992, pp. 318-322).

4. It is still a legal activity to sublet one's (actually the state's or cooperative's) apartment for several times more than the actual rent. Hence, many people leave Prague and other cities for their secondary house, renting their apartment to a foreigner.

5. Under communist law, a distinction was made between "private" and "personal" property, the former being the means of production, the latter personal goods. Thus, a house should not go beyond a certain limit of surface to be acknowledged as a "family" house. If this limit was crossed, the owner's powers were limited and taxes much higher.

6. The situation in former Czechoslovakia is much different from the "political capitalism" described by Staniszkis (1991) for Poland and Hungary. In those countries, reform attempts which started prior to 1989 gave much more power and autonomy to managers, who could use this power to convert themselves into capitalist entrepreneurs. In Czechoslovakia, the preservation of centralized economic power until the last days of communist rule ensured fairer privatization methods.

7. According to the 1990 Law on Relieving the Consequences of Some Property Injustices, only physical persons and resident Czechoslovak citizens whose property was nationalized between February 25, 1948 and January 1, 1990 were entitled to reclaim their property. Thus, bigger firms (generally over 50 employees) nationalized before this time were not included. According to the Economic Expectations and Attitudes survey of November, 1994, 28 percent of respondents got something back in restitution, most of them farm or land (72%), others a house or real estate (16%) and the rest a factory or workshop.

8. See, for instance, the extreme but temporary success enjoyed by the so-called "post box firms" (both domestic and foreign) abusing lack of control and naïveté of consumers by cheating them on a massive scale.

9. In a somewhat extreme form, those characteristics were summarized by Benáček (1994), who asserted that it is nearly impossible for an honest entrepreneur to survive and prosper. According to him, the Czech economy is fueled by hidden economic forces. Black marketeers, crooks and tax evaders could be as responsible for the Czech "economic miracle" as the macroeconomic policy.

10. See Oxenstierna, 1990 for a detailed description of this transformation in the former Soviet Union. Here, we should stress the specific features of the Czech economy with an unemployment rate of about 3 percent. Although some increase is expected, it should remain in the one-digit range.

11. The price index increased by 57 percent in 1991 (reflecting the liberalization of most prices), 11 percent in 1992, 21 percent in 1993 (reflecting a new system of taxes including VAT) and 10 percent in 1994.

12. According to the Law on Subsistence Minimum, assistance is given to all citizens whose incomes do not reach a certain level and who are considered able to increase their incomes due to their age, health or other serious reasons. Eligibility is reviewed by social security offices in districts subsequent to individual requests and after testing the household's income and living situation. The subsistence minimum income is to meet the basic needs both of individuals and households. It was set at about half of the average household income. The subsistence minimum is increased each time the rise in the cost of living of households below the legal poverty line surpasses 10 percent.

13. For our comparison we used the Subjective Poverty Line (SPL) as measured by the Minimum Income Question which is: "What minimum income would your household require to meet basic needs?" (For calculation of SPL see Goedhart, Halberstadt, Kapteyn and Van Praag 1977).

14. Households whose respondent answered "definitely yes" to the question "Do you feel your household is poor?" were classified as poor.

15. We should stress that due to various political considerations, the Law on Conflict of Interests has not yet been approved by the Czech Parliament. After the last increase, the Prime Minister's salary is 38,500 CRK monthly ($1375, which is 17.5 times the minimum wage) while a minister's is set at 28,500 CRK ($1020, which is 13 times the minimum wage).

16. After the Prime Minister Václav Klaus' statement that he "does not know any dirty money," legislative and policy activity in this direction somewhat froze. However, a law which aims to control "dirty money" is currently being prepared.

17. The new Czech banks offer high interest rates (10-14% for long-term savings), thus increasing the risk for customers who in the beginning did not realize that a bank can go bankrupt. After the first bankruptcy (Bank Bohemia), a huge public debate was initiated that led to the introduction of a state guarantee on savings to a certain limit (100,000 CRK).

18. The popular perception of the social market model is far from the original concept of W. Eucken, A. Müller-Armack and Kreis Ordo, in which the state was supposed to be a guarantor of the market economic order. The popular perception is much closer to a "third way," where the state provides large social guarantees

and redistributes incomes. It obviously reflects the existing German and Austrian model that includes large welfare provisions (Barry 1993).

19. According to the "Economic Expectations and Attitudes" survey, whereas in June 1992 50 percent of the respondents opted for the right, 33 percent for the middle and 17 percent for the left, corresponding figures for November 1993 were 39 percent, 42 percent and 19 percent.

20. Here we are referring to some results of the two comparative surveys "The Dismantling of the Safety Net and its Political Consequences" and the ISSP module "Social Inequality—1992."

21. As part of the Austro-Hungarian Monarchy until 1918, the Czech lands represented its industrially most developed constituent. Pre-war Czechoslovakia numbered among the top 10 developed countries in the world. Czechoslovakia had been left almost intact by the war and the pre-war level of production was regained in two years.

22. The Czech lands were a typically middle class society. From a sociological perspective, they were viewed (perhaps with a certain exaggeration fashionable for the time) as extremely equalized, as "almost one homogeneous stratum of urban manual workers and employees with very similar living conditions and mentality corresponding to the unified mass culture of today" (Ullrich 1937, p. 43).

23. The social protection system is based on three "pillars:" social insurance, state social support and social assistance. The new social insurance system, launched in 1993, includes de-etatization and independent funding. Instead of full revenue financing, the state will act merely as a guarantor. This system should also stimulate the establishment of complementary individual pension systems based on citizenship. State social support includes targeted and differentiated aid for households whose incomes are over the poverty line but which fall into financial hardship. The system aims to contribute to their survival but not to fully cover newly emerging costs. The construction of benefits is derived from a minimum income level (the legal poverty line). Social assistance is oriented towards households with incomes below the poverty line and is aimed at the highest possible level of de-centralization. The regulations and administration have to ensure better targeting and means testing: only those who are not able to overcome financial hardship themselves will be eligible. In order to make social assistance more flexible for households in need, a new, more effective network of institutions providing social support is to be established.

REFERENCES

Atkinson, A.B., and Micklewright, J. 1992. *The Economic Transformation of Eastern Europe and the Distribution of Income.* Cambridge: Cambridge University Press.

Barry, N. 1993. "The Social Market Economy." *Social Philosophy & Policy* 10 (Summer): 1-25.

Benáček, V. 1994. *Small business and private entrepneurship during transformation: The case of the Czech republic.* Working Papers No. 53. Prague, CERGE/EI.

Berger, P.L. 1986. *The Capitalist Revolution.* New York: Basic Books.

Earle, J.S., R. Frydman, A. Rapaczynski, and J. Turkewitz. 1994. *Small Privatization. The Transformation of Retail Trade and Consumer Services in Czech Republic, Hungary and Poland.* London, Central European University Press.

Featherman, D.L., and R.M. Hauser. 1984. *Opportunity and Change.* New York: Academic Press.

Goedhart, T., V. Halberstadt, A. Kapteyn, and B.M.S. Van Praag. 1977. "The Poverty Line: Concept and Measurement." *The Journal of Human Resources* 12: 503-520.

Kornai, J. 1992. *The Socialist System. The Political Economy of Communism.* Oxford: Clarendon Press.

Kreckel, T. 1992. *Politische Soziologie der sozialen Ungleichheit.* Frankfurt/M.: Campus.

Machonin, P. et al. 1969. *Československá společnost. Sociologická analýza sociální stratifikace.* (Czechoslovak society. A sociological analysis of social stratification) Bratislava: Epocha.

Machonin, P. 1969. *Československá společnost. Sociologická analýza sociálnií stratifikace.* (Czechoslovak society. A sociological analysis of social stratification). Bratislava: Epocha.

Marx, K. 1965. *Capital* (Vol. 1). Moscow: Progress Publishers.

———. 1966. *Critique of the Gottha Programme.* Moscow: Progress Publishers.

Matějů, P. 1993. "From Equality to Equity? The Czech Republic Between Two Ideologies of Distributive Justice." *Czech Sociological Review* 1: 251-275.

Mincer, J. 1974. *Schooling, Experience and Earnings.* New York: Columbia University Press.

Oxenstierna, S. 1990. *From Labor Shortage to Unemployment? The Soviet Labor Market in the 1980s.* Universitet Stockholm.

Sewell, W.H., and R.M. Hauser. 1975. *Education, Occupation and Earnings.* New York: Academic Press.

Sik, E. 1994. "From the Multicolored to the Black and White Economy: The Hungarian Second Economy Under the Transformation." *International Journal of Urban and Regional Research* 18: 46-70.

Staniszkis, J. 1991. *The Dynamics of the Breakthrough in Eastern Europe: The Polish Experiment.* Berkeley: University of California Press.

Ullrich, Z. 1937. "Sociální struktura dneška" (Social structure today). In *Populační, hospodáršky, ideový, politický dnešek,* by A. Boház et al. Demografia: Praha.

Ullrich, Z. 1937. "Sociální struktura dneška" (Social structure today), in A. Boháč et al., *Populační, hospodarský, ideový, politický dnešek.* Demografia: Praha.

Večerník, J. 1991a. "Distribuční systém v. Československu: Empirická fakta, výkladové hypotézy." (The Distribution system in Czechoslovakia: Empirical observation, explanatory hypotheses). *Sociologický časopis* 27: 39-56.

———. 1991b. "Earnings Distribution in Czechoslovakia: Intertemporal Changes and International Comparison." *European Sociological Review* 7 (December): 237-252.

———. 1995. "Changing Earnings Distribution in the Czech Republic. Survey Evidence from 1988-1992." *Economics of Transition* 3: 355-377.

DIVISIONS AND CONFLICTS IN POLAND

Lena Kolarska-Bobinska

Increasing social differentiation is one of the fundamental consequences of democratization and privatization in Poland. It is both a goal and a side effect of the ongoing changes. As a goal, social differentiation is an element of the ideology and economic policy of liberal and conservative parties. They view social differentiation as an incentive for more efficient work and entrepreneurial activity. Social differentiation is also a side effect of structural changes in production, investment, and privatization.

Growing differentiation concerns the objective indicators of social status as well as group attitudes and interests. Some types of social differentiation already existed in the 1980s. The differences in attitudes after five years of change are therefore not due solely to the transformation of the economy. During the transformation process, however, the social abysses deepened and changed their character.

International Review of Comparative Public Policy,
Volume 7, pages 177-187.

ISBN: 0-7623-0153-8

VISIONS OF THE FUTURE SOCIETY

In the 1980s the intelligentsia, the professionals and the managers held rather nonegalitarian views and perceived the market system as a means to realize their interests. Unskilled and some skilled workers exhibited egalitarian preferences. They supported the values of the socialist system and rejected only the manner in which the communist authorities chose to implement these principles. "Socialism yes, but not warped," was a popular concept in the early 1980s. The market system was therefore at odds with the preferences of many workers, although they supported it verbally. However, this verbal support was more an expression of protest against the privileges of communist authorities and the politicization of the economy than an acceptance of the principles of the market economy.

By supporting nonegalitarian principles during the 1980s, many Poles expressed their dissatisfaction with the falling standard of living, the empty shelves in shops, and the inefficiency of the centralized economy. While the public had no precise idea about the shape the future system in Poland should take, it was absolutely certain about the kind of living conditions it was not willing to tolerate.

One can therefore conclude that during the 1980s all social groups were eager to see an effective economy functioning on rational principles which enabled them to live better lives in a just and democratic system. Each social group had its own interpretation of these notions but the differences between them were not clear. This was due to the fact that they were overshadowed by the public's dominant opposition toward the communist authorities. The post-1989 changes crystallized social attitudes and strengthened the differences in attitudes and interests between various groups.

According to data presented by H. Domanski, the beginning of the 1990s saw an increase in the relative distance in the hierarchy of income of workers and employees compared to the intelligentsia and managers (Domanski 1994). In 1992, income per capita in workers' families (relative to the national average) was lower than in 1987. When calculated in this manner, the incomes of the intelligentsia employed in non-technical fields (i.e., teachers, doctors etc.) increased by 150 percent while the managers' incomes increased 250 percent.

Indeed, due to its higher level of education, the intelligentsia seems to have the least difficulty adjusting to the changes. Its members are most likely to take additional jobs and set up new businesses. The people in this group enjoy not only the best position in the labor market, but also have the best chance to assure the well-being of their children. Persons with secondary and university education are fairly pleased with the general direction of the transformation process and rather optimistic about their own futures and the future of the country as a whole. They support the Balcerowicz plan and continue to favor privatization and foreign investment in Poland.

Growing unemployment affects workers most strongly. Over half of the workers declare that their per capita family income was less than the social minimum (CBOS 1994b). They also experience changes on the ladder of social prestige most clearly; the social force which the Communists both praised and feared the most became an "obstacle to reform" for many politicians during the transformation process. Indeed, workers and farmers give the lowest marks to their own predicament and the general direction of the development of the situation in the country. They also show a low level of tolerance for various market solutions.

Society at large has a relatively clear picture of the groups which have benefited from, and those which have been harmed by, the transformation.

Unskilled workers, farmers and skilled workers are perceived as those who have paid the highest price for the introduction of the market economy. The intelligentsia, managers and priests, besides "swindlers" and private entrepreneurs, are perceived as those who have benefited most.

In conjunction with the entrenchment of reforms, there are more groups which, according to the people, are benefiting from the changes than those which are incurring losses. Moreover, with time, specific groups are coming to be perceived more frequently as winners rather than losers. This, however, does not change the fact that the perceived hierarchy of groups is very stable. Society is oblivious to group mobility.

PERCEIVED SOCIAL DIFFERENCES AND MECHANISMS OF SOCIAL ADVANCEMENT

Does the worker—farmer—intelligentsia division dominant during the days of communism still apply? A survey conducted in the late

1970s and early 1980s on the residents of Warsaw, revealed that 29 percent of those polled perceived social groups and classes in terms of their profession or employment, 21 percent in terms of wealth, 14 percent on the basis of power, while 13 percent identified them in terms of education (Zaborowski 1988).

There are reasons to presume that the role of income and material well-being was considerably reinforced in the perception of social structures during the 1980s. In the 1987 study "Social Structures II," when respondents were asked to identify their place on the social ladder and the factors which make them different from other persons, they most often indicated their standard of living (45%) and income (35%) (Janicka 1993).

In framing the question in this manner (i.e., using a scale), respondents were able to indicate financial problems more frequently than with the open questions asked in the surveys conducted by W. Zaborowski in 1979 and CBOS in 1994. The frequency with which financial problems were mentioned in the latter case is nonetheless high. The introduction of the market economy made social consciousness focus entirely on economic divisions. The 1994 CBOS research results are quite telling in that respect.

In 1994, wealth was pointed out as the main criterion of social division by 72 percent of respondents (CBOS 1994d). Wealth and income differences were perceived as a dichotomy between rich and poor (40 percent), and as a poor-medium-rich continuum (32%). The next, most often mentioned division (15%) is difficult to grasp. It is identified by using several criteria at the same time in the framework of the typical Marxist class division of workers, peasants and the bourgeoisie. Education as a criterion of social division was cited by 7 percent, profession or type of employment by 5 percent, power by 4 percent (CBOS 1994d).

Perceptions of economic differentiation are accompanied by an ever stronger influence of the individual's financial situation on the formation of interests and attitudes. Under communism, education and one's socio-professional position, rather than income, constituted the basis of attitudes. The differences between the incomes of various groups were minimal and the hierarchy in incomes did not overlap with the hierarchy created by other factors determining status (i.e., prestige or power). Moderate economic differentiation and the discrepancies between the status determining factors minimalized the influence of income on people's attitudes.

At present, the cohesion of social status factors is increasing. This means that groups are found in a given location in the social hierarchy due to several factors at the same time (Slomczynski 1994). This contributes to the growing internal cohesion and homogeneity within groups and deepens inter-group differences.

In the first phase of the market reforms the attitudes of many Poles were influenced by their visions of the future. Fear from the changes bore greater influence on attitudes than did objective social status. However, all CBOS data indicate that with time status factors began to affect attitudes although a greater role is still being played by subjective evaluations of one's own material situation.

At present, income per capita in the family exerts a significant influence, not only on systemic preferences, but also on one's attitude toward the government, strikes and all questions which may have a direct or indirect influence on the situation of the family.

The perception of differentiation includes not only criteria normally used to identify social groups and classes, but also channels of social advancement and mobility. This concerns one's own mobility, as well as prospects for intergenerational advancement, that is, ideas about eventual advancement for one's children.

In the last couple of years, the market system has been associated with the blockage of social mobility due to recession and unemployment. The slow pace of privatization during the first phase of the reforms promoted neither individual nor group advancement. Most affected are workers and their children—unemployment is most rampant among young people with vocational training.

Table 1. What Does Polish Society Look Like, What Kind of Groups are Being Composed and how do they Differ?

Most often mentioned criteria for group differentiation	
Wealth—dichotomic division (two opposing groups)	40%
Wealth—non dichotomic divisions	32%
Wealth Total	72%
Class differentiation	15%
Personal characteristics; behavior, skills, predisposition	14%
Attitudes toward work; employed-unemployed	9%
Education, knowledge, abilities	7%
Profession, type of employment	5%
Possession of power	5%

Source: CBOS, May 1994.

Many farmer-come-workers have been forced to return to their farms after having lost their jobs in the city.

Polish society has a nonegalitarian vision of the transformation. Poles are convinced that the changes are in favor of the already privileged (including the swindlers) while the ordinary citizen has to suffer.

In the 1980s, market mechanisms were accepted by many as an impartial means of allocation of income and wealth—the antithesis of privileges based on political patronage and insider knowledge. The market was supposed to reward "the best" on the basis of their effort and initiative. At present, the Polish public is disturbed not so much by wealth itself, but rather by the illegal manner in which wealth can be accumulated.

Social differences require specific political legitimation, especially when they are widening. However, the emerging democratic system in Poland and its political elite have not yet produced an ideology that may justify social differences.

A model of a future class structure has not been developed nor have mechanisms of social mobility which are both widely accessible and legal. Elites assumed that the rejection of the communist regime sufficiently legitimized the new nonegalitarian system and growing social differentiation.

Popular perceptions of change contradict the ideology of "people's capitalism" which legitimized social differences in many Western countries. At this juncture, a fundamental question arises: could the ideology which originated in the nineteenth century be applied at all in Eastern Europe? In an era of multinational corporations, the idea of a "rags to riches" career seems somewhat naive. It seems that although this idea cannot be automatically applied to the new system in Poland, many elements of "people's capitalism" would facilitate the acceptance of nonegalitarian reforms. However, instead of indicating the real channels of social mobility and the actual opportunities for the realization of personal interests, elites concentrated on convincing society in general that capitalism will benefit the economy and the country.

PERCEIVED CONFLICTS

The conviction that the majority of Poles are losers and that only a few are benefiting from the reforms may elicit strong intergroup conflicts. Will the notion of a class society in which one group benefits at the cost of others become popular?

Opinion polls indicate that no significant changes have occurred in the way the structure of conflicts is perceived in Poland following 1990 (CBOS 1992; CBOS 1994a; Institute of Sociology and Philosophy 1991). Recently, as in the 1980s, political tensions are the most frequently perceived social conflicts in the country. Political conflicts tend to crop up within a wide range of relations between various groups (i.e., between parties, politicians, former Communists and Solidarity), as well as between the government and society. Conflicts between the rich and the poor, the rural and the urban milieus, and so forth, constitute a very small part of perceived tensions.

While conflicts in the political sphere dominate social consciousness, respondents noted different types of conflict with varying frequency at different points of time. The "us" (society) vs. "them" (government) division perceived in the 1980s disappeared entirely in the 1990s. This gave way to conflicts between the various structures of state authority as well as within the various groups of Solidarity. Two years later, in 1992, the "us"—"them" dichotomy came back to life in full vigor. Even stronger, however, was the perception of conflict between politicians and parties struggling for power. In addition, there was also the revival of the conflict between Solidarity and the government.

The conflict between the rich and the poor was noted less often than other conflicts but with an increasing frequency: in 1990—4 percent, in 1992—9 percent, while in 1994—21 percent of respondents mentioned conflicts rooted in economic inequalities.

The fact that political conflicts are noted by the public more often than social and economic ones—although the latter are perceived as the main source of differentiation—may be explained in the following way:

1. One may conclude that the very notion of conflict is understood by the people as something which applies to relations in the political arena or those between the authorities and society, rather than to relations within the civil society itself. The clashes between the authorities and society and within the political system itself most often produce obvious conflictual behavior documented by the mass media.

In May 1994, over half of society felt that conflicts between the most important political institutions have great influence on their lives; thus they follow the clashes with disquiet (CBOS 1994e).

2. This may mean that the fundamental manner in which the structure of public life is perceived by the public did not undergo an essential change during the first five years of the transformation. Under communism, the economy was closely tied to politics. The government is still perceived as the main actor: it sets the rules of taxation, the pay and pension rates in the public sector and decides on increases in the cost of utilities and fuels. The government decides on privatization, the issue price of shares, sets customs duties, wage ceilings and refrains from helping enterprises in bankruptcy. Close to 60 percent of the Polish public feels that the state of the economy is dependent on the political situation, while 63 percent feel that the decisions of politicians have a strong influence on the fate of individuals (CBOS 1994c). As opinion polls indicate, attitudes toward the government are closely tied to evaluations of the personal circumstances of respondents rather than to their views on the economic or political conditions of the country. In this context, the instability of the political system may be perceived as a source of personal uncertainty.

In the future, the government may be blamed for growing social differentiation. The people may then think that the government helps the rich get richer and lends no aid to the poor. As a consequence, social frustration may be directed against the government rather than other social groups.

EMERGING SOCIAL STRUCTURE

Privatization is beginning to act as a factor creating new social structures which divide, for example, the intelligentsia in yuppies, businessmen and state employees. The same applies to workers. The new divisions have not crystallized yet. It is still difficult to identify any specific homogeneous social group of wealthy people. Poles become more aware of social differentiation, but not of new social classes and strata. Moreover, newly emerging groups have little awareness of their distinct interests. This is why traditional group identities are stronger than new divisions and interests. These become evident when considering the variety of social fears. Regardless of their place of employment, members of the intelligentsia are more disturbed than are others by the drop in their standard of living, incompetent decision makers and environmental pollution. Skilled workers are most afraid of losing their jobs, while unskilled workers fear living in poverty.

One can identify group interests related specifically to employment as well as interests of broader social groups, that is, farmers or workers. This can be illustrated by a survey on attitudes of employees in the private, state and recently privatized sectors (CBOS 1993a). When selecting interests which they would like political parties to promote, employees chose their own narrow sectoral interests over broader group interests. For example, employees in state industries were keen to support political parties which were willing to protect these industries, while private sector employees favored parties supporting the development of ties between Poland and Europe in order to promote trade. Employees in the recently privatized firms prefer parties promoting the development of the private sector as well as the protection of state enterprises. However, apart from "sectoral" interests, all groups expressed concern over welfare issues, law and order, and the good governance of the country.

A more rapid pace of privatization would likely deepen sectoral divisions and, as a consequence, pluralize economic and political interests. It would also provide channels of social mobility. However, politics in Poland seem to reinforce old socio-economic and political divisions (i.e., those between "Solidarity" and the ruling post-communist elite as well as between farmers and other groups).

As a result of the pluralization of interests over the last five years, the sides in the old "us" vs. "them" conflict lost their homogeneity. "They" (the authorities) became an amalgam of individuals and parties with rather unclear identities; "we" means individuals and groups searching for a new place in the changing world.

The new government coalition of 1993 including peasant and post-communist parties, led to a reinforcement of previous socio-economic divisions. The revival of the old rhetorical division became evident during the parliamentary debate on the 1994 budget. It reinvigorated the almost forgotten rural-urban split: the interests of farmers versus the rest of society. Following the 1993 electoral victory of the left, some came to perceive the representatives of farmers and rural residents as "them" while others saw former Communists in this manner.

Despite five years of reform, "old" political divisions have not disappeared. As indicated by our surveys, the views of former Solidarity and Communist Party members are still fundamentally at odds (CBOS 1993b).

The Solidarity members from 1980 remain more vehemently anti-communist and more egalitarian in their economic views than the rest of society. Nor has the fifteen year period significantly altered the attitudes of former party members; they still espouse slightly more nonegalitarian attitudes and are quite pleased with the 1993 electoral victory of the left.

Due to the fact that Solidarity represents the interests of the workers and employees, while in the case of state industry the ruling post-communist is the employer itself, the overlap of political and economic differences is inevitable. This in turn leads to the politicization of conflicts in the economy.

It seems that the revival of old divisions will cause political conflicts to dominate the social imagination, and in turn, marginalize social perceptions of the differences created by the market.

REFERENCES

CBOS (Center of Public Opinion Research). 1992. *Konflikty i podzialy w polskim spoleczenstwie* (Conflicts and divisions in Polish society). CBOS (October).

CBOS (Center of Public Opinion Research). 1993a. *Pracownicy przedsiebiorstw panstwowych, prywatnych i sprywatyzowanych o zmianach ustrojowych w Polsce* (State-owned sector employees, commercialized-sector employees and private sector-employees on transformation in Poland). CBOS (July).

CBOS (Center of Public Opinion Research). 1993b. *Co zostalo z dawnych podzialow? Analiza pogladow bylych czlonkow PZPR i czlonkow "Solidarnosci" z 1981 roku* (What is left of the old division? An analysis of opinions of former members of PZPR and members of "Solidarnorbsrbc"). CBOS (October).

CBOS (Center of Public Opinion Research). 1994a. *Spoleczna wizja systemu politycznego Polski* (A social visions of a Polish form of government), CBOS (February).

CBOS (Center of Public Opinion Research). 1994b. *Strajki i ich uczestnicy* (Strikes and their participants). CBOS (April).

CBOS (Center of Public Opinion Research). 1994c. *Wplyw polityki na gospodarke i zycie obywateli* (Influence of politics on the economy and the life of citizens). CBOS (April).

CBOS (Center of Public Opinion Research). 1994d. *Konflikty "stare" czy "nowe"* ("Old" conflicts or "new" ones). CBOS (May).

CBOS (Center of Public Opinion Research). 1994e. *Opinie o uprawnieniach instytucji wladzy centralnej i konfliktach na "gorze"* (Opinions about authorization of central government and about conflicts "at the top"). CBOS (May).

Domanski, H. 1994. *Spoleczenstwo klasy sredniej* (Middle Class Society). Warsaw: Institute of Sociology and Philosophy, Polish Academy of Sciences.

Institute of Philosophy and Sociology. 1991. *Polacy '90. Konflikty i zmiana* (Poles' 90: Conflicts and Change). Warsaw: Institute of Philosophy and Sociology, Polish Academy of Sciences, ISP PAN.

Janicka, K. 1993. "Factors of Structuralization of Polish Society in the Social Consciousness at the End of the Eighties." *Polish Sociological Review* 3(103).

Slomczynski, K. 1994. "Class and Status in Eastern European Perspectives." In *The Transformation of Europe, Social Conditions and Consequences,* edsited by M. Alestalo, E. Allart, A. Rychard, and W. Wesolowski. Institute of Philosophy and Sociology.

Zaborowski, W. 1988. *Postrzeganie struktury spolecznej przez mieszkancow Warszawy* (Perception of social strucure by Citizens of Warsaw). Warsaw.

PART III

UNEMPLOYMENT, DECENTRALIZATION OF SOCIAL POLICY AND HEALTH CARE REFORM: CASE STUDIES OF THE TRANSFORMATION

VOCATIONAL SCHOOL GRADUATES ON THE LABOR MARKET IN POLAND

Elżbieta Drogosz-Zabłocka

INTRODUCTION

The transition from a centrally planned to a market economy has resulted in a drop in output and a fall in employment. An increased demand for jobs requires that both those in employment and those seeking employment adjust to the needs of the economy by:

- changing occupation and occupational specialization,
- changing place of employment and residency,
- increasing the quality (through further education) and intensity of work, being disciplined and showing respect for official hierarchy,
- increasing mobility and learning new skills.

International Review of Comparative Public Policy,
Volume 7, pages 191-201.

ISBN: 0-7623-0153-8

Our survey of the careers of vocational school graduates concerns all the above-mentioned aspects, although particular attention was paid to educational problems.

DESCRIPTION OF THE RESEARCH PROJECT

Subject and Aims

This project aims at evaluating the possibility of employment in acquired vocations and assessing occupational mobility—understood as the will and the capability to change vocation and vocational specialization. We wanted to illustrate the young people's reasons for not undertaking or giving up jobs in acquired vocations, as well as for their readiness to change vocation when the possibility of finding employment arises in a vocation different from that acquired at school. We were also interested in the extent to which the system of vocational training is maladjusted to the needs of the labor market and how it hinders occupational mobility. We asked whether the reasons lie in external factors (e.g., housing) or in the attitudes of vocational school graduates themselves.

This project sought answers to the following questions:

- Do graduates undertake jobs in line with their vocational training. What positions do they occupy and what tasks do they perform?
- How many graduates do not start working in acquired vocations and what are the reasons?
- Are graduates willing to change their vocation?
- How do graduates assess their own vocational preparation in the context of their jobs?

Characteristics of the Research Field and the Most Important Problems of the Labor Market in Poland

The research project was carried out in municipal districts: Działdowo, Kutno and Maków Mazowiecki situated in Central Poland. Of these three districts, Kutno is the largest—in 1991/92 the number of inhabitants amounted to 51,000, Działdowo is the next—20,500—and Maków Mazowiecki is the smallest with a population of 10,500. These towns are located in three different voivodships (counties): Ciechanów, Płock and Ostrołęka. As far as the number of inhabitants is concerned, the three districts are below national average. From the point of view of urbanization and employment structure, the Ciechanów Voivodship (Działdowo) and the Ostrołęka Voivodship (Maków Mazowiecki) are agricultural areas. The Plock Voivodship (Kutno) is included among industrialized regions.

In 1993 the unemployment rates were as follows: The Ciechanów Voivodship—20.9 percent; the Płock Voivodship—19.7 percent; the Ostrołęka Voivodship—18 percent. If we calculate these rates without including those employed in agriculture, the numbers increase more than twofold to 40.9 percent, 40.6 percent and 45.8 percent, respectively. These are among the highest unemployment rates in the country.

One of the reasons for the high unemployment in the Działdowo district is the decline of local state enterprises, including state farms. In June 1993 in the town of Działdowo there were 5,140 unemployed and in the surrounding district (commune)—2,577. Both in the town and the commune the majority of unemployed were women—over 70 percent. Most of the unemployed are young people under 35 years of age. At the end of 1992, vocational school graduates constituted 5.2 percent of the unemployed.

Kutno is the second biggest town in the Płock Voivodship. In December 1992 the number of professionally active people there was 16,000 of which 40 percent were employed in industry, 12.8 percent in health service and 9.8 percent in transport. In June 1993 in Kutno there were 6,538 registered unemployed, which is 27.9 percent of all professionally active people in the town. The labor market in Kutno is primarily based on large state enterprises which did not manage to adapt to the new conditions of competition and the loss of traditional markets. Like in Działdowo, the situation of young people is very difficult here.

The employment structure in the third town, Maków Mazowiecki, is peculiar. Most people are employed in health service (23.4%), trade (23.1%), industry (17.4%) and education (12.4%). Institutions financed out of the state budget employed 35.5 percent of the total number of employed. At the end of 1993, in Maków Mazowiecki 1,430 unemployed were registered and the rate of unemployment was 21.6 percent. Among the main causes of this unemployment were the closing down of two state enterprises and reduction of employment in others.

The towns are faced with the problems of an ill-balanced labor market. The unemployed have practically no employment opportunities, and the disabled live in poverty. Organization culture is poor and the new business ventures are scarce.

Sample

The sample consisted of 1,087 graduates from 1992, out of which 315 were from Działdowo, 404 from Kutno and 368 from Maków Mazowiecki.

Questionnaires were sent to graduates from the following schools:

- 6 basic vocational schools (mechanical, construction, electrical, agricultural, trade, services),
- 2 secondary vocational schools (lyces): trade and agriculture,
- 2 secondary medical schools (nurses and midwives),
- 2 secondary business schools: finance and accounting, management and organization,
- 5 secondary technical schools: machine building, agriculture,
- 2 post-secondary medical schools (nurses and midwives).

The structure of post-primary vocational education in the voivodships under research does not differ significantly from the national average, although in the Ciechanów and Ostrołęka Voivodships more primary school leavers continue their education in basic vocational schools. In these voivodships about 80 percent of the total number of post-primary school graduates go on to vocational schools.

Methods and Design

The mailed questionnaires consisted of two parts: (1) information on the place of residence, parents' education, type of school completed and qualifications, reasons for school choice and plans for the future; (2) possibilities of workplace choice, supplementary courses completed, additional qualifications, assistance in job-seeking, congruence of job performance and vocation learnt at school, assessment of knowledge and skills in the light of

Table 1. The Structure of Post-primary Education 1992/1993 (students enrolled in schools)

	Total	*Secondary Schools General*	*Basic Vocational Schools*	*Secondary Vocational Schools*	*Post-Secondary Vocational Schools*
Poland	2,079,816	26.7%	36.9%	33.1%	3.3%
Ciechanów Voivodship	23,171	25.0%	43.7%	30.0%	2.7%
Ostrołęka Voivodship	22,039	20.6%	42.5%	35.6%	1.3%
Płock Voivodship	29,022	26.9%	34.2%	35.1%	3.8%

Source: Education in the school year 1992/1993. Central Statistical Office (1993).

job performance. Moreover, in the second part of the questionnaire, graduates were asked what should be done to improve the occupational start of young people and for the development of their careers.

The project was carried out from March to June 1993. 360 questionnaires were sent back by the respondents which constitutes 33.1 percnet of the total number of questionnaires. 345 duly completed questionnaires, that is, 30.8 percent, were classified for further analysis.

Graduates from the following schools responded to our questions:

- basic vocational schools—216 responses (62.6%),
- secondary vocational schools—66 responses (19.1%),
- secondary technical schools—39 responses (11%),
- post-secondary schools—21 responses (6.1%).

Most responses came from the Ciechanów Voivodship (159). 58.6 percent of the respondents were female and 41.3 percent male.

SOCIAL ENVIRONMENT AND DIFFERENCES AMONG GRADUATES

The Place of Residency

The place of residence is closely connected with the pupil's educational start; it influences his or her course of education and future career. In the sample there were 118 graduates who lived in towns and 227 who lived in the countryside. Most graduates from the countryside were registered in the Ostrołęka Voivodship (72.8%) [Ciechanów Voivodship (62.3%), Płock Voivodship (58.2%)]. These data agree with urbanization rates for the voivodships in question.

This research project shows that town dwellers continue their education after primary school 10 percent more often than those from the countryside.

104 respondents to the questionnaire lived in towns in which the school was located. The majority (70%) had to commute daily, out of which 51.3 percent had to travel more than 10 kilometers. Commuting causes waste of time, limited use of libraries and after-school activities, lack of time to help parents in farming, lack of friends and increased tuition costs. The greater the distance from a big town (a regional center), the more often a syndrome of social and cultural discrimination arises. Occupational mobility of these graduates (understood as the readiness for and the capability to change vocation and specialization) will be weaker than in the case of graduates living in towns. These statistics also say something about the network of vocational schools. It is fragmentary, with urban areas being better provided. In rural areas post-primary schools are lacking and young people continuing their education have to travel daily.

Parents' Education

It seems likely that the education of parents influences their children's choice of post-primary school to a great extent and, in consequence, determines their careers as well as their educational and professional aspirations.

The parents of our respondents had a low level of education: 54.5 percent of the mothers completed primary school or several grades of primary school (primary school in Poland consists of 8 grades), 22.6 percent completed basic vocational school, 5.8 percent secondary general school, 12.6 percent secondary technical school or vocational lycée. Only 3.8 percent (9 persons) completed schools of higher education. Similar data were obtained with respect to fathers. 50.5 percent of the fathers completed primary school or several grades thereof, 35.5 percent (12% more than by the mothers) completed basic vocational school, 2.4 percent secondary general school (less than half of the rate for mothers), 9.6 percent secondary technical school and vocational lycée. Only 1.7 percent completed higher schools.

Reasons for Occupational Choice

One point in the questionnaire concerned direct forms of motivation. The respondents had to choose the three main reasons from among ten possible answers, or to mention additional reasons. The respondents were not asked to arrange them in any order of importance—we considered the one most frequently mentioned as the most important reason.

The main reason for choosing a particular school was a conviction that the vocation learnt there would help in finding employment, which was selected by 46.1 percent of graduates. This reason was most often declared by graduates from basic vocational schools (52.3%). Basic vocational school graduates from 1992 had made their school and career decision in 1989, that is, at the same time as major socio-political changes began in Poland, but before unemployment had become a serious problem. Graduates from secondary vocational schools (vocational lycées or technical schools) had made their decision in 1987 (for 5 year schools) or in 1988 (for 4 year schools), that is, under political circumstances in which all graduates had been given a guarantee of employment. Hence this reason was most probably quoted as very important because of the present situation in the labor market, and it could not have influenced career choice at that time.

The next reason most often cited (16.2%) was the possibility of obtaining a certificate of maturity (final exam in secondary schools) and continuing education in higher schools. This reason was given by graduates from secondary vocational and secondary technical schools.

The third place among the reasons for career choice was taken by a predilection for the future job (15.4%). The fourth place was taken by the location of the school (proximity of school to place of residence)—12.5 percent.

When asked "What school would you choose if you were to make a career choice once again?" 60.3 percent of graduates repeated their original choice although, when explaining the reasons, the majority of them referred to the perspective of getting an interesting job, and not just to a possibility of employment. The greatest number of repeated choices, however, was noted in services and commerce and in these cases graduates explained that these were the only vocations with any guarantee of employment.

SCHOOL PREPARATION FOR WORK

Evaluation of Knowledge and Skills Acquired at School

Graduates were asked to evaluate to what extent their school fulfilled their expectations with respect to:

- theoretical preparation for work
- practical preparation for work
- preparation for the development of one's own abilities and interests
- ability of co-operation
- ability of self-assessment
- decision making skills
- job seeking ability
- occupational mobility.

School preparation with respect to the above-mentioned abilities and skills was assessed as definitely sufficient by 21 percent of the respondents, as rather sufficient by 37.4 percent, as definitely insufficient by 9.7 percent, as rather insufficient by 14.7 percent. ("No comment" was chosen by 7.9% of graduates and 9.3% left this question unanswered.)

This surprisingly positive judgment of the effectiveness of vocational schools differs considerably from the evaluations prepared on the basis of graduates' unemployment statistics provided by educational authorities, labor offices and labor market researchers.

There were considerable differences in judgment by graduates from different vocational schools. The most negative judgment was presented by secondary technical school graduates—29 percent chose the option "definitely insufficient" and "rather insufficient." The most positive judgment was presented by secondary economic and medical school graduates—26.7 percent opted for "definitely sufficient."

Among the different skills and abilities, the following were viewed as "definitely insufficient" or "rather insufficient": occupational mobility, job seeking ability and the preparation for the development of one's own abilities and interests in general. Almost 50 percent of the respondents are of the opinion that the school did not prepare them to move around in the labor market. Theoretical teaching still prevails in vocational schools. Graduates stated that they were best prepared in vocational theory—35.9 percent of positive judgments.

At the same time, a great number (49.8%) of opinions about preparation for the needs of the labor market were negative.

The Value of Education

Among graduates the opinion prevails that education ought to guarantee appropriate living conditions for the school leaver and his/her family—28.9 percent, realization of personal interests—18.4 percent, improvement of knowledge—13.1 percent, higher earnings—12.3 percent. Only a few graduates declared that education was able to help achieve a good position in society—6.7 percent or social approval—4.4 percent.

Females, more often than males, are of the opinion that education ought to help realize personal interests (F - 21.3%, M - 16%) and gain social approval (F - 5%, M - 3.5%). Males put more stress on proper living conditions for themselves and their families (M - 30.1%, F - 27.6%) and on higher earnings (M - 17%, F - 9%).

These differences in expectations are culturally determined. According to the social and cultural patterns of Polish society, the responsibility for the well-being of the family is still ascribed to males and education is still combined with career.

It should be added that in comparison with the results of the research conducted in the 1980s, the value of education has changed considerably in Poland. Education is to serve the family's well-being rather than help realize ambitions and interests.

GRADUATES AT WORK

Careers of Vocational School Graduates

Ten months after the completion of vocational schools, graduates comprised the following groups:

- higher school students—4.7 percent
- post-secondary school students—1.6 percent
- unemployed receiving unemployment benefits—61.6 percent
- unemployed not receiving unemployment benefits—9.4 percent

- employed—12.9 percent
- graduates in military service—3.5 percent
- disabled—0.3 percent
- secondary technical school students (upon the completion of basic vocational schools)—6.0 percent.

Overall, 71 percent of graduates were out of employment, 12.3 percent continued their education in schools of different types and only 12.9 percent were employed. No more than 7.8 percent of graduates had the opportunity to choose between different places of work. Job offers are characterized by low wages, often paid in installments. Graduates complain that employers are not willing to employ young people as they need experienced workers.

Reasons for Giving Up Vocations Acquired at School

90.8 percent of the respondents had no opportunity to choose their first place of work. The most frequently given reasons for this situation are:

- a high percentage of unemployment in town and in the voivodship—29 percent
- lack of job offers—15.9 percent
- lack of jobs in line with acquired vocations—15.4 percent
- no extension of work contracts signed for the period of training—5.2 percent.

When we compare the situation in the three voivodships it appears that the Ostrołęka Voivodship offered the best opportunities of finding work—8.6 percent; the worst chances occurred in the Płock Voivodship—7.5 percent.

Readiness to undergo retraining is declared by 51.6%; males (56%), more often than females (44%). All graduates questioned would like their new vocations to guarantee employment. The most sought after vocations are: salesman, broker, trade worker—these vocations are mainly preferred by women. Males prefer the following vocations: car mechanic, carpenter, bricklayer, computer scientist, craftsman.

Young people are attached to the traditional model of work. They prefer regular employment to casual work.

CONCLUSIONS

(1) The main reason underlying career choice, and—correspondingly—educational choice, was a conviction that the vocation acquired at school would help find employment. In comparison with research projects carried out in the eighties, the motivation has changed considerably. In the eighties, the main reasons were personal interests and job-satisfaction, while practical reasons prevail at present.

(2) Due to unfavorable conditions in the labor market and passive attitudes displayed by graduates, only 12.9 percent of graduates found employment, 61.6 percent were registered as unemployed in labor offices, 9.4 percent were unemployed though not registered, the majority of which had ceased to receive unemployment benefit. These statistics seem alarming.

(3) Graduates display assertive attitudes toward the state and the employers, they are attached to a traditional model of work, demand a guarantee of regular employment consistent with what they have learnt at school.

EMPLOYMENT AND LIFE CHANCES OF THE LONG-TERM UNEMPLOYED IN HUNGARY

Agnes Simonyi

Experts consider the high rate of long-term unemployment to be a typical feature of the unemployment that developed and rapidly increased in Hungary in the nineties. In 1993, 302 thousand persons exhausted their benefit entitlement period. The average benefit period of those still eligible has decreased but it is still quite long. (According to the data of the National Labor Market Center this was 231 days in April 1994.) Long-term unemployment is a new phenomenon in the Hungarian economy and society and it results in a new state of life for hundreds of thousands and their related family members.

For this study, those people who have exhausted their benefit entitlement possibly are considered long-term unemployed. This could be a period of one or possibly even two years. The Hungarian labor administration considers those registered over 180 days

International Review of Comparative Public Policy,
Volume 7, pages 203-214.

ISBN: 0-7623-0153-8

(i.e., those registered over half a year) to be long-term unemployed but for our research purposes, the exhaustion of the benefit was considered to be a major change in the life of the unemployed. Within the benefit entitlement period it is difficult to judge to what extent the benefit makes one uninterested in an efficient job search. In other words, it is difficult to determine to what extent the benefit system itself prevents the unemployed from finding a job or taking one with unsatisfactory conditions. The situation of permanent unemployment without benefit entitlement, however, indicates the long-term nature of the conditions of those forced out of the labor market.

This survey was carried out in a small region of Hungary: in the town of Szolnok and in two of its neighboring villages. Its primary aim was to explore the basic problems of long-term unemployment and to describe the types of adjustment possibilities rather than to make a representative statistical survey. 75 interviews were conducted with unemployed persons who have exhausted their benefit entitlement period.

INTERVIEWING THE UNEMPLOYED

Those interviewed were willing to openly discuss family problems, living conditions, working careers, qualifications, circumstances of their dismissals, grievances at work or at labor offices and their job search efforts. It was surprising that those interviewed spoke frankly—with only a few exceptions—about illegal work, additional incomes and about occasional jobs. There was only one encounter with a "taboo." This occurred when an unemployed person who wanted to become a businessman was asked about his future plans and ideas.

The interviews were conducted in unheated adobe houses, in multistorey family houses equipped with cable aerials, in housing estate "night-shelters" and in decent downtown apartment buildings. In several cases we were sitting in partially finished houses talking with unemployed persons in their 30s and 40s who had begun construction in the late eighties but were unable to finish partition walls and plastering. We were in houses built a few years ago, where furniture, a washing machine, or a video could not be afforded, but also in apartments where the owners had already started selling the furniture and the durable consumer goods. We visited one person who—at the suggestion of the local Social Service Center—was supported by relatives she had taken into her house because they had no apartment of their own but did have permanent jobs. We knocked at locked gates and doors in vain until, following the neighbors' directions, we had found the unemployed person, in most cases single or with a small child, at his or her parents', relatives' or friends' homes, where the house is heated and the dinner can be cooked jointly.

Since we were trying to establish a relationship of "confidence" during the interview, we did not aim at recording figures of material wealth, incomes and reserves. In a limited scope survey like this, instead of accurately declared incomes, it was considered to be more revealing to collect "stories" about the situation of the unemployed: how they exchanged the worn out shoes of a growing adolescent child months after they purchased it presenting a quality complaint; how one pays the rent for lodging "in kind" by preparing and serving the candle-lit dinners of the "landlord;" how a couple announces divorce officially and becomes entitled to the benefit while they continue to keep a common house; and, how someone decides between undergoing a knee operation which would result in a disabled pension entitlement or riding a bicycle for some more years.

There was not only a variety of different situations, but the ways in which these were judged, perceived and lived were very different. Additionally, there was a great difference between the sizing up of hopes and prospects even in those groups of the interviewed who had very similar circumstances. In the same type of rundown apartments we met happy families, depressed people, people applying for allowances and assistance, and also people who did not apply but whose eligibility for assistance was reported by the district nurse. There were people who thought they were only temporarily "shelved" and were optimistic about their chances for a new start, but there were others who had already experienced the trap of long-term unemployment—qualifications, experience becoming obsolete, the distrust of employers toward an applicant who is growing older and older and is going to be unemployed for a longer time. In our research we experienced various attitudes: the reluctant acceptance of a lasting situation, the entire submission to it, the readiness to live with it for a long time, but also the intentions to recuperate strength and resources to break out as well as the first faltering "steps out."

ON THE UNEMPLOYED

Among those interviewed, the number of long-term unemployed men (54.6%) slightly exceeded that of women (45.4%). Regarding age: the middle-age group is primarily represented in the sample (2/3), young people under 25 make up only 12 percent of the interviewed, while the ratio of those close to early retirement is one-fifth.

Two-thirds of the interviewed had professional qualifications. Those with secondary school certificates made up 17 percent of the interviewed. 13 percent of the sample were unskilled.

Nearly half of those interviewed were breadwinners and had children. One third was raising 1-2 children, 13 percent, 3 or more children.

Three quarters of those interviewed lived in an urban environment. Slightly over a quarter of them lived in villages or in rural areas of the town outskirts. One quarter of those interviewed lived in good circumstances, in houses or apartments in good condition and in markedly good urban or rural environment. Nearly 30 percent lived in similarly good houses or apartments, but in a worse environment; in neglected living quarters far from the city center or in villages with unpaved roads. 31 percent of those interviewed lived under bad circumstances, regarding both the condition of the house or the apartment and the settlement conditions as well. Within this ratio, the housing conditions of 10 percent were found significantly dilapidated.

We were able to compare our sample according to age and qualifications with the total of registered unemployed in the Local Labor Center, and within this, with those local long-term unemployed who maintain their registration even after the exhaustion of the benefit entitlement period. Our findings show that those interviewed were somewhat older and more qualified than the local unemployed who had exhausted their benefit entitlement period altogether.

JOB OPPORTUNITIES, JOB SEARCH, LABOR UTILIZATION

The long-term unemployed that we interviewed are trying to find jobs, not only through their contacts with the labor office, but also through friends and newspaper advertisements. Our experiences show that although neighborhood relations are more intensive among the people in the villages and in the rural outskirts of towns and thus among the unemployed as well, the chances of having access to information on job opportunities are worse due to the scarce and basically homogeneous sources of information. Although in the urban environment the unemployed have a more restricted scope of life, a life "enclosed within four walls," the rare and casual acquaintances and contacts (with neighbors, in the parking lot, in shops, in discount shops, at bus stops, at news-stands, in social institutions) assure them access to more varied sources of information to facilitate their job search.

With only a few exceptions, those interviewed attempted to take jobs offered by the labor offices, but in most cases the job had already been filled when they were contacted. In a smaller number of cases it turned out that the unemployed would be incapable to fulfill the professional requirements of the employers or the employer did not offer acceptable working conditions to the unemployed. The following calculation was found in almost all interviews: will the income earned by the offered job exceed the sum of the benefit as much as to cover the travel, food and clothing costs of going to work? None of the interviewed persons found a financially satisfactory job during their benefit entitlement period.

The intensity of the search was quite varied. Those who have had only one or two "not suitable" or "already filled" job offers from the labor office, or those who had only inquired their acquaintances about jobs, are considered to have a *low intensity job search.* To illustrate those who demonstrate *high intensity job search,* here is an example from our interviews:

The railway worker tried but failed to finish a welding course. He then managed to finish another requalification course and qualified as an electric fork-lift driver. He exhausted his benefit in several stages, found jobs for longer and shorter periods of time and then was made redundant. He worked as a presser for an apparel company, as garden help in a chemical factory, then he assembled Kinder eggs in another company. After that, he applied for a light manual job requiring his fork-lift driver skills and also for a course on self-management organized by the local job-club.

Similar job search procedures were related by women with office jobs who were trying in vain to find similar jobs after finishing various secretarial, manager and word processing courses within the system of active labor market programs organized by the local office.

Efforts made for self-employment or for starting a venture can also be considered an intensive search for job. Eight persons out of the interviewed, 10 percent of the total, made attempts in vain in some commercial, catering, artisanal or animal breeding business and ended up with failure and financial losses. Out of nine people under 25 who were involved in the survey, eight were doing occasional jobs in commerce, services or agriculture for a few months or only for days. After the exhaustion of the benefit entitlement period, however, only eight persons (10%) of those interviewed had jobs, two of them became entrepreneurs, a third person became a partner in a venture.

Those capable of the shift from unemployment to entrepreneurship have unanimously stable financial and housing conditions and a *family background* which made it possible to utilize the family members for a flexible combination and extension of time and energy input as well as their assets (house, garage, car, etc.). At the same time, there were some persons who, in their long-term unemployment status, were providing assistance to a family member (parent, child, brother or sister) with better chances in some entrepreneurial activity by taking care of the children, housekeeping, or procuring supplies. It can be assumed that in other cases the persons were recuperating resources in the unemployment period and even the unemployment benefit was part of the family capital accumulation to start some kind of a business venture.

One entrepreneur, a highly qualified agricultural expert, after exhausting his entire benefit entitlement period, opened a retail store in the courtyard of the family house. The single man in his 30s procures and sells goods by dividing the labor with his parents although there is heavy competition from two dozen recently opened similar stores in the village. Another entrepreneur managed to obtain, through former connections of his wife, a low-cost lease in a garage at their living quarter, where the couple first opened a shoe store and then a greengrocer store which is operated with the involvement of several family members (parents, children, in-laws). In the shop they also sell the produce of the family plot outside the town.

Another person interviewed belonged earlier to the "retail and catering elite" emerging in the originally state-owned or cooperative network of shops. With not only several post-secondary commercial school qualifications, but also with a degree from Marxist political studies, he had been running successful shops and catering services from the mid-seventies. The lease of his last shop was withdrawn. As an entrepreneur he was entitled to an unemployment benefit for only 4 months. At the time of the interview he was seeking partners and capital for his new ambitious ventures well exceeding his own resources—(which were significant compared to those of other unemployed). In the meantime, in the cellar of his house, his distant family members are running a "pub" which they report to be unsuccessful.

PREVIOUS JOB CAREERS

Two types of careers can be distinguished among those interviewed who suffered several failures in their job search. One is the employee with several previous jobs and tasks. This "leading nowhere" employee career is typical of men and women working in unskilled or semi-skilled jobs who wander from town to town and back for decades. There are also skilled workers among them who did not work in their own trade for a long period of their working life. In some cases, they even gained other company qualifications that they never used either. About 10 percent of those interviewed belonged to this group.

In the group described above, we found some long-term unemployed who earlier had successfully "commuted" between different part-time artisan activities, small industries and the internal subcontracting groups of "intra-enterprise working associations." All of these were more or less related to the activities, the markets and the technical equipments and instruments of their main workplace. These experienced skilled workers (mostly in the area of the construction industry and of the public community services), qualified primarily for machine maintenance and installation, had neither the necessary capital nor the resources to start their own venture. They were not capable of exploring new markets apart from those created by the collapsed large companies that had served as a background of their jobs.

Another type of the long-term unemployed interviewed, unlike the previous group, worked for the same employer all or for most of his working life. They often worked 10-15 or even 30-35 years for the same company. The experience and the qualifications of this group significantly devalued as they were closely related to their former employers, and job search and adjustment to the labor market are alien to their former employee attitude. The former low-ranking military officers who became long-term unemployed represent a special subgroup of this working career.

Nearly one quarter of those interviewed claimed various health problems. In these cases their problems very often hindered their job search and the ability to accept certain working conditions. However, for many of them, the articular, gastric, circulatory or nervous diseases also provides the "security" of becoming disabled and entitled them to disabled pension after their benefit entitlement period is exhausted.

WAY OF LIFE IN THE STATE OF LONG-TERM UNEMPLOYMENT

Our research confirmed common wisdom that prolonged unemployment is accompanied by a social decline which is less tolerable than the financial losses suffered. Nearly all interviewed persons experienced the rapid decline of their social prestige. In many cases this was also accompanied by the devaluation of their family role and in the perceived (or only presumed) loss of prestige with the children and the spouse.

Savings

The economic pressures of unemployment resulted in the minimization of food and medicine consumption; mostly for single people and single parents raising children. Others still had certain reserves to mobilize.

Out of the 75 subjects interviewed, 5 sold their car. Three had to swap their bigger, good location apartments with high overhead costs for smaller ones, on the one hand to repay their debts, on the other hand to obtain cash.

The main possibilities for saving are the "Polish market" and the discount stores. In order to cut down on transport costs every day "mobility" is seriously considered. They have to learn again the saving techniques of daily housekeeping: not to throw away food leftovers, to substitute costly ingredients, to mend clothes, and so forth. The young people interviewed know much less about these saving techniques, whereas the middle-aged group might learn these methods from their parents who are in their 50-60's. There was a teenage woman who complained how expensive canned baby food was—sooner or later she will have to learn how to prepare baby food at home. Several people indicated that they had given up entertainment—mostly going to cinemas—and buying new clothes. The families with younger children also mentioned that the children stay home from expensive school excursions.

For those unemployed who formerly had intellectual or "white collar" jobs or who worked as junior or middle level executives, the more economical way of life means not only the lowering of their demands but also a decline in social status. They consider giving up visits to the Budapest Opera and theaters or purchasing books as relegation from the middle class. In this group we did not find people starting a business venture even in those cases where there were available reserves to start with.

Occasional Incomes

One-third of those interviewed are pursuing some kind of activity that formerly belonged to the "second economy" but cannot be considered black (illegal) but rather gray or informal. In most cases, this means vegetable and fruit growing or poultry and pig husbandry in their own houses or rented plots located near the town. Occasionally, and in smaller quantities, the food produced is marketed, too. Some people take their garden flowers to the market as well. For those unemployed living in housing estates, the following informal activities were registered in the interviews: house or child caretaking, elevator maintenance, repair activities for men, dressmaking, housekeeping, care for the elderly. Some long-term unemployed men mentioned various trade activities, for example, purchaser ("bag-trading") and commission agent (in real estate business). Young people in good physical condition found occasional jobs in the security services.

Those who do occasional jobs are in the middle age groups as well as in the group of young people living and dividing household with their parents. The skilled and semi-skilled workers previously involved in the second economy are trying to keep in touch with small entrepreneurs. It is not only the construction industry that offers restricted opportunities to this group of the long-term unemployed.

Several of them, men and women alike, find occasional incomes in the market niches of trade and services.

The possibility of finding occasional work was at the same time minimal among those young men and women (between 20 and 30 years of age) who, after marriage, are living far away from their original family environment. They are not only inexperienced in finding a job, but they have not yet created work place relations of their own and cannot rely on any inherited network (neither the labor market of "black," "gray" and "voluntary" works).

Allowances

A quarter of the interviewed persons had their lives based on the social assistance system of allowances and benefits. Beside the old age pensions, pre-pensions, early retirement, disabled pensions, unemployment benefits, child care allowances, "targeted" social support schemes offer stable income to these families. The rules of eligibility are well known among them but they sometimes have difficulties having their needs recognized by the different authorities. The minimum security thus obtained is complemented by occasional incomes for "smaller works" around the house or in the neighborhood.

Not only unskilled unemployed can be found in this group. Qualified workers are also included who have lost their stable jobs in the big firms, together with those having secondary or high level of education and those who became jobless in local public administration or in the large industrial, agricultural or commercial enterprises. In the past decades, these public sector employees had always calculated with the advantages of social and enterprise welfare, early retirement, sickness pay, disabled pension, and child care when changing their jobs. These allowances, especially in the case of larger families, were important factors complementing wages or offered alternative income according to the short or long-term interests of the families (child care, household economy, etc.). For the long-term unemployed relying on the system of assistance became a forced necessity that reinforces the submission of these people.

FAMILY STRATEGIES OR LACK OF THEM

After having examined the job search and labor utilization strategies of the long-term unemployed, together with their way of life, two questions were formulated as to the life of such families: (1) How are the ways of adapting to unemployment connected with the family relations? (2) How are the internal relations changing within the families; how are the members' roles rearranged?

The answer to the first question is unambiguous. Similar to other research projects—ours underlines the role of the family in handling the unemployment situation. The worst material, physical and human situations (the appearance of psychosomatic diseases and their worsening) were registered with those long-term unemployed who lived alone or without the spiritual, moral and financial support of a wider and more stable family background. Sharing the responsibilities of problems in a larger circle, the family dinners at weekends, the division of certain household activities (shopping, cooking, conserving, feeding animals, mending garments, etc.) among the family members, all that means a more even distribution of the financial and material burdens and strengthens the feeling of security. We experienced that in one quarter of our interviews. It seems that multigenerational large families can better counterweigh, if not compensate for, the losses and insecurities due to unemployment within the family.

A similar stability can be obtained by long-term unemployed women who undertake the old/new functions of the housewife. This is an involuntary choice open for working women of lower middle class groups. Among those interviewed, with 5 women who became "housewives" through unemployment, good financial and housing conditions were found. At the same time, they expressed their will to start working again in case of a suitable job.

In the families of the interviewed, regular monthly earning and the family member assuring it, have special importance. In several cases, not only the traditional male head of the family is performing that role, but the wife or the adult single child as well. Family allowance or social assistance after one or more children, unemployment compensation or other allowances are additional to this stable income. Such situations, however, are rather badly tolerated—with alcoholism, with several health problems—by the once family-head male unemployed who cannot contribute to the family incomes by informal and occasional works. (It is difficult to conclude whether inability to utilize one's labor force leads to health and other complaints, or growing alcoholism and health problems paralyze the reintegration even to the informal economy.)

The answer to the second question is more perplexing. Research experiences of the past decades concerning employee attitudes and behaviors have showed that the strategies of work and life were based on calculations concerning all the resources and tasks of the families. These cover the family economy and infrastructure (time, energy, capacities, skills, money, lodging, car, household plot, etc.), and also the tasks and services necessary for the short and long-term family goals (child care, education, shopping, housekeeping, home services, house building, etc.).

Under the pressure of unemployment the patterns of "family resource management" have changed. In some cases the system falls apart immediately when, for example, the couples divorce, or when the wealthier grandparents assist one of the children and leave the others to their fate—as we found among our interviews.

In other cases, disintegration is a gradual process. Eating up the reserves, moving to always smaller and worse apartments and houses, accumulating debts and back rents, having more and more health problems—in this way, tension is growing among the older members of the family who need the support of the younger as well as among the young ones expecting the help of their elders. The efforts to get rid of the burdens of the others lead to individual solutions of adaptation. A young woman interviewed in our research, after her own and her husband's long-term unemployment, succeeded in finding her way again by the side of a new partner in life and in business. In other cases, the job search failures of the unemployed and their former spouses or of their children who moved away from home was followed by growing alcoholism and deviant behavior.

In one quarter of the families we experienced decisive steps to enhance and strengthen family cooperation, to recreate links among those family members who do not live together.

At the same time, in certain cases, we found that even local neighborhood relations may offer similar support to the long-term unemployed through voluntary help, joint economic shopping and housekeeping, joint newspaper reading and through the distribution of important information on the job market.

ON THE BORDER OF STATE AND CIVIL SOCIETY IN HUNGARY:

SOME ASPECTS OF SELF-GOVERNANCE IN THE PERIOD OF TRANSITION

Julia Szalai

The idea of self-governance enjoyed a high priority in the programs of the new political parties in Hungary before the first free elections in 1989. It had its historical roots in liberal thought and seemed to be justified by major social developments of the late-1980s. By this time, the gradual dualization of the social order had been realized. The continuous strengthening of the informal economy contributed to a massive accumulation of capital in both the material and cultural senses. By the very same development, the informal society opened up new pathways of social mobility and created new sources of hidden influence in the important fields of production and distribution. Nevertheless, given the prevailing communist arrangements, its entire

International Review of Comparative Public Policy,
Volume 7, pages 215-231.

ISBN: 0-7623-0153-8

potential was forced into informality and the representation of alternative interests lacked any legal and political guarantees. Ongoing informal bargaining behind the scenes gradually eroded the strength of central control. The peaceful transition, that is, the replacement of the old political order through negotiations was an open acknowledgment of the prevailing state of affairs on both sides. It expressed a general readiness for the redefinition of the political order through a set of agreements between the Communist Party and its potential successors. The dual principles of free elections and local self-government seemed to guarantee not only the extension of democratic participation, but also to assist the rise of efficiency in both decision making and the allocation of resources. The municipal elections of fall 1990 were held in an atmosphere of self-confidence: time appeared to be ripe to establish a system, the resources of which originate in the cumulated knowledge, expertise and capital in the hands of the civil society.

Although the unity of political will was unquestionable, serious conflicts were foreshadowed in the process of the preparations for the local elections. It became clear that the concept of self-governance lies at the junction of diverse and sometimes conflicting expectations.

From a *political* perspective, the new local governments were seen as institutional guarantees for an equitable share in *power* and *authority*. The legacy of a centralized bureaucratic order put this political claim into the context of independence and equality in realizing community rights. Thus, the new act on self-governments aimed at significantly curtailing the scope for interference from above and put an emphasis on the institutional warranties of local autonomy. From an *institutional* perspective, future local governments were seen as parts of the system of *public administration*. Thus, the issue was the proper definition and clear separation of "central," as opposed to "decentralized" tasks in order to raise administrative efficiency and to assure accountability. In this regard, much of the authoritative functions of the former local councils had to be suspended and replaced by a redefined and legally regulated relationship between the *citizen* and the *state*. From an *economic* perspective, the local organs were seen as providers of a great number of public services, that is, as units of *production* and *distribution*. In this context, a new system of financing had to be established and clear rules of collective property rights had to be formulated; both of which were compatible with the tasks of restructuring and marketizing the economy as a whole. Finally, from a *social* perspective, local governments were seen as representatives of the *needs* and *interests* of the community which was going to elect them. In this respect, central command on entitlements had to be replaced by a political consensus on the range and standard *of legally acknowledged basic needs* that would be met locally. This included the definition of the duties of local governments in delivering social welfare and of their responsibility in income redistribution. In short, the reshaping of local governance brought all the key-aspects of systemic transformation to the forefront: old authority had to be replaced by modern administration, subordination by representation, bureaucratic orientation by entrepreneurial innovation, command by service and central dependency by self-determination. Behind all these precepts, the focal issue remained democracy.

Below I will go on to discuss the attempts by the newly elected local bodies to identify their priorities among the competing requirements. Given the conditions of a general economic crisis and necessary cuts of central subsidies, the basic question is of an economic character: how did local governments cope with the obvious shortage of capital and financial means which are so important in safeguarding their autonomy? In other words, did local competition for resources lead to a broadening of civic participation, or, on the contrary, did it bring about sharp conflicts of social exclusion? How did the new local governments interpret their dual functions as "entrepreneurs" and agents of "social justice and equity"? Did the extension of local democracy strengthen social cohesion or deepen social disintegration to the detriment of the weakest groups of the community?

* * *

This paper is based on a number of sources. First, a nationwide survey of 75 local governments was conducted to discover the role of political aspirations, professional commitments, expertise, individual and collective interests and, last but not least, socio-cultural traditions in shaping the actual decision making in matters of local politics during the period 1990-1992. Secondly, although the obvious dilemmas were already clear from the dry fiscal data, a set of interviews were held with local decision makers in planning, investment and finance. The actual decision making process was traced from the accounts of the regular sessions of the municipal assembly in a middle-sized Hungarian town, Eger, between winter 1991 and fall 1993. The closer analysis of 267 items on the agenda gave us an opportunity to outline the priorities of the local representatives, and to gain an insight into the deeper structure of interests. Finally, the examination of the press reports in the regional daily newspaper ("Hevesi Hírlap") on the activities of the municipal government of Eger from the date of its formation (October 30, 1990) to fall 1993 helped us assess public response to the changing power relations in the community.

ON PEOPLE'S EXPECTATIONS AND THE OUTCOME OF LOCAL ELECTIONS

The high expectations concerning the transformation of local governance rapidly eroded a few months after the parliamentary elections of spring 1990. Subsequent opinion polls showed general disinterest and a definite regression of presumable participation in the municipal elections scheduled for October of the same year. First, the public did not trust in their gaining direct control over matters that counted most. The general experience of the preceding years of economic decline had been of unstoppable impoverishment and an increase in visible inequalities. Thus, the expectations turned to macro-level economic policy which should have halted the crisis and assisted an upward turn in immediate consumption. In this context, once important local claims for an improvement of the infrastructure, a better utilization of public services and a bigger slice of the public funds were ranked lower on the priority lists. They were outstripped by claims for taming inflation, raising real incomes and ensuring job-security—all beyond the scope of local power. Second, while people disliked the "council system" of socialism, an increasing number of the settlements (especially, the smaller ones) did have favorable experiences with their municipal management in the late years of Kadarism. Local administration became gradually depoliticized and professionalized. Its relationship with the public concentrated on matters of business and local welfare in exchange for the lack of political rights of the community. Thus, the political will to replace the old officials with new ones was far from ubiquitous.

Third, the parliamentary elections seemed to guarantee the essence of the systemic changes, that is, to put an end to communism—and in general, people did not aspire for more. A few months of experience was enough to generate quite widespread disappointment with party-politicking, which was frequently characterized in the press as "the mere substitution of one-party rule with multiparty dictatorship." People did not expect to gain a chance to countervail it with local elections. In this political climate of disillusionment and pessimism, they rapidly lowered their expectations. Broad commitment to the program of a given party, and personal popularity—the leading values prior to the parliamentary elections—lost their attraction in people's eyes. Instead, they wanted to see locally born professionals whom they could trust to maintain the continuity of management and administration (Kurtán et al. 1992).

The actual outcome of the elections confirmed these trends. The analysis of some basic socio-demographic characteristics of the municipal representatives and mayors (Vajda and Farkas 1991) showed that people elected the members of the most consolidated, "settled," middle-aged professional (male) elite of their community who had proved their abilities in one or other administrative posts, production or public service. Party affiliation ceased to matter: the local elections brought about the victory of "independents." The leading slogan of the campaigns was to "defy the 'particularism' of party-politics and, instead, to represent the common and 'undivided' interest of the community." In this climate, it is no surprise that former local council members had a lead which no other occupational groups could catch up with: they constituted no less than a third of all the newly elected representatives, and more than half of the mayors.

These features of the municipal elections were clearly demonstrated in Eger as well. The local press introduced the mayor with the following words of pathos: "Dr. R. Gy. has an Eger-based family which roots 270 years back in history. His grandfather was an engineer who left an unforgettable seal on the city by urging and later introducing electrification and drainage. Dr. R. Gy.'s father was a popular lawyer who educated his son to become a medical doctor. The famous water-polo player, scholar and medical chief in pediatrics was recommended by several political parties and individuals as the best candidate to become our mayor:... 'let us elect a mayor who can do the most to benefit our city, who will certainly work for a prosperous future. Let us elect this man, who enjoys general esteem and will serve the common consent, mobilizing professional competence and employing knowledge of foreign languages, whose honesty cannot be questioned, who is known to be full-heartedly devoted to his community".[1]

His rival, Dr. V. Gy. was no less suited for the post. As an engineer, he represented professionalism, pragmatism and entrepreneurial aptitude. True, he came from a less "noble" family, but he was a popular figure who owed prestige and high position to adroitness, hard work and discipline. His religious education—a clear disadvantage under socialism—turned out to be a source of exceptional honor amid the revitalized conservatism in a city known as the bastion of the Catholic church in Hungary.

The two rivals' party-affiliation was clearly incidental—a fact openly admitted by both of them. "Liberalism" meant no more for Dr. R. Gy. than "national conservatism" for Dr. V. Gy. They shared the same values, culture and aspirations. It came as no surprise that the "liberal victory" of the local elections was questioned in the municipal government within a few months. Four months after the elections, 12 out of the 31 representatives established the Faction of Local Patriots, chaired by Dr. V. Gy., who gained the tacit consent of his friend the Mayor the following day. The new faction was founded with the deliberate goal to give priority to "values of patriotism" above "narrow party-interests." This initiative gave birth to the biggest civic association in the town, attracting more than 250 members within a year. By crossing party lines, local politics was shifted toward corporatism. True, the formal structure of the municipal government was maintained, but "civil agreements" that avoided cumbersome voting procedures gained legitimation. The boundaries between "elected" and "associated" opinion-leaders became unclear, and nobody could follow who was acting in which capacity. By 1993 the elected representatives became (if they were not already) chairmen of the most influential local associations; presidents of the numerous single-issue foundations; managers of the most powerful, recently privatized companies; activists for the town's international relations; and professional advisors to city planners and local social service agencies.

Although the example of Eger is singular in its clarity, reports from other municipal governments showed similar fluidity in local politics. As the nationwide survey showed, some 35-40 percent of the representatives had left their original party faction by 1993 and, simultaneously, a great number of non-elected members were drawn into the work of the various committees of the local assembly. True, the non-elected professionals are not always afforded the right to a formal vote. The boundaries between the local government and its civic context loosened up—with gains and losses alike. On the one hand, increased corporatism corrodes responsibility and accountability. On the other, it expands involvement in local matters and improves the chances for the broader public to gain some influence on community decisions. Regardless, these developments seem to reinforce the traditional bargaining patterns of late Kadarism.

LOCAL POLITICS, FINANCES AND ACCESS TO PROPERTY

Decentralization of authority was accompanied by a grandiose program of property distribution in the hope of creating stable bases for local economic activities, and freeing the central government from its welfare functions. The sheer size of the central administration was regarded as the major obstacle to marketization. It had to get rid of its vast redistributive functions and cease serving as a paternalistic agency. In an attempt to meet this major goal, central social spending had to be cut and the government budget had to be gleaned of extensive schemes for subsidies which, besides being dysfunctional, proved to paralyze economic adjustment and disorient the market. Instead, new and identifiable agents had to be entrusted with the tasks of social provision. Thus, contribution-based social security became the major source of central revenues while targeted welfare programs and compulsorily delivered public services were delegated to the local governments. With the same momentum these governments were made owners of municipal infrastructure. It was also hoped that decentralization would bring about additional economic advantages by reducing bureaucracy and mobilizing resources.

Despite the ideological and political coherence of the new regulations, the reality disproved the liberal expectations. Increased local independence has not reduced the claims for central redistribution. On the contrary, it has legitimized an intensified hunger for state funds and reinforced central administration. Instead of an "either-or" relationship between privatization and centralized redistribution, recent developments show a complementary link between the two processes. An increased share in central funds became a prerequisite of increased marketization, and vice versa. The much hoped clear separation of "economic" and "social" functions proved to be illusory. Statism turned out to be a decisive and inseparable component of the transition.

Although factors such as the lack of legal institutions to protect property, the general shortage of working capital and the pressures from below induced by the increase in unemployment and poverty might be only transitory elements of the transformation, they were immediate causes of increased insecurity. Local governments tried to countervail these by an intense search for central assistance. The paternalistic traditions of conflict resolution also inspired the local agents to overcome their discord by seeking justification and help from above. The most important reasons lay, however, in the historical dualism of the "state-controlled" and "semi-private" spheres.

The heritage of the new local governments is a set of unfulfillable obligations rather than wealth in the classical sense of the word. Although they are expected to run autonomous economic activities with the help of "their" newly acquired property, the actual form and composition of these assets block any such attempts. First, due to the decade-long neglect of investments in public infrastructure, the greater part of this property has been run down.

Second, the property rights are far from being clear. This fact is an ironic consequence of gradual modernization of public services through the informal economy. In the last phase of Kadarism, a growing part of childcare, education, health-care and investments in sewerage or water-supply were provided through a complicated exchange of informal work and favors. From this perspective, the inherited assets belong as much to the new municipal governments as to the parents of the local school, for example, who had voluntarily built the school's swimming pool; or to those firms which bought expensive equipment for the local hospital in an informal exchange with the local council which lobbied on their behalf for extra investment funds; or to the commuting workers of the neighboring village who had contributed with money and work to the municipal kindergarten in an exchange for the reinforcement of their position in the local firm that employed them. Thus, the claims for the decentralized assets were justifiable from all directions. In an attempt to preserve social peace by fulfilling all these justifiable claims, the central coffers had to be opened. "Communal property" remained an empty concept. Instead, property-rights have become segmented. Looked upon from an administrative perspective, the municipality remained the "owner" in charge of management. Looked upon from that of finance and investment, it is partly the central government who payed maintenance and upgrading, partly the users through their continuously rising contributions. However, in terms of actual functioning, frequently an external buyer (a private firm, an agency, a non-profit organization, a club, the police, any of the local associations, etc.) is the owner in an unclear bartered lease on premises, equipment or services from any of the "formal" proprietors. As a consequence, ownership has proved to be a slippery category, meant more in terms of unspoken agreements than in clear rules of contract and command. This is why, nowadays, one cannot tell by opening the door of a local nursery, whether one will find kids in daycare or the office of a nearby factory, paying rent to the headmistress who found this the best solution to raise the salaries of the staff (not to mention the additional advantage of tax evasion). In a similar way, libraries, schools, community centers, local movie theaters and museums, even medical offices have reduced their primary service in favor of creating space, time and capacity for all kinds of entrepreneurial activity. The municipalities have no resources to raise earnings, thus they give their reluctant consent to individualistic solutions of all kinds. The institutions are impoverished in budgetary terms, thus they reduce the standards of their services to liberate assets for the market. The users have no money to buy alternative private services thus, at best, they form associations around the public institutions to canalize central, municipal and individual donations and to keep some vague control. The outcome is a delicate balance among all the interested partners, financed by all of them—at the expense of all of them.

Third, the designation of the local self-governments as the "natural" heirs of public infrastructure creates also conflicts from a historical perspective. In coping with chronic underfinancing over the past decades, a massive concentration of institutions took place in urban settlements. Smaller villages gradually lost their local services, including even schools, health centers and public transport. The new municipalities argue that without extra help, they are unable to render even the rudimentary services. At the same time, those in a better position argue that without extra help, they are unable to meet the needs of the public beyond the boundaries of their own community. Added to this, increased local patriotism finds its compromise in paternalism.

As a consequence of these complex pressures from below, substantial cuts in central spending became a utopia. Statistics show a continuous increase in government expenditure which results in a dramatic growth of budget deficit: within four years, it has increased by 7,700 percent. Such a speedy growth of indebtedness has led to an increase in the recentralization of incomes: instead of releasing taxes and contributions, revenue collection has become more stringent in recent years. Recentralization has led to dependency, which is manifested in a quick rise of redistributed resources in the budgets of the municipalities.[2] The old story seems to go on.

But does it really go on in the same way?

One has to answer with a definite "no." Much to the refutation of simplistic fiscal reasoning, the recentralization of local resources has not been accompanied by a slow-down of marketization.

While in the past, the concentration of resources served to maintain the authority of the center (supervised by the Communist Party); today, it is a sign of weakness. Instead of representing a long-term program of social development, the government attempts to find a balance between the many pressures from below, which originate in justifiable local demands and long-oppressed civic interests. Today's recentralization is in a sense an effort in synchronization: informal marketization and privatization take open and institutionalized forms.

In real terms, these developments are manifested in a particular duality of local economic management. While the revenue side of the municipal budgets shows a high degree of structural uniformity (with the above-mentioned dominance of centrally redistributed resources), looked upon from the perspective of actual economic strategies, one sees a surprising variety of solutions.

On the grounds of the nationwide survey, three distinct strategies can be differentiated.

The first is characterized by an unbroken continuation of "socialist traditions." Impoverished small villages belong to this type, in which both the social and the economic bases for genuine economic autonomy are lacking. As a consequence, these municipalities see their role in the perfection of bureaucratic efficiency. The elite is mainly comprised of old-fashioned administrators, who had been brought up in communist party schools and undergone the training programs of the old trade unions which gave them little expertise. Due to their earlier career, they are irrepressible in administrative negotiations, but lack economic sensitivity. They are good in organizing mass events and campaigns but feel insecure when thinking in terms of investment and returns. In general, they "fear" money and, instead, distribute assistance in kind. They prioritize institutions above individuals and attempt to meet the needs in terms of quantitative equality of access to public provisions. They regard themselves as mere "welfare agents" and claim more paternalism from above. They see no way out of poverty except through more rigorous control over their own poor. The effort to tighten authority often concludes in sharp local conflicts, leading to the exclusion of certain local citizens from social services on "moral" and "administrative" grounds. As a consequence, all agents become united in a deep nostalgia for dictates from above; the poor want centrally prescribed protection, while the local elite desires the affirmation of its intervention by the center in order to keep law and order.

The second strategy is a clear opposite of the first one. It is followed by "entrepreneurial" municipalities which represent a turn toward marketization. Using the freedom of local decision making, they see their role mostly in economic terms. They bravely sell or rent their "own" property, and invest centrally redistributed funds in private business. Legal obligations to meet basic needs are understood with great innovation. These municipalities inspire public institutions to become "private" managers of their services and are ready to finance civic initiatives in this direction. They set up a great number of foundations (to start small enterprises rather than pursue cultural or social aims), and welcome similar activities from the population. As welfare agents, they lay emphasis on the slow-down of the impoverishment of the local middle class. Thus, in their social spending, they focus on various support schemes for housing and education and, simultaneously, try to limit individual welfare assistance by rigorous means-testing. They are no less reluctant to lobby for central funds than the representatives of the first group. However, their arguments are different. Instead of claiming old-type provisions, they request support for job creation and investment. In fact, they are major users of central retraining funds, targeted investment funds for infrastructure, and so forth, the number of which has multiplied during the last few years. As for the local political structure, these municipalities are usually ruled by the strong regional economic lobbies, which see their primary role in inspiring economic recovery of the firms they represent. Thus, they keep social spending under strict budgetary control. In an attempt to avoid social conflicts, they "sell out" the welfare tasks to various charitable agents who, in an exchange for municipal support, take over the full responsibility for assistance and in-kind services for the poor.

As a consequence, these local societies show trends of segmentation. The poor become increasingly ghettoized, oriented toward special services only "for them" and excluded from the normal opportunities of the more fortunate majority. Sharp divisions are also reflected in local politics. In contrast to the general rule of corporatism, in these local governments power is monopolized by a closed circle of community leaders who frequently clash with the population. Inhabitants do not appear in their civic capacity. Instead, local needs are represented by protests and strikes organized by local trade unions and other workplace based organizations. This is the case with the old centers of mining and heavy industry where the local government had always been dependent on large state firms, many of which went bankrupt during the last few years. Thus, municipal policy is less concerned with "local patriotism" than with the classical dispute of capital and labor.

The third strategy can best be described as a kind of "social entrepreneurship." Most numerous in its occurrence, this strategy reflects deliberate efforts for the maintenance of double footing. Its representatives are in favor of privatization, though they support it only in a gradual, strictly controlled form. They prefer to make modest gains through renting the assets than to make quick profit by selling them. Instead of investing with an eye on higher returns in the future, they seek prompt increase in municipal revenue. Instead of raising local taxes, they show caution in spending, always withholding enough reserves at immediate disposal for unforeseeable events. Although they have detailed development plans for the future, they tend to focus on the instantaneous fulfillment of popular needs of all kinds. In an attempt to gain ample social support, they allocate the municipal resources according to a wide range of purposes, articulated by the corporatist bodies of decision-making. The main goal is the maintenance of social peace. These local governments are also relatively generous in supporting civic initiatives, though with municipal participation and control. The more "statist" an association or a foundation is, the more willing they are to subsidize it. In their relationship with the agencies of central administration a similar precaution can be detected. They are in favor of long preparations for social programs and ask for funding from above only with strong backing on a local level. They spend a lot on publicity and prioritize services which broad social groups might be interested in. They are less willing to subsidize economic activity directly, investing instead in education, training and infrastructure. Besides commitments to local patriotism, this strategy reflects the cultural traditions and earlier careers of the local representatives, among whom physicians, teachers, health assistants, social workers, priests, and medium-level bureaucrats are represented in great numbers. As former subjects of systematically neglected public services, they are fully aware of the fact that modernization plans need joint efforts by all relevant agents. Besides supporting the social policy institutions with direct subsidies, they raise the purchasing power of the public through a wide range of assistance programs to various target groups. This latter issue is frequently brought up in their negotiations with the center for funding. Instead of requesting subsidies for special schemes, they bargain for an expansion of the centrally guaranteed incomes of local governments to cover yet "unacknowledged" public needs. For this purpose, they mobilize all kinds of informal networks: locally elected politicians, famous actors born in the locality and successful businessmen are entrusted to lobby for them. In short, established traditions of paternalism and statism are combined with a modern entrepreneurial spirit with great ingenuity.

The site of our in-depth research, Eger, is an obvious example for this third type. As regards occupational background, most of the 31 municipal representatives come from the public sphere, with an expertise mainly in education, cultural management and health-care.[3] They see their main task in regaining the old prestige of their historic town and leading it back onto the road of prosperity. In concrete terms, they attempt to achieve these goals by investing in education, promoting domestic and international tourism, and developing the town to become an acknowledged international sports center. Industrialization is not on their agenda; instead, they try to support commercial and other services. As part of this policy, urban development enjoys a high priority both in spending and in the way in which they try to mobilize the population. (Our interviewees mentioned with great pride that the town won a first prize in an international competition for "Flowery cities," and this led to a rise in revenue from tourism.) The representatives regard themselves as the "ambassadors of Eger," using their international contacts to draw foreigners (and foreign capital) to the town. At the same time, they do not neglect domestic P.R. Famous writers, scholars and politicians, even the Prime Minister are their frequent guests, who, having enjoyed hospitality, do not disregard the "national interest" in supporting Eger's yearly water polo championship, or the organization of local "Wine weeks" with smaller or larger donations.

The analysis of the decision made in the regular sessions of the municipal assembly shows the balance indicated above between the maintenance of solvency and gradual privatization. The budget came up as an issue in 25 percent of the cases. Less frequently, it was discussed in the context of options for raising local revenue. In most cases it was mentioned in the discussions about the fulfillment of yet unacknowledged needs of particular groups or institutions (claims for raising the funds allocated to local schools, kindergartens, homes for the elderly, and so forth; financial "injection" to local transport; a general subsidy scheme for house maintenance; subsidy to all families with school children at the start of the school year; municipal contribution to in-school catering, extra subsidy to primary schools taken over by the church, etc.). As a rule, these claims are introduced by one or another invited representative of the social group in question. By late 1992, 75 regularly invited and paid professionals helped the work of the 31 representatives in nine ordinary, and 12 *ad hoc* committees, which were set up "as a reflection of the local needs to be represented"[4] (as the mayor put it in a public interview).

Nearly equal in its occurrence on the agenda, the second most frequent issue is privatization (21 percent of all discussion items). Two topics have dominated the scene: the sequence of buying up emptied workers' hostels, communist party buildings, transferring ownership of half-used community houses, and so forth, in order to meet the claims of the Catholic church for restitution; and the recurrent issue of selling off municipal apartments.

As to the first topic, restitution proved to be a profitable move. First, by giving back several buildings to the Catholic church with remarkable generosity, the municipality collected extra funds from the central budget, which had been separated for this purpose by the nationalist-conservative government in power at the time. Second, the support of religious charity assisted in expanding the local welfare schemes and in maintaining control over the most problematic social groups. Third, the pioneering role in restitution made government politicians inclined to lobby for the realization of Eger's dream, a first-class international swimming-pool.

While the local assembly shows great flexibility and generosity toward all forms of institutional privatization (including support for foundations and associations of all kinds), it approaches "genuine" privatization with great hesitation. All attempts to start "big business" in town have been blocked to date. Instead, the municipality envisions the support of small entrepreneurship, emphasizes "fairness" in privatizing land, buildings and equipment among a great number of applicants, and rejects any risky, though grandiose endeavors. This attitude characterizes its policy also in the privatization of the municipally owned apartments. Although the issue came up several times, and the more business-oriented representatives raised strong arguments for speeding up sales, the references to "social justice" proved to be stronger. Privatization has proceeded exceptionally slowly, giving way only to the claims of the best organized and most vocal groups of the inner-city area. Instead of a direct sale to the inhabitants, a company was set up under municipal control and entrusted with a "thorough preparation, in which the officials pay attention not only to the dry financial aspects of profit and maintenance costs, but also to considerations of the 'appearance of the town' and our indisputable commitment to the needs of the poorer residents."[5]

The attempts to avoid sharp local conflicts are also clear from the discussion of daily administrative matters. Great emphasis is given to publicity, and the representatives try to achieve compromises with all the interested partners in advance. As a result, classical political discords rarely come up for discussion in the sessions. Neither do "welfare issues" appear on the agenda. Instead, the sessions are dominated by the authorization of well-prepared projects and institutional programs, merely giving the impression of unbiased representation, expertise and well-rooted agreements. This is what a great majority of our interviewees emphasized as their major achievement. "Obviously, sometimes we have serious conflicts. This is natural: we are different, with different aspirations and different interests. However, it is our conviction that some form of compromise can always be found. Furthermore, it is useless to go to the public with odds and ends, and to quarrel all the time. Instead, we invite each other for wine and try to come to terms at the 'white table.' It is better. And you should see how proud we are when our 'enemy' of yesterday presents our ideas with full conviction in the open session a few days later! You'll never forget it. Of course it goes without saying that next time, I am the one who is obliged to give way to him first. These are the unwritten rules of courtesy and fairness. We all hate conflicts."[6]

The balance sheet of municipal actions is generally positive. Professionalism in local administration has definitely increased and, according to the records, a delicate equilibrium can be maintained between the contrasting economic and social interests of the population. True, the great breakthrough is still awaited: the much-desired boom has not come yet. Nevertheless, small-scale privatization of all kinds is progressing, reaching a wide circle of inhabitants at least through the growing diversity of consumption.

CONCLUSIONS

The example of Eger belongs to the success stories of the past years of local democracy. The secret source of this achievement is to be found in the unbroken trend of double footing in the preceding years and decades. However, what is favorable here might be dangerous elsewhere. Peaceful transition in Hungary has brought about a high degree of fragmentation in the representation of interests and sharp competition for the diminishing resources. As a consequence, insecurity has increased on all levels. Nevertheless, most of the communities have in a way managed to come to terms with their own set of conflicts. Perhaps, this is the way of progress. It is not unilinear, and it is certainly not without serious losses. It reinforces paternalism, but helps to avoid authoritarianism.

NOTES

1. Hevesi Hírlap, October 21, 1990.
2. While the various transfers from the central budget amounted to "only" 53 percent of the revenues of municipalities in a nationwide aggregation in 1990, their share grew to 63 percent by 1992. The corresponding ratio in Eger is even higher: in 1992, it was 70 percent.
3. By professions, the composition is as follows: 7 teachers, 4 physicians, 4 lawyers, 2 free-lance writers, 1 journalist, the director of the town museum, 5 civil servants, 4 small entrepreneurs, the head manager of one of the hotels, and two pensioners.

4. The "ordinary" committees are as follows: Medical care, Social welfare, Education and sports, Urban development, Budget and local economy, Tourism and small-trade, Cultural needs, Financial control, Legislation and legal representation. Some examples of the "ad hoc" committees: Sale of municipal assets, Church and religion, Housing management and privatization, Construction, Publicity and local relations, and so forth.

5. Interview with Mr. H.L., deputy-mayor in charge of municipal finance and economy.

6. Interview with Mr. M.A., Chairman of the Welfare Committee.

REFERENCES

Kurtán, S., P. Sándor, and L. Vass, eds., 1991. "A politikai közvélemény 1990-ben (Political Opinions in 1990). In *Political Yearbook of Hungary*. Budapest: Hungarian Centre of the Foundation of Democracy Studies.

Vajda, Å., and J. Farkas. 1991. *Két választás Magyarországon 1990-ben* (Two Elections in Hungary in 1990). Budapest: Central Statistical Office.

DILEMMAS OF THE TRANSFORMATION FOR PUBLIC HEALTH INSURANCE IN HUNGARY:

MALFUNCTIONS OF THE SYSTEM OF PRICE SUBSIDY FOR DRUGS

Peter Vince

INTRODUCTION

Expectations and illusions related to the market economy are now experiencing their heyday in East-Central Europe. It is still an open question as to what proportion of the transformation processes can be regulated by market mechanisms. Experience shows that apart from regular economic transactions, the limits of the influence of market forces are becoming increasingly vague.

International Review of Comparative Public Policy,
Volume 7, pages 233-245.

ISBN: 0-7623-0153-8

This question arose in the study of the Hungarian Health Insurance Fund (HIF) and the system of price subsidies for drugs (PSD). HIF is an institution in which market forces could only play a limited and subordinate role. HIF is currently being taken out of the hands of government administration to be run independently; this leaves little space for the market to come into play anyway. HIF implements income redistribution independently of market norms, intentionally correcting the effects of market requirements.

At the same time, HIF is increasingly incapable of isolating itself from market effects. The tightening of its budget constraints and the establishment of manifold connections within the framework of PSD with companies producing and selling pharmaceutical products is forcing HIF further into a situation where it must consider the impacts of market norms. The different agents running the PSD system are therefore connected to both the market and non-market spheres.

On the micro-levels of the Hungarian economy, privatization and the liquidation of former monopolies are coming to bear while the macroeconomic financial imbalances are growing. Under such conditions the organizational and regulatory system of HIF is also undergoing a fundamental transformation.

At the beginning of this paper, I will describe the formation of the Health Insurance Budget and the trends in drug prices. Then the importance of the criteria of PSD will be discussed. The following section deals with the conflicts between HIF and the agents acting on the drug market. Various regulatory factors will also be analyzed, which indicate that unjustified demands fall on HIF. Finally, the main conclusion of the study: that HIF is afflicted by serious malfunctions will be presented.

Apart from statistics and other written sources of information, the study was made on the basis of consultations and interviews with the HIF management and other specialists in the field, various government agencies and companies producing and selling pharmaceutical products. The conclusions resulted from the observations to be made from their conflicting statements. This case study belongs to an analytical school often referred to in Hungarian sociological and economic literature. It relies on the results of an earlier work by the author (Vince 1993).

THE FUNCTION AND FINANCES OF THE PSD SYSTEM

The budget of the Health Insurance Fund Administration (HIFA)—the administrative apparatus of HIF—finances the PSD system. The main objective of the PSD system is to influence the structure and quantity of drug consumption. HIFA has many different roles in financing the PSD system. In Hungary, everyone is entitled to a price subsidy for drugs on products prescribed by a physician. The scale of the PSD varies, and drugs are classified in different keys (categories) of subsidies. These keys of subsidies are not determined by HIFA, but by the Ministry of Welfare. Another task of HIFA is to bargain on drug prices with the companies which produce and sell them. HIFA can only subsidize the drug prices which have been calculated on the basis of these price agreements. Finally, HIFA transfers the subsidies to retailers so that the customer does not pay the whole price, but a subsidized price (drug fee) at the pharmacy.

The HIFA budget is established from year to year according to a repeated scenario. The budget plan compiled by HIFA was always cut by the government and this version was presented to Parliament. The government modified HIFA's budget plan annually; the estimated deficit and expenditures were decreased, the incomes and revenues were increased. In practice, however, it always became evident that these figures were unrealistic and could not be satisfied. This process of passing the budget may also have led to its mid-year modification, to drug price increases and subsidy reductions to limit the growth of the budget deficit. In spite of these efforts, HIFA's budget deficit was larger than estimated every year.

The price subsidy for drugs became one of the most important items on the growing HIFA budget deficit. In 1993, more than half of this deficit was caused by exceeding drug subsidy estimates.

PSD expenditures exceeded forecasts on a growing scale from one year to the next. This is connected to the methods used to calculate the forecasts: from 1991 on *every year the PSD budget lagged behind the actual expenditures of the previous year.* In each new budget the impacts of increasing drug prices, widening choice and growth in trade was not taken into account despite the very strong impact that they made. The choice of drugs rapidly expanded with imported products far exceeding the price levels of domestic producers. Imported drugs penetrated fast, forcing up the price levels of drugs. The share of foreign products was one quarter of the value of the turnover in the domestic drug trade in 1990, rising to almost half the value of turnover by 1993. The effects of the devaluation of the Hungarian currency and inflation were also significant in the drug price increase. This resulted in a 250 percent consumer price increase in drugs between 1990 and 1993. PSD increased by 200 percent in the same period. Customers paid 70 percent more for subsidized drugs in the period between 1992 and 1993 alone. The average level of PSD decreased from 91 percent in 1992 to 88 percent in 1993.

The trend of rising drug prices in turn increased HIFA's PSD expenditure. This led to a series of conflicts between HIFA and the government (more precisely, the Ministry of Welfare). The necessity of reducing PSD expenditure was put firmly on the agenda. A reduction in expenditure could be achieved by decreasing PSD, that is, by an increase in drug prices paid by the customer. However, raising drug prices is a socially sensitive issue. Thus, the government postponed this decision for fear of anticipated negative public reaction. *The government tried to shift the burden of accumulated tension from postponing modifications to PSD onto the budget of HIFA*. This was an inconsistent attitude because while the government did not allow the level of PSD to be reduced, neither was it willing to accept the growing deficit this brought about in the HIFA budget. HIFA did not reduce its subsidies, so its only alternative was to regularly exceed its budget forecasts.

THE PSD SYSTEM: CONTINUITY AND CHANGE

The Functioning of PSD

The slow reduction in the level of subsidies can be explained by the continuity of the basic features of the subsidy system. The construction of the PSD system has not changed in the last few years and neither have those participating in or influencing its formation. The various facets of, as well as the methods employed for the allocation of subsidies on drugs have altered in many respects over the same period.

PSD is administered by HIFA and the Ministry of Welfare. The regulations are made by the Ministry of Welfare with the agreement of HIF.

In the formation of drug subsidies the Ministry of Welfare regulates two factors. One is the scale of subsidy keys (categories) determined as a percentage of consumer price, the other is the principle of classification of drugs according to the subsidy keys. The subsidy keys in force have not changed (100%, 95%, 80%, 0% of consumer prices) with respect to the falling living standards, but new keys—offering lower (50% and fixed) subsidies—have in the meantime been introduced. The broadened selection of subsidy keys to date has already resulted in subsidy savings. In 1992 "50%" and "fixed" subsidy key drugs represented 2.8 percent of the drug trade, and 9.2 percent in 1993.

The purpose of these changes was to reduce the level of subsidies and avoid excessive consumption of drugs. A combination of consumer price increases and excessive consumption has resulted in a level of demand in subsidies which HIFA can no longer finance.

Criteria of Price Subsidies for Drugs

The most important element of the PSD system is to determine the criteria for classifying the keys of subsidies. The classification has three main criteria which always prove to be irreconcilable with each other. The first aspect which is taken into consideration in the classification of drugs is related to the patient using the drug. This reflects a *social policy* preference depending on the social background or age of the patient, as well as on for how long the drug is prescribed. (Drugs taken by the elderly and children have a high level of subsidy, regardless of the type of illness.) The second criterion of classification includes *medical, therapeutic* factors. Here the classification of drugs is determined by the type, seriousness and length of the illness. In the third group belong *financial* criteria.

In the period between 1992 and 1994 a significant restructuring began in the hierarchy of these criteria with a view to *pushing into the background those social policy considerations which had carried so much weight in the past.* It is quite evident that all three criteria cannot be equally enforced at the same time.

The restructuring has been lent impetus by the rapid penetration of imported products into the market. Partly medical and partly social policy considerations were the underlying reasons for these modern and expensive imported products being given higher subsidies in the early 1990s than domestic drugs with exactly the same remedial effects. This helped to give the population easier access to imported drugs. Although, in 1992 it had already become clear to HIFA that it could not continue financing the same level of subsidies.

From 1992 there were more moves to modify subsidies, or rather to raise drug fees. In August 1992, of the 1300 drugs in circulation, 300 became subject to subsidy reductions. These were drugs considered to fall into the range of excessive consumption. HIFA did not manage to get the Ministry of Welfare to accept that subsidy reductions for expensive foreign drugs should be greater than those for similar domestic products. However, the subsidy reduction introduced at the beginning of 1994—affecting another 300 drugs—largely followed this principle.

From HIFA's point of view getting these changes accepted was not an easy task. The partners were opposed to even negotiating the issue. The Ministry of Welfare was against any changes because of expected increases in drug prices: it insisted on the enforcement of social policy criteria. The same standpoint was adopted by employee representatives at the Self Government of HIF elected in 1993. Foreign pharmaceutical companies also attacked the changes because they expected the deterioration of their market position following the subsidy reductions.

The budget deficit of HIFA in 1992 and 1993 finally induced action to be taken; measures to reduce subsidies had become unavoidable. The principle was thus adopted that among drugs with the same remedial effect, the ones being cheaper should enjoy larger subsidies. *Financial considerations played a decisive role in these measures*, while social policy criteria were clearly neglected. Yet these moves also meant that *the influence of medical criteria became restricted*, due to cut backs in subsidies for effective modern but expensive drugs.

HIFA'S RELATIONS WITH AGENTS IN THE DRUG MARKET

Modifications in the PSD system influenced not only HIFA's budget imbalance but the position of its partners, that is, domestic and foreign pharmaceutical producers and drug wholesalers and retailers. HIFA has a dominant role in the drug market. As subsidies cover an average 80 percent of the price of drugs, companies producing or selling drugs have to accept that their largest "purchaser" controls the market.

HIFA's relations with drug producers and wholesalers consist of bargaining on drug prices and transferring subsidies to drug retailers. The position held by domestic producers in the market has changed fundamentally; almost half the market share has been seized by foreign pharmaceutical producers since 1990. The consequence is growing competition between producers. Another significant change was due to the end of a traditional monopolist structure in the wholesale of drugs. The smallest structural changes so far have been in the retail end of the drug trade because the privatization of pharmacies continues at a very slow pace.

Weakening Ties with Domestic Drug Producers

HIFA's relations with domestic pharmaceutical companies were not restricted to formal bargaining on drug prices in the past. It was *mutual interest and interdependence that characterized their cooperation* because domestic firms dominated the market. In the bargaining on drug prices both sides took into account not only pricing but the financial possibilities, resources and interests of their partners. Domestic producers, for example, took into consideration the tight budgets imposed on HIFA by the government. Domestic producers thus practiced self-moderation with regard to price increases. In return, HIFA kept in mind that pricing should ensure a profitable operation for the companies and that the main suppliers' financial position should remain stable.

The market share of domestic drug producers fell as rapidly as imports increased in the 1990s. The reason for this is that although imported drugs are more expensive, they broaden the choice of effective remedial products. This and the ongoing privatization of domestic pharmaceutical companies forced HIFA to reconsider its traditional relations with the suppliers. However the relations forged in the past will not vanish without trace in the future. The main source of income for domestic producers will remain the subsidies. Therefore it is in their own interest to continue to practice self-moderation in the future as well. In return, HIFA may provide them with more favorable PSD classifications than foreign suppliers. It is also in the interest of HIFA not to completely sever its strong informal links with domestic companies, because these could contribute towards the preservation of its influence.

Changes in the Financing of PSD

HIFA's relations with drug retailers are based on the financing of price subsidies for drugs. HIFA transfers the subsidy to drug retailers. This transaction is necessary because the buyer pays a drug fee and not the full consumer price at the pharmacy. The regulation of financing and transferring subsidies is not a neutral financial matter but plays an important role in the budget imbalances of HIFA.

The functioning of the PSD system has created financial conditions which completely differ from the conventional patterns of retail trade. According to general commercial practice retail margins should cover the costs and profits. In the drug retail trade, however, the price subsidy of drugs supports not only the customer but also the drug retailers. In addition to retail margins, the price subsidy for drugs has become an extra source of income for drug retailers. This form of regulation has a peculiar consequence: *HIFA has been forced to take on another role, one quite different from its basic function.* It has had to participate in the financing of commercial operations while constantly struggling with its own financial difficulties.

Since 1989 price subsidies have been transferred before the real subsidy demand was formulated, that is, before the time of purchase at the retail outlet. Regulations for the payment of subsidies were modified several times between 1989 and 1994, but the basic feature of payment in advance has remained unchanged. This procedure is unilaterally advantageous for drug retailers. The advance payment of price subsidies for drugs has made it possible for retailers to use HIFA's money to cover operational costs (e.g., those of stockpiling). Besides this, retailers have been presented with the opportunity to make investments with returns in the short-term. The interest-free advance payment of subsidies made it unnecessary for the retailers to use bank loans. Between 1989 and 1994 the only change in the system of subsidy transfers was that the period of advance payment has been reduced.

In May 1994 PSD financing changed: *HIFA was to pay subsidies after and not in advance of purchase of drugs.*

In the case of newly established privately owned pharmacies the post-purchase transfer system was not introduced; in the first year of operation the system of advance payment was maintained. HIFA had to carry the burden of supporting new private ventures. *Thus, HIFA was again forced into a role it was not originally intended for: to support privatization and enterprise formation.*

POWER RELATIONS AND CONFUSION OF ROLES

To what extent does the formal, organizational independence of HIF mean *real independence from the state administration? How far has the process advanced in which the basic function of HIF could be separated from ones not originally intended*? A few answers will be given to these questions by reviewing the PSD system.

Clash of Interests

The first step in the reorganization of the Social Insurance Fund (SIF) in 1989 was that the elaboration and passing of its budget was separated from the state budget. Another important change was the separation of the budgets of the two sections of the Social Insurance Fund Administration (SIFA) in 1992—Pension Insurance Fund Administration (PIFA) and Health Insurance Fund Administration (HIFA). In principle, the election of the autonomous Governing Body of HIF in 1993 marked the end of government control and the beginning of supervision by representatives of employers and employees.

Apart from organizational independence, the legal and regulatory conditions of separation and independence were very poor, at least as far as the PSD system is concerned. *HIFA has too much influence and too many obligations, while having unjustifiably little authority over the functioning of the PSD system.* The following lists the jurisdiction and obligations of HIFA with regard to PSD:

The establishment of HIF's autonomous Governing Body was not followed by redistribution and modification of authorities between the Ministry of Welfare and HIFA. The Ministry of Welfare will continue to decide—as it did in the past—on the key issues of the PSD system: that is, on the construction of PSD, on the principles of classification of drug subsidy keys, on the scale of price margins in the drug trade and on the method of transferring subsidies to retailers. Although the consumer prices of drugs are not determined by a government authority but through an agreement between pharmaceutical companies and HIFA, the regulation of subsidies remains a responsibility of the Ministry of Welfare. The state administration, therefore, decides on HIFA's utilization of PSD resources.

HIFA's rights are incomplete, nevertheless it has an unusual power vis-à-vis the suppliers. It is HIFA and not the wholesale companies which agree on drug prices with the producers. HIFA is not the purchaser. The "only" legal grounds it has is that its subsidies cover the majority of drug prices. *The drug sector is on the whole characterized by the fact that those who have the money at their disposal* [*traders and HIFA*)—due to government regulations—*cannot determine, or only within limits, the way they use their own resources.*

Market norms cannot be applied in this sector. HIFA is naturally not to be mistaken for market agents such as the manufacturing or trading companies in the sector. It has completely different functions: it redistributes incomes between various groups of the population independently of market criteria and interests attached. At the same time, HIFA's activity is at the juncture between the various agents of the economy. Its partners are producers and traders on the one side; these are effectively able to assert their interests (to make profits) although their competitiveness is shaped by the decisions of HIFA. On the other side, HIFA subsidizes the drug consumption of insured citizens, and grades and selects their conflicting interests within the PSD system. Next to the state budget, HIF has the largest volume of income in the Hungarian economy. It shares control of the drug sector with the state administration. In shaping the position of drug producers, traders and insured citizens, it cooperates to some extent with the state administration. At the same time, the assertion of different interests leads to conflicts with the government on a day-to-day basis.

Additional Functions of HIF

The authority of HIFA is too narrow in certain areas and unjustifiably wide-ranging in others.

HIFA's task is to monitor and assert its influence on the drug sector. It has the resources (its own budget) to perform this task. The Ministry of Welfare, however, which strives to enforce different views, does not receive any money from the state budget. *Thus, the state administration can only assert its own interests by the utilization of HIF resources, that is, by maintaining its authority over HIF.*

Among the additional functions of HIFA, the most important sphere of authority is its agreement on drug prices with pharmaceutical companies. Bargaining on drug prices gives HIFA room to maneuver and represent its interests. It can provide subsidies with varying conditions according to the price offers made by the pharmaceutical companies. If a company gives a discount or moderates its claim for a price increase, HIFA can in return guarantee not to reduce its subsidies for a certain period. HIFA has a large degree of freedom when it comes to decisions on drug prices and subsidies. It is helped by rather loosely formulated regulations which determine the price subsidy of drugs. It is in the interest of HIFA to maintain its bargaining position. However, it does not only pursue its own interests; its role is essential for the time being because there is no other institution or market agent which could put a restraint on drug producers' endeavors to increase prices.

HIFA is interested in continuing to cooperate with domestic drug producers, a relationship that has been maintained over the span of many decades. This form of cooperation assures the supply of cheaper drugs and, at the same time, the protection of the domestic pharmaceutical industry. This, however, does not belong to the basic functions associated with HIF, but to the legacy of the old system of economic management. The characteristic feature of this system was that the importance, influence and prestige of an institution could not be based purely on its accomplishments or the positive social implications of its work. Prestige and influence was won not just by completing its "basic activities," but by taking on additional functions. *The example of HIF demonstrates how essential additional functions were as prerequisites to the maintenance of an institution's ability to survive.*

Among the additional functions some have lost their significance in the last few years. One striking example, which was in evidence as recently as the beginning of the 1990s were *direct* HIFA grants of subsidies to manufacturing and trading companies struggling with financial difficulties. This support complemented the *indirect* subsidies to drug retailers provided by advance payments. The former, direct means of support no longer survives. The latter has become much smaller in scale. Indirect support for retailers in the past was justified by the need for a wide choice of drugs and the reduction of frequent shortages of drug supply. Drug supply in the last few years has become more balanced as a consequence of import liberalization. This has significantly weakened the motives for subsidizing retailers.

Restrictions of Authority

HIF has a very restricted margin of authority to complete its functions in other areas. The Ministry of Welfare has the right to regulate the drug sector as a whole. *It has often used its authority to interfere with the interests of HIF.*

The Ministry of Welfare is responsible for social and health policies. Its interest is primarily to moderate consumer price increases and maintain high levels of subsidies. The financial consequences of enforcing these criteria, however, have led to a growth in the budget deficit of HIFA. Another criterion of the government was to ensure a balance in drug supply. This aspect resulted in imposing regulations for subsidy financing and giving preference to new privately owned pharmacies. The implementation of the Ministry's social and health policies is borne by HIF.

One of the major components in determining the scale of subsidy for drug prices, the trade margin, is also regulated by the Ministry of Welfare, contrary to general commercial practice. This regulation makes it possible for the Ministry of Welfare to influence revenues in the drug trade.

Limitations of the Health Insurance Fund

The HIF budget became independent of the state budget in 1989. It has not led to the discontinuing of all of HIF's previous functions as a state agency. The establishment of the autonomous Governing Body of HIF in 1993 put an end to state control over HIF, although for the moment *it does not enjoy complete legal guarantees of independence.*

The independence of HIF is rooted in two recent developments. One is the reduced importance of administrative functions, such as direct subsidizing of the pharmaceutical industry and retailers, financing welfare provisions, and distributing PSD according to social policy criteria. Another sign of its independence is that HIF can formulate its own views more decisively while its autonomous Governing Body can represent these more vigorously in negotiations with the government. HIF's tight budget position forces it to re-examine the system of PSD and reduce the level of subsidies. Representing these issues has given rise to conflicts of interest with the state administration which tries to delay these changes. The results of these clashes of interest show that HIF does not hold sufficient legal guarantees of its independence: its financial position and any effective decisions on the system of PSD come under the jurisdiction of the Ministry of Welfare. The formal conditions of independence in regulation and the division of decision making powers have not yet been defined, but the informal positions of HIF—due to the growing prestige of its autonomous Governing Body—appear to be strengthening.

ACKNOWLEDGMENT

The research project was sponsored by the Active Society Foundation, Budapest.

REFERENCES

"Act on Health Insurance Fund Budget." 1993. *Magyar Közlöny* 185.

Collection of Regulations of the Drug Sector. 1993. Gyógyszertári Központok.

"Health Insurance." 1994. *Heti Világgazdaság*, August 24.

Hungarian Statistical Yearbook. 1992. Budapest: Központi Statisztikai Hivatal.

Information on Financing Price Subsidies for Drugs. 1993. Budapest: Pharma FELAX.

Information on the System of Price Subsidies for Drugs. 1994. Budapest: Országos Egészségbiztosítási Pénztár.

Monthly Review of Statistics. 1994. Budapest: Központi Statisztikai Hivatal, No. 1.

Review on Economic Trends 1993-1994. 1994. Hungary: Ministry of Finance.

"Statements of the Association of Hungarian and Foreign Pharmaceutical Producers." 1993. *Pharmorient* (June-July).

"Statement of National Social Insurance Fund on the Concept of Price Subsidies for Drugs." 1993. *Népjóléti Közlöny*, No. 2.

Statistical Reviews of the Social Insurance Fund 1990-1993. Budapest: Országos Társadalombiztosítási Föigazgatóság, 1990, 1991, 1992, 1993.

Vince, P. 1993. *What Do We Pay for in the Drug Prices*? (Mit fizetünk meg a gyógyszerek árában?), No. 6. Hungary: Közgazdasági Szemle.

Working Papers of the Health Insurance Fund Administration. 1993. Budapest: Országos Egészségbiztosítási Pénztár.

Working Papers of the Health Insurance Fund Administration. 1994. Budapest: Országos Egészségbiztosítási Pénztár.

World Bank. 1994. Budapest: *Health Reform in Hungary: Taking Stock*. World Bank and Health Insurance Fund.

Yearbook of Social Insurance. 1990, 1991, 1992, 1993. Budapest: Országos Társadalombiztosítási Föigazgatóság.

Printed and bound by CPI Group (UK) Ltd, Croydon, CR0 4YY

16/09/2026

14963399-0001